THE CAMBRIDGE BIBLE COMMENTARY

NEW ENGLISH BIBLE

GENERAL EDITORS
P. R. ACKROYD, A. R. C. LEANEY
J. W. PACKER

PSALMS 51–100

PSALMS 51–100

COMMENTARY BY

J. W. ROGERSON

Senior Lecturer in Theology, University of Durham

AND

J. W. McKAY

Lecturer in Theology, University of Hull

CAMBRIDGE UNIVERSITY PRESS

CAMBRIDGE

LONDON · NEW YORK · MELBOURNE

Published by the Syndics of the Cambridge University Press
The Pitt Building, Trumpington Street, Cambridge CB2 IRP
Bentley House, 200 Euston Road, London NW1 2DB
32 East 57th Street, New York, NY 10022, USA
296 Beaconsfield Parade, Middle Park, Melbourne 3206, Australia

First published 1977

PRINTED IN GREAT BRITAIN
AT THE UNIVERSITY PRESS, CAMBRIDGE

Library of Congress cataloguing in publication data
Bible. O.T. Psalms. English. New English. 1977. Psalms.
(The Cambridge Bible commentary, New English Bible)
Includes bibliographies and indexes.
CONTENTS: [1] 1–50. – [2] 51–100. – [3] 101–150.
1. Bible. O.T. Psalms–Commentaries. I. Rogerson, John William.
II. McKay, John William. II. Title. III. Series.
BS 1430.3.R63   223'.2'077   76-27911
ISBN 0 521 21464 5 hard covers (Psalms 51–100)
ISBN 0 521 29161 5 paperback (Psalms 51–100)

GENERAL EDITORS' PREFACE

The aim of this series is to provide the text of the New English Bible closely linked to a commentary in which the results of modern scholarship are made available to the general reader. Teachers and young people have been especially kept in mind. The commentators have been asked to assume no specialized theological knowledge, and no knowledge of Greek and Hebrew. Bare references to other literature and multiple references to other parts of the Bible have been avoided. Actual quotations have been given as often as possible.

The completion of the New Testament part of the series in 1967 provides a basis upon which the production of the much larger Old Testament and Apocrypha series can be undertaken. The welcome accorded to the series has been an encouragement to the editors to follow the same general pattern, and an attempt has been made to take account of criticisms which have been offered. One necessary change is the inclusion of the translators' footnotes since in the Old Testament these are more extensive, and essential for the understanding of the text.

Within the severe limits imposed by the size and scope of the series, each commentator will attempt to set out the main findings of recent biblical scholarship and to describe the historical background to the text. The main theological issues will also be critically discussed.

Much attention has been given to the form of the volumes. The aim is to produce books each of which will be read consecutively from first to last page. The introductory material leads naturally into the text, which itself leads into the alternating sections of the commentary.

The series is accompanied by three volumes of a more general character. *Understanding the Old Testament* sets out to provide the larger historical and archaeological background, to say something about the life and thought of the people of the Old Testament, and to answer the question 'Why should we study the Old Testament?'. *The Making of the Old Testament* is concerned with the formation of the books of the Old Testament and Apocrypha in the context of the ancient Near Eastern world, and with the ways in which these books have come down to us in the life of the Jewish and Christian communities. *Old Testament Illustrations* contains maps, diagrams and photographs with an explanatory text. These three volumes are designed to provide material helpful to the understanding of the individual books and their commentaries, but they are also prepared so as to be of use quite independently.

P. R. A.
A. R. C. L.
J. W. P.

CONTENTS

The footnotes to the N.E.B. text   *page* x

✻   ✻   ✻   ✻   ✻   ✻   ✻   ✻   ✻   ✻   ✻   ✻   ✻

Name, content and place of the book in the
    Old Testament   1
Psalm titles, authorship and growth of the Psalter   3
History of interpretation   6
The character of the N.E.B. translation   8
Literary and poetic characteristics of the psalms   10
The contents of the Psalter   13

✻   ✻   ✻   ✻   ✻   ✻   ✻   ✻   ✻   ✻   ✻   ✻   ✻

Book 2 (cont.)

    Psalm 51   15
    Psalm 52   21
    Psalm 53   24
    Psalm 54   27
    Psalm 55   29
    Psalm 56   36
    Psalm 57   41
    Psalm 58   44
    Psalm 59   48
    Psalm 60   53
    Psalm 61   57
    Psalm 62   60
    Psalm 63   64
    Psalm 64   68
    Psalm 65   71

Psalm 66   *page* 75
Psalm 67   80
Psalm 68   82
Psalm 69   92
Psalm 70   102
Psalm 71   104
Psalm 72   111

Book 3

Psalm 73   117
Psalm 74   124
Psalm 75   130
Psalm 76   133
Psalm 77   135
Psalm 78   139
Psalm 79   152
Psalm 80   155
Psalm 81   159
Psalm 82   163
Psalm 83   165
Psalm 84   169
Psalm 85   173
Psalm 86   177
Psalm 87   181
Psalm 88   184
Psalm 89   188

Book 4

Psalm 90   198
Psalm 91   202
Psalm 92   206

CONTENTS

Psalm 93   *page* 208

Psalm 94   211

Psalm 95   216

Psalm 96   219

Psalm 97   222

Psalm 98   225

Psalm 99   227

Psalm 100   229

✻   ✻   ✻   ✻   ✻   ✻   ✻   ✻   ✻   ✻   ✻   ✻   ✻

A NOTE ON FURTHER READING   231

INDEX   233

THE FOOTNOTES TO THE
N.E.B. TEXT

The footnotes to the N.E.B. text are designed to help the reader either to understand particular points of detail – the meaning of a name, the presence of a play upon words – or to give information about the actual text. Where the Hebrew text appears to be erroneous, or there is doubt about its precise meaning, it may be necessary to turn to manuscripts which offer a different wording, or to ancient translations of the text which may suggest a better reading, or to offer a new explanation based upon conjecture. In such cases, the footnotes supply very briefly an indication of the evidence, and whether the solution proposed is one that is regarded as possible or as probable. Various abbreviations are used in the footnotes:

(1) Some abbreviations are simply of terms used in explaining a point: *ch(s)*., chapter(s); *cp*., compare; *lit*., literally; *mng*., meaning; *MS(S)*., manuscript(s), i.e. Hebrew manuscript(s), unless otherwise stated; *om*., omit(s); *or*, indicating an alternative interpretation; *poss*., possible; *prob*., probable; *rdg*., reading; *Vs(s)*., version(s).

(2) Other abbreviations indicate sources of information from which better interpretations or readings may be obtained.

Aq.   Aquila, a Greek translator of the Old Testament (perhaps about A.D. 130) characterized by great literalness.

Aram.   Aramaic – may refer to the text in this language (used in parts of Ezra and Daniel), or to the meaning of an Aramaic word. Aramaic belongs to the same language family as Hebrew, and is known from about 1000 B.C. over a wide area of the Middle East, including Palestine.

Heb.   Hebrew – may refer to the Hebrew text or may indicate the literal meaning of the Hebrew word.

Josephus   Flavius Josephus (A.D. 37/8–about 100), author of the *Jewish Antiquities*, a survey of the whole history of his people, directed partly at least to a non-Jewish audience, and of various other works, notably one on the *Jewish War* (that of A.D. 66–73) and a defence of Judaism (*Against Apion*).

Luc. Sept.   Lucian's recension of the Septuagint, an important edition made in Antioch in Syria about the end of the third century A.D.

Pesh.   Peshitta or Peshitto, the Syriac version of the Old Testament. Syriac is the name given chiefly to a form of Eastern Aramaic used by the Christian community. The translation varies in quality, and is at many points influenced by the Septuagint or the Targums.

Sam. Samaritan Pentateuch – the form of the first five books of the Old Testament as used by the Samaritan community. It is written in Hebrew in a special form of the Old Hebrew script, and preserves an important form of the text, somewhat influenced by Samaritan ideas.

Scroll(s) Scroll(s), commonly called the Dead Sea Scrolls, found at or near Qumran from 1947 onwards. These important manuscripts shed light on the state of the Hebrew text as it was developing in the last centuries B.C. and the first century A.D.

Sept. Septuagint (meaning 'seventy'; often abbreviated as the Roman numeral LXX), the name given to the main Greek version of the Old Testament. According to tradition, the Pentateuch was translated in Egypt in the third century B.C. by 70 (or 72) translators, six from each tribe, but the precise nature of its origin and development is not fully known. It was intended to provide Greek-speaking Jews with a convenient translation. Subsequently it came to be much revered by the Christian community.

Symm. Symmachus, another Greek translator of the Old Testament (beginning of the third century A.D.), who tried to combine literalness with good style. Both Lucian and Jerome viewed his version with favour.

Targ. Targum, a name given to various Aramaic versions of the Old Testament, produced over a long period and eventually standardized, for the use of Aramaic-speaking Jews.

Theod. Theodotion, the author of a revision of the Septuagint (probably second century A.D.), very dependent on the Hebrew text.

Vulg. Vulgate, the most important Latin version of the Old Testament, produced by Jerome about A.D. 400, and the text most used throughout the Middle Ages in western Christianity.

[...] In the text itself square brackets are used to indicate probably late additions to the Hebrew text.

(Fuller discussion of a number of these points may be found in *The Making of the Old Testament* in this series.)

PSALMS

✳ ✳ ✳ ✳ ✳ ✳ ✳ ✳ ✳ ✳ ✳ ✳ ✳ ✳ ✳

NAME, CONTENT AND PLACE OF THE BOOK
IN THE OLD TESTAMENT

The name 'psalms' comes from the Greek Septuagint translation of the Bible via the Latin Vulgate (see *The Making of
the Old Testament*, pp. 147-54). The Greek word *psalmos*
denoted the twanging of a stringed instrument with the
fingers, and later came to mean a song sung to the accompani-
ment of a plucked instrument. In turn, *psalmos* is a translation
of the Hebrew *mizmōr*, which also appears to have denoted
both the playing of instruments and the singing of songs.
Strictly speaking, then, the title 'psalms' means 'songs'.
The name for the book in the Hebrew Bible is *tehillīm* or
sēpher tehillīm, meaning 'praises' or 'book of praises'.

In actual fact, neither 'songs' nor 'praises' adequately describes the content of the Psalter. In it, we find expressed by
both the individual and the congregation, prayers for help
and thanksgivings for deliverance in the face of sickness,
despair, desertion by friends, and physical danger. We find
hymns of praise to God as creator and judge of the world, as
the one who has chosen his people Israel and his dwelling in
Zion, and who has guided, supported and punished his people.
We find entreaties that God will speedily and effectively
establish his rule throughout the world, at the same time
that it is acknowledged that he is already the universal king,
controlling the forces of nature, and shaping the destinies of
the nations. We find prayers for the well-being of the king,
and traces of ceremonial used at the king's coronation and the
periodic renewal of the divine covenant with the house of
David. We find extended meditations on Israel's past history,

I

and on God's gracious revelation of his law and his will to his people. We find the whole range of human emotions in their relation to God, from extreme pessimism and doubt to simple and certain trust. Even this lengthy catalogue is not complete, thus showing the impossibility of describing the Psalter and its contents in one word or short phrase. At the end of this introduction, an attempt is made to tabulate the contents of the Psalter.

The psalms stand either in first or second place in the third section of the Hebrew Bible, the Writings (see *The Making of the Old Testament*, pp. 118–24). The English Bible has a different order for the books, with Psalms following the Pentateuch and the historical books (including Ruth, Esther and Job). This arrangement derives from the way the books of the Old Testament were grouped together in the early Christian centuries. The underlying principle was probably that the psalms (believed to be substantially by David) should precede the books attributed to Solomon (Proverbs, Ecclesiastes, Song of Songs) which in turn should precede the prophetic books bearing the names of Isaiah, Jeremiah and Ezekiel. In other words, these books appear in the order of the historical sequence of the lives of those who were believed to have been their authors.

Although there are 150 psalms, there are two major ways of numbering them, the Hebrew and the Greek. The N.E.B. follows the Hebrew numbering, while among Bibles and commentaries used by Roman Catholics, the Greek numbering has been familiar. The major differences are that Pss. 11–113 and 117–146 in the Hebrew numbering are 10–112 and 116–145 in the Greek numbering, and these differences arose from uncertainty about how to regard the verses contained in Pss. 9, 10, 114, 115, 116 and 147 (according to the Hebrew reckoning). The Greek numbering was almost certainly correct in regarding Pss. 9–10 as one psalm (and note that the N.E.B. regards them as one psalm, numbered 9–10) but it was probably incorrect in regarding Pss. 114 and 115 as one psalm, and in dividing 116 and 147 each into two psalms. On the other hand, modern scholarship is virtually unanimous in regarding Pss. 42 and 43 as originally one psalm, against both the Hebrew and the Greek numberings.

PSALM TITLES, AUTHORSHIP AND GROWTH OF THE PSALTER

The preface to the Library Edition of the N.E.B. Old Testament (p. xiv) notes that in the Hebrew, many psalms have titles or headings. The N.E.B. translators decided not to include them in the translation because (i) they are almost certainly not the work of the authors of the psalms, (ii) where they are historical notices they are deduced from the text of the psalm itself and rest on no reliable tradition, and (iii) where they are musical directions, they are mostly unintelligible. However, it is to be noted that the N.E.B. retained the 'doxologies' at the end of Pss. 41, 72, 89 and 106 which mark the conclusion of Books 1–4 of the Psalms respectively, as well as the notice 'Here end the prayers of David son of Jesse' at 72: 20. It can be said of all these that they are no more the work of the authors of the individual psalms than are the psalm titles. Like the titles, they were added at various times as the psalms were collected together to form the Psalter as we have it, and it is odd that in the N.E.B. they were retained where the titles were omitted.

Although the N.E.B. translators are correct in saying that the musical parts of the psalm titles are today unintelligible and that the historical notices are no more than guesses, the titles have something to contribute when we try to deduce how the psalms were collected together. The following psalms are associated with David through the phrase *le dāwīd* in the titles: 3–41 (except 33, and 10 which is a continuation of 9; see above), 51–65, 68–70, 86, 101, 103, 108–110, 122, 124, 131, 133, 138–145. Pss. 42–49, 84–85 and 87–88 are associated with the sons of Korah, while 50 and 73–83 are associated with Asaph. These account for almost all of the 'named' psalms; there are thirty-four nameless or 'orphan' psalms.

3

It will be observed that the 'Davidic' psalms fall predomin-
antly in the first half of the Psalter (fifty-five of Pss. 1–72 are
'Davidic') while the 'orphan' psalms are found mainly in the
second half. This may indicate that in the first instance,
collections of 'Davidic' psalms were made, and that in the
later stages of the compilation of the Psalter, anonymous
psalms were added.

The meaning of the Hebrew phrase *le dāwīd* has been much
discussed. Traditionally, it was taken to denote Davidic
authorship. In modern scholarship, it has often been taken
to mean 'belonging to the Davidic collection', while a third
view is that the phrase was meant by those who added it to
denote authorship, but that these editors were not guided by
any reliable tradition. There is probably some truth in all
three of these views.

The Old Testament contains several references to David's
skill as a musician and singer (e.g. 1 Sam. 16: 17–23; 2 Sam.
1: 17–27; Amos 6: 5) and it is reasonable to assume that
David was the author of some of the psalms, even if we have
no means of discovering exactly which. It is also possible that
from early times these psalms were headed *le dāwīd*. Later
scribes are also likely to have claimed Davidic authorship for
psalms by prefacing them with this title, although reliable
tradition was lacking. That the phrase *le dāwīd* might also
indicate a collection can be argued as follows. Beginning with
Ps. 42, we have the Elohistic Psalter (Pss. 42–83), so called
because an editor or editors seem to have altered the divine
name in the psalms from an original 'the LORD' to 'God'
(Hebrew *'elōhīm*, thus the term 'Elohistic'). This can be seen
if Ps. 14 is compared with Ps. 53 in the English; and the edit-
ing is crudely apparent in the Hebrew of Ps. 80, though not
in the English translation. This editorial treatment of the
divine name begins immediately after the first block of
'Davidic' psalms (3–41), and it is thus reasonable to assume
that Pss. 3–41 once existed as a separate collection from 42–83,
because they escaped this editorial work. Further, since all but

one of Pss. 3–41 are entitled *le dāwīd*, it is reasonable to say that the title indicates a collection as well as authorship. If we examine the psalms ascribed to the sons of Korah, we see that most of them have an interest in Zion, the temple and worship, from which it is usually concluded that the sons of Korah were a band of temple singers. For the name Asaph, see 1 Chron. 16: 4–7; 2 Chron. 35: 15.

With the help of these points, the following suggestions can be made about the growth of the Psalter. (i) There first existed several separate collections of psalms: two Davidic collections (Pss. 3–41 and 51–72 – cp. 72: 20) probably containing genuine psalms of David and others attributed to him; a Korahite collection (Pss. 42–49, 84–85, 87–88) and an Asaphite collection (Pss. 50, 73–83). (ii) An Elohistic Psalter was compiled from three collections – the second Davidic, part of the Korahite, and the Asaphite, to form the group of psalms, 42–83. This collection was subjected to editorial revision in which the divine name 'the LORD' was changed to 'God' (*'elōhīm*). It is also possible that the Elohistic Psalter extended as far as Ps. 88, and that the editorial alteration of the divine name proceeded no further than Ps. 83. (iii) The first Davidic collection and the Elohistic Psalter were joined together. (iv) Numerous further additions were made, about which we can only guess. It is probable that Ps. 1 was composed to be the beginning of the whole Psalter, and possible that Ps. 119 at one point marked its conclusion. If this is so, then Pss. 120–134 which are each entitled 'A song of ascents' would have been attached as a block following on from Ps. 119, and Pss. 138–145 may have been a small group of Davidic psalms which were added at a late stage to the Psalter. (Pss. 135–137 lack titles, and it is impossible to say why or when they were placed after Pss. 120–134.)

The division of the Psalter into five books (Pss. 1–41, 42–72, 73–89, 90–106, 107–150) presumably dates from the time of the completion of the Psalter, probably in the third century B.C. It is usually held that the Psalter was divided into five books on analogy with the five books of the Pentateuch. However, we have already suggested that long before the Psalter was complete, Pss. 3–41 and 42–83 probably existed as separate collections, and in the commentary on Ps. 72, it is suggested that the doxology of 72: 18f. was added to that psalm before the Psalter was divided into books by means of doxologies. Ps. 72: 18f. may have served as the model for the other doxologies.

Although we know little about how the psalms came to be arranged in their present order, the process may not have been entirely haphazard. Pss. 105 and 106 are clearly complementary, and the unrelieved pessimism of Ps. 88 is immediately followed by the affirmation 'I will sing the story of thy love, O LORD' in 89: 1.

HISTORY OF INTERPRETATION

It has long been recognized that the psalms are rich and varied in content, including praise, prayer and lament. Commentators in all ages have recognized their applicability to many situations in the religious life of the individual and the community, and it is probable that even in the Old Testament period, psalms were reinterpreted in the light of new situations. Thus, Ps. 79, which speaks of enemies defiling Jerusalem and its temple, is never quite explicit enough to enable us to identify the events for certain, and the reason may be that reinterpretation and spiritualizing of the psalm have obscured its references to the events which first called it forth. In 1 Chron. 16: 8–36, parts of Pss. 96, 105, 106 and 107 are quoted in respect of the institution of praise to God by David, after he had brought the Ark to Jerusalem.

Alongside, and not necessarily instead of, what we might call the spiritual interpretation of the psalms, there has been the historical interpretation. Traditional Jewish interpretation understood many of the psalms in the context of the life of David, and this approach was expressed already in some of the psalm titles. Thus the title of Ps. 51 reads 'To the choirmaster. A Psalm of David, when Nathan the prophet came to him after he had gone in to Bathsheba', linking the psalm with the incidents related in 2 Sam. 11–12. When, in the eighteenth and nineteenth centuries, critical scholarship began to abandon belief in the Davidic authorship of the psalms, the historical approach continued, but now many psalms were understood in the context of the history of ancient Irsael. If psalms spoke of Israel or Jerusalem surrounded by enemies, they were referred to the known crises of Israel's history, especially the siege of Jerusalem in 701 B.C. by the Assyrian king Sennacherib. An extreme form of this approach connected some, or even all, of the psalms with events of the Maccabaean revolt and the rule of the Hasmonaean dynasty (169–63 B.C.).

In the present century, psalm studies have been dominated by the form-critical and cultic interpretations. The former, associated with the German, Hermann Gunkel, sought to classify the psalms into types according to their formal structure, and then to suggest a context in the religious life of Israel for the types. The latter, associated with the Norwegian, Sigmund Mowinckel, attempted to reconstruct the worship of the Jerusalem temple, especially as it centred around the king, and it was based on material about worship among ancient Israel's neighbours, as well as upon allusions in the psalms themselves. Subsequent scholarship has criticized these pioneering efforts. Gunkel's psalm types have been considerably modified, and doubt has been cast on the validity of some of Mowinckel's reconstructions. However, the work of these scholars has left a permanent mark on the interpretation of the psalms. Classification of psalms into types on the basis of their formal pattern or structure may be subjective, and unconsciously use content as well as form; but it is useful to consider as a group the so-called individual laments (e.g. Pss. 3–7, 13–14, 17, 22, 25–26), the psalms of the kingship of God (Pss. 47, 93, 96–99), or the psalms of Zion (Pss. 46, 48, 76, 84, 87, 122), to name only three groups. Also, attempts to reconstruct the worship of the Jerusalem temple have drawn attention to important features of ancient Israelite religion, such as the role of the king, and the covenant between God and the house of David.

7

No commentator, then, can fail to be indebted to the form-critical and cultic approaches to the psalms; but the usefulness of the approaches can be exaggerated. For example, to label a psalm as an individual lament is sometimes to say nothing that could not be observed by an intelligent reader, and further, if psalms are tied too closely to a particular suggested 'original setting', this may obscure the fact that the psalms were certainly reinterpreted within the Old Testament period, and seen in a fuller perspective in later Jewish and Christian interpretation. Also, concentration on the 'original setting' may sometimes make it difficult for the reader to regard a particular psalm as anything more than interesting information about obsolete ceremonies from a remote and alien culture.

In the present commentary, the writers have tried to strike a balance between the spiritual, historical, form-critical and cultic approaches, seeing value in each where appropriate. The writers have also tried to bring out the religious teaching of permanent value which they believe the psalms to contain.

THE CHARACTER OF THE N.E.B. TRANSLATION

For the translator of the Old Testament, the psalms present some major difficulties. First, it is often not clear from a given psalm what exactly it is about; it may be open to two or more interpretations depending on how a difficult Hebrew word or phrase is regarded. Sometimes, the translator will translate a psalm according to a general view of its meaning which he has arrived at not so much by looking at the psalm as a whole, but by studying the difficult Hebrew word or phrase, and comparing it with similar phrases elsewhere in the Old Testament or in ancient Near Eastern literature. Alternatively, he may let the content of the psalm as a whole override the way in which he translates a difficult word or phrase. In such cases, translators will not claim absolute certainty for their translation; it will represent the best that they feel they can do in a difficult case.

A second reason for the difficulty in translating the psalms arises from the use and re-use of the psalms in Old Testament times, and later in the synagogue and in the church. The psalms can be understood at so many different levels that really adequate translation is impossible. One result of this is that translations of the psalms have different characters, depending on the general approach adopted by their translators. If one compares Ps. 84 in the N.E.B., the Authorized Version and the Psalter of the Book of Common Prayer, the different characters of these renderings are clearly apparent. The Prayer Book version, dating from 1540, preserves some of the early Christian Greek and Latin interpretations of the psalms, with modifications from continental Reformation sources. It presents Ps. 84 as a description of worship and pilgrimage in such a way that the earthly Jerusalem about which the psalm speaks is a veiled symbol for the heavenly Jerusalem, and the pilgrimage to Zion is a symbol for that pilgrimage which is the whole of the religious life of an individual. The Authorized Version is much more literal, and in its attempt to give a faithful rendering of the Hebrew, it sometimes produces nonsense, as in verse 5, where it has 'Blessed is the man whose strength is in thee; in whose heart are the ways of them.' On a superficial reading, the Authorized Version conveys less than the Prayer Book version. The N.E.B. adopts the view that the psalm was sung in connection with a pilgrimage to Zion in ancient Israel. It achieves a consistency of interpretation with the occasional help of a radical treatment of the Hebrew text, but unlike the Prayer Book version, allows no hints that the psalm could be seen in a wider perspective. The difference between these translations of Ps. 84 is not that one is more 'correct' than the others. At one or two points, the N.E.B. is doubtless more correct from the point of view of Hebrew than the Prayer Book version, but at the same time the N.E.B. contains some conjectures that are at best only possibilities. The proper way to assess a translation is to examine it in the light of its overall approach, and in the case of the N.E.B., this approach seems to have been to render the psalms according to what the translators believed to be the setting of individual psalms in the life of ancient Israel.

Because in the present commentary the writers have sought to see the psalms in a wider perspective than their suggested original setting in ancient Israel, they have regarded the N.E.B. as a witness to the original Hebrew, but they have felt free to criticize the N.E.B. translation, and to draw attention to more traditional approaches to interpretation, where they have felt that the N.E.B. implies too narrow a view, or a misleading interpretation.

LITERARY AND POETIC CHARACTERISTICS OF THE PSALMS

The psalms are poetry, and they employ several literary devices. Some of these characteristics are apparent, even in translation. Nine psalms, 9–10, 25, 34, 37, 111, 112, 119 and 145, are acrostic psalms, in which individual lines or verses, or groups of verses, begin with successive letters of the Hebrew alphabet. Possibly, the psalmists regarded Hebrew as a special language because in it God had allowed his law and the record of his mighty deeds to be written. The alphabet perhaps symbolized the whole of the Hebrew language, and so, in composing psalms in which verses began with each successive letter of the alphabet, the psalmists were reminding themselves of the marvellous fact that the oracles of God had been recorded in Hebrew. The acrostic principle is at its most elaborate in Ps. 119, where each group of eight verses begins with a successive letter of the alphabet.

In some psalms, refrains can be noticed. In Pss. 42–43 the refrain

      'How deep I am sunk in misery,
        groaning in my distress:

> yet I will wait for God;
> I will praise him continually,
> my deliverer, my God'

occurs at 42: 5, 11; 43: 5. In Ps. 46: 7, 11 the refrain

> 'The LORD of Hosts is with us,
> the God of Jacob our high stronghold'

is found. Refrains such as that in Ps. 46 and at 80: 3, 7, 19 suggest that they were congregational responses, while in Ps. 136, the fact that every second line is

> 'his love endures for ever'

suggests that this psalm, at least, was used antiphonally, perhaps with the congregation responding every other line with the refrain. In an ancient Hebrew manuscript discovered in caves near the Dead Sea, Ps. 145 appears with a refrain after each verse.

Hebrew poetry is not characterized by rhyme, but by stress and sense. Unfortunately, we do not know how Hebrew was pronounced in biblical times, and what is written in the commentaries about stress must inevitably rest a good deal upon conjecture. In any case, no translation can reproduce the stress in the Hebrew. The sense aspect of Hebrew poetry can, however, be recognized in translation. Often, the sense of a line is exactly reproduced in the next line:

> 'what is man that thou shouldst remember him,
> mortal man that thou shouldst care for him?' (8: 4)

> 'O LORD, who may lodge in thy tabernacle?
> Who may dwell on thy holy mountain?'   (15: 1)

Sometimes, the sense of the first line is taken up and slightly expanded in the second:

> 'The LORD is righteous in his acts;
> he brings justice to all who have been wronged' (103: 6)

or the sense of the first line may be followed by an opposite
sense:

> 'The LORD watches over the way of the righteous,
>> but the way of the wicked is doomed.' (1: 6)

Another device is for the sense to be repeated, until it reaches
a climax:

'O LORD, the ocean lifts up, the ocean lifts up its clamour;
the ocean lifts up its pounding waves.
Mightier far than the noise of great waters, than the breakers
of the sea,
Is the LORD who is on high.' (93: 3f. The N.E.B. is here
adapted to follow the order
of the Hebrew more closely.)

Sometimes, the poetry employs metaphor:

> 'A herd of bulls surrounds me,
>> great bulls of Bashan beset me.
>> Ravening and roaring lions
>> open their mouths wide against me' (22: 12f.)

or simile:

> I am like a desert-owl in the wilderness,
> an owl that lives among ruins.
> Thin and meagre, I wail in solitude,
> like a bird that flutters on the roof-top. (102: 6f.)

These are just some examples of the literary and poetic devices
that are used in the Psalter, and the psalms can be much better
appreciated if we bear them in mind as we read the biblical
text. The psalms are religious texts, but their writers were
literary craftsmen. They not only strove to find the best
possible language in which to utter their prayers and praises;
they also probably appreciated that poetry alone was the
medium in which it was possible to come closest to the task of
expressing the unspeakable mysteries of God in the language
of men.

THE CONTENTS OF THE PSALTER

(Some psalms appear under more than one heading. This usually means that they are adaptable for use in different situations, but occasionally it means that the psalm's interpretation is open to debate.)

A. *Hymns*

In praise of God for what he is, good, loving, faithful, etc.: 100, 103, 111, 113, 145, 146, 150.

To God the creator: 8, 19, 24, 29, 104.

To God the bounteous provider: 65, 84, 144, 147.

To the Lord of Israel's history: 68, 78, 105, 111, 114, 117.

To God both as creator and as Lord of history: 33, 89, 95, 135, 136, 144, 148.

To God the mighty, the victorious: 68, 76, 149.

On the final victory of God and his people: 46, 47, 48, 68, 93, 96, 97, 98, 99.

'The LORD is king': 47, 93, 96, 97, 98, 99.

'Songs of Zion' (cp. 137: 3): 46, 48, 76, 84, 87, 122.

Suitable for use by pilgrims: 84, 121, 122, 125, 127.

B. *National psalms*

Prayers for deliverance or victory: 44, 60, 74, 79, 80, 83, 85, 89, 108, 126, 129, 137, 144.

Prayers for blessing and continued protection: 67, 115, 125.

General prayers for mercy or restoration: 90, 106, 123.

Psalms that call the people to obedience: 81, 95.

Royal psalms: 2, 18, 20, 21, 45, 72, 89, 101, 110, 132.

Other psalms that include prayers for the king: 61, 63, 80, 84.

Other psalms that make reference to the king: 78, 122, 144.

C. *Prayers of the individual in time of need*

For protection, deliverance or vindication in the face of persecution: 3, 5, 7, 12, 17, 25, 35, 40, 41, 54, 55, 56, 57, 59, 64, 70, 86, 120, 123, 140, 141, 142, 143.

For use in time of suffering and dereliction: 6, 13, 22, 28, 31, 38, 39, 42–43, 69, 71, 77, 88, 102, 143.

For justice or personal vindication: 7, 17, 26, 35, 69, 94, 109.

For forgiveness: 6, 25, 38, 51, 130.

Expressing a deep longing for the nearness of God: 22, 25, 27, 38, 42, 51, 61, 63, 73, 77, 84, 130, 143.

Expressing confidence or trust: 4, 11, 16, 23, 27, 52, 62, 91, 121, 131.

Suitable for use in a night vigil: 5, 17, 22, 27, 30, 46, 57, 59, 63, 108, 143.

The 'Penitential Psalms' in Christian tradition: 6, 32, 38, 51, 102, 130, 143.

D. *Thanksgiving psalms*

For national deliverance: 118 (?), 124.

For personal deliverance: 18, 30, 34, 66, 116, 118, 138.

For forgiveness: 32.

For the knowledge of God's continuing love and care: 92, 107.

See also above: A. *Hymns.*

E. *Psalms giving instruction or containing meditations on various themes*

On the Law: 1, 19, 119.

On the qualities required in the citizens of God's kingdom: 15, 24, 101, 112.

On corruption in society: 11, 12, 14, 53, 55, 58, 82, 94.

On the lot of mankind, the problem of evil and suffering, the ways of the godly and the wicked: 1, 9–10, 14, 36, 37, 39, 49, 52, 53, 58, 62, 73, 90, 92, 94, 112.

On God's judgement: 50, 75, 82.

On God's blessings: 127, 128, 133.

On God's omniscience: 139.

F. *Psalms generally accounted Messianic in Christian interpretation*

The royal Messiah: 2, 18, 20, 21, 45, 61, 72, 89, 110, 118, 132.

The suffering Messiah: 22, 35, 41, 55, 69, 109.

The second Adam, fulfiller of human destiny: 8, 16, 40.
Psalms describing God as king, creator, etc., applied to Jesus
   in the New Testament: 68, 97, 102.

G. *Special categories*

Acrostics: 9–10, 25, 34, 37, 111, 112, 119, 145.
Songs of ascent: 120–134.
Hallel: 113–118.
Hallelujah: 146–150.

✳   ✳   ✳   ✳   ✳   ✳   ✳   ✳   ✳   ✳   ✳   ✳   ✳

BOOK 2 (*cont.*)

WASH ME, WHITER THAN SNOW

51

Be gracious to me, O God, in thy true love;   1
in the fullness of thy mercy blot out my misdeeds.

Wash away all my guilt   2
   and cleanse me from my sin.
For well I know my misdeeds,   3
and my sins confront me all the day long.
Against thee, thee only, I have sinned   4
and done what displeases thee,
so that thou mayest be proved right in thy charge
   and just in passing sentence.

In iniquity I was brought to birth   5
and my mother conceived me in sin;
yet, though thou hast hidden the truth in darkness,   6
through this mystery thou dost teach me wisdom.
Take hyssop[a] and sprinkle me, that I may be clean;   7
wash me, that I may become whiter than snow;

[a] *Or* marjoram.

8   let me hear the sounds of joy and gladness,
       let the bones dance which thou hast broken.
9   Turn away thy face from my sins
           and blot out all my guilt.

10 Create a pure heart in me, O God,
        and give me a new and steadfast spirit;
11   do not drive me from thy presence
       or take thy holy spirit from me;
12   revive in me the joy of thy deliverance
           and grant me a willing spirit to uphold me.

13   I will teach transgressors the ways that lead to thee,
       and sinners shall return to thee again.
14 O LORD God, my deliverer, save me from bloodshed,*a*
       and I will sing the praises of thy justice.
15   Open my lips, O Lord,
       that my mouth may proclaim thy praise.
16   Thou hast no delight in sacrifice;
       if I brought thee an offering, thou wouldst not
           accept it.
17   My sacrifice, O God, is a broken spirit;
       a wounded*b* heart, O God, thou wilt not despise.

18   Let it be thy pleasure to do good to Zion,
           to build anew the walls of Jerusalem.
19   Then only shalt thou delight in the appointed
           sacrifices;*c*
       then shall young bulls be offered on thy altar.

[a] *Or* from punishment by death.
[b] *So Pesh.; Heb.* a broken and wounded.
[c] *Prob. rdg.; Heb. adds* a whole-offering and one wholly consumed.

* This is the fourth and most moving of the 'Penitential Psalms' (see p. 14, section C). The title reads 'A Psalm of David, when Nathan the prophet came to him, after he had gone in to Bathsheba', and scholars have noted certain points of contact between this psalm and 2 Sam. 11f. The Bathsheba affair was a glaring stain on the record of one who is otherwise upheld by tradition as a figure of godliness (cp. 1 Kings 15: 5). But David was forgiven by God when he repented (2 Sam. 12: 13) and the title reminds the sinner that he too may be cleansed and restored to the way of righteousness. Following his opening plea (verse 1) the psalmist confesses his sins (verses 2–4), pleads for cleansing (verses 5–9) and renewal (verses 10–12), offers himself to God in thanksgiving (verses 13–17), and prays for the restoration of Jerusalem (verses 18f.). The conclusion is enigmatic. It does not cohere well with the rest of the psalm and must have been added some time after the fall of the city in 586 B.C. This could mean that the whole psalm eventually came to be used as a national plea for forgiveness and restoration. Alternatively, the individual may have been taught to see his own sin as a further augmentation of the national heritage of sin that had caused the disaster and hence to pray for his city as well as for himself. Notwithstanding, the psalm remains penitential and is a most eloquent witness to man's inner consciousness of sin and his deep longing for forgiveness and the joy of God's presence.

1. *Opening plea. Be gracious:* his prayer is for kindness that cannot be deserved. *true love:* Hebrew *ḥesed*; this word describes the loving relationship that exists in the covenant between God and his people. God's *ḥesed* is seen in his faithfulness to his promises of protection and blessing; the Israelite's *ḥesed* is his loyalty and obedience to God's demands. The psalmist has broken his part of the covenant, but he knows that God keeps faith (cp. 2 Tim. 2: 13), that despite his errancy and unworthiness, he still belongs to the family of God and can rest his hope in God's faithful love and compassion (cp. Luke 15: 17f.). The Hebrew word for *mercy* suggests the tender

warmth of feeling that a mother may have for her child. In this verse and the next three different expressions are used for sin and forgiveness, but the parallelism suggests that the writer is employing a stylistic device to emphasize his need for thorough cleansing, rather than making a doctrinal statement about the nature of his sins (cp. Ps. 32: 1f.). *blot out:* as it were from some heavenly record-book (cp. Exod. 32: 32; Dan. 7: 10). *misdeeds:* deliberate acts of rebellion.

2–4. He prays for cleansing and confesses his sin.

2. *Wash away:* the Hebrew suggests the picture of a dirty garment being vigorously scrubbed and pounded (cp. verse 7). *guilt* implies deliberate wrong-doing. *cleanse:* a verb used in the levitical rituals for declaring a man clean after the healing of a skin-disease (Lev. 13: 6, 34), though it does have more general applications. *sin:* wandering from God's way.

3. Feelings of perpetual and inescapable (*all the day long*) guilt or oppressive (*confront me*) inner tension resulting from awareness (*I know*) of sin are a necessary prerequisite to true repentance.

4. *Against thee, thee only:* all sin is ultimately against God and breaks man's relationship with him. Thus David repented of his sin against Uriah with the words 'I have sinned against the LORD' (2 Sam. 12: 13). *so that:* the N.E.B. translation implies that the psalmist committed his sins so that God's justice could be glorified, but this interpretation is totally alien to the mood of the psalm. The clause must stand as the conclusion to all that goes before it in verses 1–4: 'I make this confession, asking for forgiveness and acknowledging my sin, so that . . .' His confession is thus an acknowledgement that God's punishment was justified.

5–9. Though his very nature is sinful, God can purify and restore him.

5. The psalmist's concern is not to confess his parents' sins, nor to condemn the processes of conception and birth. His intention is to express his own very personal feelings of utter degradation, his consciousness of deep corruption in his whole

being that has been there from the start (cp. Ps. 58: 3). Nor is his confession offered to excuse his actions. Its purpose is to express grief at the recognition of his and every man's tragedy to be born into a world of sin.

6. Though no man can grasp the whole truth about himself and God, yet through *this mystery* of sin and inner torment an element of *wisdom* or understanding is imparted (cp. Job 38: 36). But the N.E.B. does not offer the most widely accepted translation and it is possible to render this verse as a prayer for purity and illumination: 'Behold, thou desirest truth in the inward being; therefore teach me wisdom in my secret heart' (Revised Standard Version).

7. *Take hyssop and sprinkle me:* literally 'purge me with hyssop'. Hyssop was a small bushy plant (probably the Syrian marjoram) used as a sprinkler in purification and cleansing rituals (Lev. 14: 4; cp. Exod. 12: 22). For the whiteness of snow as a symbol of purity, see Isa. 1: 18.

8. It is no mere priestly blessing he wants to hear. Inner *joy and gladness* are the tangible marks of God's presence and are of the very essence of religion (cp. Ps. 4: 6f.; John 15: 11). But his whole frame (*bones*) has been shattered by the awareness of God's displeasure and he longs for the healing of forgiveness that will permit his spirit to *dance* and rejoice once more.

9. *blot out:* recalling the image of verse 1 he concludes his prayer for forgiveness.

10–12. He prays for renewal.

10. *Create:* pardon is the recognition of a changed heart, but to ensure continued community with God a *new* creation is needed, a new inner life, a new *heart* and *spirit*. Ezekiel used this language to describe the new covenant (Ezek. 11: 19; 36: 26) and Jesus illustrated the point exactly in the parable of the unclean spirit (Matt. 12: 43–5).

11f. *thy holy spirit:* this expression, found elsewhere in the Old Testament only in Isa. 63: 10f., is, as the parallelism shows, a synonym for *thy presence*. But the experience of God's presence brings *the joy* of a restored relationship, together with the will and the power to endure in faithfulness (cp. Ezek. 36: 27), and is therefore comparable with the New Testament experience of God's Spirit (cp. Gal. 5: 22).

13–17. He pledges himself to a life of witness and praise.

13. God's gifts and blessings are not solely for personal enjoyment, but for the upbuilding of the community (cp. 1 Cor. 12), and part of this work is testimony to God's saving acts (Pss. 9: 1f.; 22: 22). The verb *return* is frequently used by the prophets when calling for conversion.

14. *bloodshed:* the stain of sins; there may be an implicit comparison with David's murder of Uriah. The N.E.B. footnote suggests 'impending death' as the awaited consequence of his sins. *God, my deliverer:* or 'God of my salvation' (see on Ps. 3: 2).

15. He longs to worship God, but his guilt acts like an impediment to his speech and prevents him from doing so. His prayer is therefore for pardon and for a heart to sing God's praise.

16f. There are many such passages in the Old Testament and, as here, they normally contrast the ritualistic offering of sacrifice with heartfelt dedication (cp. Pss. 40: 6; 69: 30f.). They are not to be read as repudiations of the sacrificial system, but as declarations that sacrifice is acceptable to God only if the worshipper's attitude is right. Even so, the law does not prescribe atoning sacrifices for more serious offences like murder and adultery, the sins of David in 2 Sam. 11–12. In such cases penitence is the only course open to the sinner.

17. *My sacrifice, O God:* the Hebrew reads 'the sacrifices of (= acceptable to) God'. The phrases *broken spirit* and *wounded heart* are probably synonyms expressing sorrow and penitent humility.

18f. A prayer from the time of the exile for the rebuilding of Jerusalem and the renewal of temple worship.

18. *Zion:* see on Pss. 2: 6 and 68: 15f. *the walls of Jerusalem* were rebuilt under Nehemiah about 444 B.C. It is possible to spiritualize this verse and identify the fallen city with the penitent worshipper, but it is unlikely that this was the original intention.

19. When restoration has taken place God will again 'accept' and *delight in* (cp. verse 16) sacrifices of the cult. Again it is possible to spiritualize and think of the restored penitent bringing acceptable offerings, but the ritualistic interest, highlighted by the gloss which the N.E.B. has relegated to the footnote, suggests that a priest in exile wanted to correct the 'misleading' idea in verses 16–17 that God wants only spiritual sacrifices. ✶

WHY MAKE WICKEDNESS YOUR BOAST?

52

Why make your wickedness your boast, you man of   1–2
     might,
forging wild lies all day against*a* God's loyal servant?
Your slanderous tongue is sharp as a razor.

  You love evil and not good,   3
  falsehood, not speaking the truth;
cruel gossip you love and slanderous talk.   4

  So may God*b* pull you down to the ground,   5
  sweep you away, leave you ruined and homeless,
    uprooted from the land of the living.

  The righteous will look on, awestruck,*c*   6
    and laugh at his plight:
    'This is the man', they say,   7
    'who does not make God his refuge,
  but trusts in his great wealth
    and takes refuge in wild lies.'
But I am like a spreading olive-tree in God's house;   8

[a] against: *prob. rdg., cp. Pesh.; Heb. om.*
[b] *Or* So God will.
[c] *Or, with some MSS.,* rejoicing, *cp. Pss. 58: 10; 107: 42.*

for I trust in God's true love for ever and ever.
9   I will praise thee for ever for what thou hast done,
     and glorify thy name among thy loyal servants;
          for that is good.

* Despite the opening 'Why', there is no discussion about the
injustice of life in this psalm, as there is in some others that deal
with the oppression of the faithful (e.g. Pss. 37, 49; see p. 14,
section E). The main intention here is to affirm faith in God's
care for his servants. The psalmist accuses the wicked of
deceitful slander (verses 1–4), envisages their downfall (verses
5–7) and contrasts the assurance obtained by faith in God
(verses 8–9). Hence the psalm is an expression of trust suitable
for use by anyone who finds himself at the mercy of a
'slanderous tongue'. The Hebrew gives it a title ascribing it to
David, 'when Doeg, the Edomite, came and told Saul,
"David has come to the house of Ahimelech"' (cp. 1 Sam.
21–2), thus inviting the worshipper to trust in the God who
protected David in circumstances similar to his own. The
psalm itself gives no evidence of its date of writing.

1–4. The psalmist denounces the wicked, presumably before
God rather than in their presence.

1f. The title *man of might* would normally be given to a
heroic figure, but there is sarcasm in its use here. This man,
whose *boast* should be in God alone (Jer. 9: 23f.; 2 Cor. 10: 17),
has made *wickedness* his idol; he should be rejoicing in God's
name *all day* (Ps. 89: 16), not perversely *forging wild lies*
(literally 'ruin') against *God's loyal servant* (ḥāsīd, cp. verse 9
and see on Ps. 30: 4); instead of singing the praises of God's
justice (Ps. 51: 14), his tongue speaks to inflict harm like a
sharp *razor* (cp. Jas. 3: 5–10).

3f. His sense of values is completely perverted and totally
contrary to the will of God (Amos 5: 14f.). *You love . . . you
love*: the repetition suggests deliberate wilfulness, not just
accidental attraction.

5–7. When judgement comes the faith of the righteous will be vindicated.

5. The N.E.B. follows the Septuagint in treating this verse as a prayer, but the indicative form of verses 6–7 suggests that the translation 'So God will' (N.E.B. footnote) is to be preferred. Thus the psalmist declares the certainty of judgement (cp. Pss. 9–10, 14) as a warning to the wicked and an assurance to the faithful. God will *pull . . . down* the godless *to the ground* (Hebrew reads 'for ever') like a building being demolished and leave him *ruined and homeless* (literally 'tear you from your tent'). The psalmist himself may look forward to being 'like a spreading olive-tree' (verse 8), but the fate of the wicked is to be *uprooted*. His destiny is Sheol, the land of the dead, where there can be no communion with the God whose presence means life (Ps. 49: 11–15). *the land of the living:* the sphere of God's activity, both in this life (see on Ps. 27: 13) and also in eternity (verse 8).

6. *awestruck, and laugh:* laughter tempered with awe can hardly be vindictive, though some manuscripts read 'rejoicing' (see the N.E.B. footnote), suggesting the comparison with Ps. 58: 10 where the note of awe is also lacking. God himself laughs at the folly of the wicked (Ps. 37: 13) and so the psalmist looks to the day when the faith of the righteous will be vindicated and they can join in the laughter of heaven. Cp. the extension of this notion to the picture of final judgement in Rev. 18: 20.

7. The sense of security that *wealth* and *lies* provide for the wicked is false (cp. Ps. 49: 6), for man's only trustworthy *refuge* is God. *in wild lies:* this translation finds no support in the versions. The Hebrew reads 'in his lust' and the Peshitta offers a synonym for wealth.

8f. But trust in God gives real permanence and leads to joyous praise.

8. *God's true love*, his *ḥesed* (see on Ps. 51: 1), is the basis of the *ḥāsīd's* faith (see verses 1f. above) and, unlike the wealth of the ungodly, it offers a sure and eternally enduring 'refuge' for those who *trust* in it. This truth is affirmed in a double simile.

The *olive-tree* is large, long-living, evergreen and not easily
'uprooted' (verse 5), a symbol of stability (cp. Ps. 1: 3).
Similarly, *God's house* symbolizes security, for there the guest
enjoys the protection of God himself (cp. Ps. 23: 6).

9. The psalmist's praise, unlike the slanderous utterance of
the wicked (verses 1–4), is an expression of heart-felt gratitude
for what God has done in making known his *ḥesed* (verse 8).
Thus it is good that the worshipper should *glorify* (Hebrew
reads 'hope for') God amongst his *loyal servants* (*ḥasīdīm*, cp.
verse 1), for in so doing not only is his own joy increased, but
their faith is strengthened (cp. Ps. 22: 22). ✶

THERE IS NO GOD?

53

^a1   The impious fool says in his heart,
       'There is no God.'
    How vile men are, how depraved and loathsome;
       not one does anything good!

2   God looks down from heaven
       on all mankind
    to see if any act wisely,
       if any seek out God.

3 But all are unfaithful, all are rotten to the core;
       not one does anything good,
       no, not even one.

4   Shall they not rue it,
    these evildoers who devour my people
       as men devour bread,
       and never call upon God?

[a] *Verses 1–6: cp. Ps. 14: 1–7.*

There they were in dire alarm*a*   5
when God scattered them.
The crimes of the godless were frustrated;*b*
  for God had rejected them.
If only Israel's deliverance might come out of Zion!   6
  When God restores his people's fortunes,
let Jacob rejoice, let Israel be glad.

✽ This is a variant form of Ps. 14, but apart from the substitution of the title 'God' for 'the LORD' (see further, p. 4), it is
only in verse 5 that there are any marked differences. Its theme
is the universality of godlessness. It suggests a depressing
comparison between the contemporary situation and conditions before the Flood (verses 1–3), but as the psalmist's
thoughts turn from the world to God, to the contemplation of
his power and his protective love for his people, confidence is
restored. In its present form this psalm may date from the exile
(see verse 6), but its thought is timeless.

1–3. The psalmist laments the godlessness of mankind.

1. *The impious fool* is not a simple-minded person; he could
be a very clever man, but he is one who has closed his mind
to God (cp. Rom. 1: 22). He is not a militant atheist. He may
not even be interested in the question of God's existence and
probably never states openly, *'There is no God.'* These are
words he *says in his heart*, they represent his inner disposition.
He lives and behaves as though there were no need to reckon
with any God. For him God is simply irrelevant (cp. Ps. 10: 4).
The consequence of this kind of attitude is always depravity in
some form (cp. Rom. 1: 28–32). *How vile men are:* as in Ps.
12: 1–2, the psalmist may have specific categories of person in
mind, but this and his following statements are framed as

[a] *So some MSS.; others add* there was no fear.
[b] The crimes . . . frustrated: *prob. rdg.; Heb. obscure.*

generalizations about human degradation, suggesting a comparison with the corruption that existed, according to Gen. 6: 5–13, before the Flood.

2. *looks down:* cp. Ps. 102: 19. Similarly God 'saw' the wickedness of mankind in Noah's day (Gen. 6: 5, 11) and 'came down to see' the corruption of Babel and Sodom (Gen. 11: 5; 18: 21). *if any act wisely:* unlike the fool of verse 1, the wise man will *seek out God*, for 'The fear of the LORD is the beginning of knowledge, but fools scorn wisdom and discipline' (Prov. 1: 7; cp. Ps. 111: 10). The contrast between folly and wisdom is a common feature of the wisdom literature.

3. On the generalization, see on verse 1; but verse 4 clearly indicates that *all* does not include the faithful, 'my people'. Paul cites parts of verses 1–3 in Rom. 3: 10–12 to illustrate his argument about universal human corruption.

4–7. The psalmist's thoughts now turn to judgement and with renewed confidence he offers prayer for the deliverance of his people.

4. *Shall they not rue it:* the more common rendering is 'Have they no knowledge', that is, presumably, of the punishment that awaits them. But the N.E.B.'s translation is equally possible and seems to fit the context better. Since the *evildoers*, whose oppressive acts are as natural to them as eating bread, are clearly the godless fools of verses 1–3 (cp. Ps. 10: 2–11), *my people* must be the community of the faithful.

5. The psalmist envisages a reversal of present conditions at the appearing of God. His picture is undoubtedly one that holds hope for the future, though it may be based on some past historical event, such as the deliverance from oppression in Egypt. The N.E.B. translators have introduced several emendations here in an attempt to bring this verse a little closer to Ps. 14: 5f., but it is better to retain the original readings, for the differences between the two texts are so great that they can only be explained in terms of deliberate re-editing and it is impossible to tell which is the more original. The general sense of Ps. 14: 5f. is that God protects the faithful, but Ps. 53: 5

lays greater stress on the destruction of the wicked and the
pictures, though somewhat obscure, have a more military
colour, perhaps likening the rout of the wicked to the panic-
stricken flight of an invading army from a corpse (bone)-
bestrewn battle-field. The Hebrew reads: 'There they were in
dire alarm, and there has been no alarm (like it before), for
God scattered the bones of him who encamped against you.
You put them to shame, for God had rejected them.'

6. It has been thought that this final prayer, expressed in the
form of a wish, is an addition from the time of the exile, but it
could equally be the worshipper's prayer for his people at any
time of persecution. The synonymous terms *Jacob* and *Israel*
would then denote, not the national unit, but the faithful
community that is afflicted by 'evildoers' within the territorial
borders of Israel (see on verse 4). *Zion* was the place of God's
abiding presence and hence a symbol of the source from which
Israel's deliverance might come (cp. Ps. 46: 5). ✶

GOD IS MY HELPER

54

Save me, O God, by the power of thy name,   1
    and vindicate me through thy might.
O God, hear my prayer,   2
    listen to my supplication.
Insolent men[a] rise to attack me,   3
ruthless men seek my life;
they give no thought to God.

But God is my helper,   4
    the Lord the mainstay of my life.
May their own malice recoil on my watchful foes;   5

[a] Insolent men: *so some MSS.; others* Strangers.

silence them by thy truth, O LORD.

6   I will offer thee a willing sacrifice
and praise thy name, for that is good;
7   God has rescued me from every trouble,
and I look on my enemies' downfall with delight.

* This psalm has a title in the Hebrew which ascribes it to David when he was betrayed by the Ziphites who 'came and said to Saul, "Is not David hiding among us?"' (cp. 1 Sam. 23: 19). The worshipper is thus invited to understand his own situation in the light of David's experience. The language is in fact very general and it is completely adaptable to a wide variety of occasions of oppression. Like many similar prayers for deliverance, it ends with a powerful profession of confidence that God's help is assured. It is virtually impossible to date this psalm.

1–3. He prays for rescue from his enemies.

1. *by the power of thy name:* literally 'by thy name', but God's name calls to mind his revealed character and is therefore a symbol of his presence and his power to save. *vindicate me:* or 'judge me'. God alone has the authority to pass the judgement that can silence his malicious foes (verse 5).

3. *Insolent men:* so several manuscripts and the otherwise identical Ps. 86: 14. The more widely attested reading is 'strangers' (cp. the N.E.B. footnote), perhaps referring to those outside the community of the faithful. *they give no thought to God:* because in their arrogance they think they are self-sufficient and have all but deified themselves (cp. Pss. 10: 3f.; 36: 1f.). But so obsessed are they with themselves that they have become *ruthless men*, not even shrinking from murder in the pursuit of their ends.

4–7. With assurance he anticipates his deliverance. So certain is the confidence expressed that some commentators believe these words could only have been uttered once release was effected, or at least after the utterance of an oracle promising such blessing. But verse 5 is prospective and it is more likely that the change of mood illustrates the psalmist's trust in God's faithfulness or 'truth' (cp. on Ps. 13: 5).

4. The issue cannot be in doubt, for *God is* (not 'will be') *my helper.*

5. The boomerang effect of sin (cp. Ps. 7: 16). *May . . . recoil:* the variant reading, 'he will cause to recoil', suggests more clearly the direct activity of God that the psalmist seeks, but it suits the parallelism better to read the whole verse as a prayer. *thy truth:* God's dependability, his quality of being true to his word (cp. on Ps. 25: 5). But whilst his promise means blessing for the faithful, it equally implies judgement for the wicked (see further on Ps. 69: 22–8).

6. The emphasis is on the word *willing* in the Hebrew. The psalmists constantly affirm that the disposition of the heart is more important than the ritual sacrifice (cp. Ps. 51: 16f.), but the worshipper's offering must be acceptable to God when, as here, it expresses a spontaneous gratitude. *praise thy name, for that is good:* cp. Ps. 52: 9.

7. *I look . . . with delight:* as he must do when he sees the defeat of evil; but his delight is an expression of joy at the triumph of faith rather than of vindictive gloating over the fate of his enemies. Though the theology differs little from New Testament teaching, the Hebraic form of expression sounds harsh, but at least it cautions against the modern tendency to underrate the reality of the power of evil. *

O THAT I COULD FLY AWAY AND BE AT REST

55

* 'The voice of Christ against the chiefs of the Jews and the traitor Judas' is the title given to this psalm in one manuscript of Jerome's Latin Version. Though verses 14–15 are hardly in keeping with the words of Jesus in Luke 23: 34, this late

Christian interpretation does exemplify the kind of situation in which this psalm would be appropriate. The sufferer is the object of an enmity so terrible that he longs to escape to some quiet, remote refuge (verses 1–9*b*). His whole environment is rife with hostility, but worse still, his adversaries are led by one who was once his intimate friend (verses 9*c*–15). Yet in his extremity he commits his case to God, expressing confidence that God will deliver him and bring judgement on his oppressors (verses 16–23). As in Ps. 11, where the psalmist is also tempted to flee his hostile surroundings, the lesson is that man's only sure refuge is to trust in God who ultimately 'will never let the righteous be shaken' (verse 22). The date of writing cannot be determined. ✶

1   Listen, O God, to my pleading,
          do not hide thyself when I pray.
2   Hear me and answer,
              for my cares give me no peace.
3   I am panic-stricken at the shouts of my enemies,
              at the shrill clamour of the wicked;
          for they heap trouble on me
              and they revile me in their anger.
4   My heart is torn with anguish
          and the terrors of death come upon me.
5   Fear and trembling overwhelm me
          and I shudder from head to foot.
6   *a*Oh that I had the wings of a dove
          to fly away and be at rest!
7   I should escape far away
              and find a refuge in the wilderness;
8   soon I should find myself a sanctuary
          from wind and storm,

[a] *Prob. rdg.; Heb. prefixes* And I said.

30

from the blasts of calumny, O Lord,   9
  from my enemies' contentious tongues.
I have seen violence and strife in the city;
  day and night they encircle it,   10
    all along its walls;
  it is filled with trouble and mischief,
    alive with rumour and scandal,   11
  and its public square is never free
    from violence and spite.

It was no enemy that taunted me,   12
  or I should have avoided him;
no adversary that treated me with scorn,
  or I should have kept out of his way.
It was you, a man of my own sort,   13
  my comrade, my own dear friend,
with whom I kept pleasant company   14–15
  in the house of God.

  May death strike them,
and may they*a* perish in confusion,
may they go down alive into Sheol;
  for their homes are haunts of evil!

* 1f. He beseeches God to heed his cry.
  1. *do not hide thyself:* that is, 'do not ignore me'; cp. Deut.
22: 1, 3, 4 where the same verb is used of unmerciful turning-
away from suffering.
  2. *my cares give me no peace:* literally 'I am restless in my
troubles', a phrase suggesting the agitation of a distracted
mind. His burden is more than persecution, for he feels he
could have coped with that. What tortures his mind is the
horror of a bewilderment he cannot resolve (verses 12–15).

[a] *Prob. rdg.; Heb.* we.

31

3-5. He describes the terrors that beset him.

3. *my enemies . . . the wicked:* since these include a former friend (verses 12-15) and he wishes them dead (verses 15, 23), they are clearly fellow human beings, but the language he uses shows that they have assumed nightmarish proportions in his mind. Thus he knows *panic* at the sound of their voice because it comes to him like *the shrill clamour* of witches or demons screeching curses in his ears. *they heap:* better 'they bring crashing down', again an image of terror.

4. *the terrors of death:* this phrase may simply mean 'deadly terrors' or 'terrifying thoughts about death', but in Job 18: 14 'terrors' are the underworld attendants of Death, their king (cp. Ps. 73: 19).

5. *Fear and trembling:* not awe in God's presence, but horror and anxiety that cause his whole body to shudder.

6-9b. He longs to escape to some quiet haven of rest.

6. *the wings of a dove:* the Hebrew reads 'wings like a dove', which makes better sense. The psalmist probably thinks of the rock dove with its nest among the crags of some inaccessible rock-face (Jer. 48: 28), but the simile may also suggest his own timidity in the face of hostility. 'And I said' (N.E.B. footnote) is omitted because it appears to upset the Hebrew poetic metre.

7. Cp. Jer. 9: 2.

8-9b. Like a traveller seeking shelter in a storm, so he longs for *sanctuary* from the raging of his enemies.

9a-b. The N.E.B. translation assumes a number of small vowel changes, but the Hebrew reads 'confuse, Lord, divide their speech', suggesting an allusion to the curse of Babel (Gen. 11: 5-9). His prayer would then be that the alliance of hatred should be broken up, that his enemies should be dispersed, like the men of Babel in primaeval times.

9c-11. He describes the violence and hatred in his social environment.

9c. *the city:* the psalmist's own community, not necessarily Jerusalem.

10. *they:* perhaps the enemies, but more probably 'violence and strife' personified. They are likened to watchmen patrolling the city's defences and the walls that should have betokened security are now a symbol of imprisonment and terror.

11. *its public square:* where men meet to transact business, hold legal assembly or simply for friendly conversation. To the sufferer this has become a place *alive with rumour . . . scandal . . . violence and spite*, instead of a centre of order and justice filled with friends.

12–15. More bitter than all else is the treachery of a former friend.

12. *I should have avoided him:* this translation suits the parallelism, but the Hebrew reads 'I should have borne it.' The taunt of an acknowledged enemy is bearable because expected, and steps would normally be taken anyhow to keep *out of his way*, but it is not so with a friend.

13. *a man of my own sort:* one he had treated as his equal in all respects. The multiplication of synonyms for *friend* emphasizes the enormity of the betrayal.

14f. Worst of all, he was of the brotherhood of the faithful, a religious man. His treachery is open rebellion against God and must be judged as such. The psalmist therefore prays that he and his associates should be punished according to the principles of covenant justice, that they suffer the same fate as Korah and his confederates who rebelled against Moses. They too went *down alive into Sheol* when the ground beneath them split open (Num. 16: 31–3). The picture is one of swift judgement. *may they perish in confusion:* transposed from the end of verse 14. The more usual translation is 'we walked in the throng', referring to the band of pilgrims at the great festivals *in the house of God* in Jerusalem. *

33

16 But I will call upon God;
    the LORD will save me.
17 Evening and morning and at noon
    I nurse my woes, and groan.
18 He has heard my cry, he rescued me
    and gave me back my peace,
when they beset me like archers,[a]
    massing against me,
19 like Ishmael and the desert tribes
    and those who dwell in the East,
who have no respect for an oath
    nor any fear of God.
20 Such men do violence to those at peace with them
    and break their promised word;
21 their speech is smoother than butter
    but their thoughts are of war;
their words are slippery as oil
    but sharp as drawn swords.

22 Commit your fortunes to the LORD,
    and he will sustain you;
he will never let the righteous be shaken.
23 Cast them, O God, into the pit of destruction;
    bloodthirsty and treacherous,
they shall not live out half their days;
    but I will put my trust in thee.

* 16–21. The psalmist tells of his certainty that God hears him, but his hurt is so deep that he reverts to the theme of betrayal.

16. The true solution to his problems is not to flee in fear before them (verses 6–9), but to bring them in trust to God.

[a] when . . . archers: *prob. rdg.; Heb. obscure.*

17. *Evening and morning and at noon:* hardly a reference to set hours of prayer, but a comprehensive expression meaning 'continually, at every moment of the day'. Evening stands first because the twenty-four-hour day was generally reckoned to start at sunset.

18. *He has heard:* it is through faith that the sufferer is assured of his deliverance, for the context clearly shows that it is not yet realized (cp. Ps. 13: 5).

18c–19. The Hebrew may be rendered 'from the hostilities against me, for there are many against me. (19) God will hear and afflict them, even he who is enthroned from of old.' The N.E.B. translators have used some ingenious conjectures to obtain their allusions to *archers* and *the desert tribes* of *the East*. Ishmael was a people in north-west Arabia, and its caravans are known to have passed through Israel and traded with Egypt (Gen. 37: 25). Here they simply typify the marauders of the East who frequently raided along the desert borders, sometimes penetrating well into Israelite territory like the Midianites and Amalekites in Judg. 6: 3–6. Their sole objective was to obtain plunder, and in pursuing this end they observed neither oath nor treaty. *who have no respect for an oath:* literally 'in whom there are no changes'. The N.E.B. understands 'changes' as exchanges of promise and mutual obligation, but the whole phrase could equally imply that these men are so set in their sinful ways that they never contemplate any changes in their life-style.

20f. His thoughts have been brought back to his faithless friend. *Such men . . . them . . .:* literally 'He . . . him . . .' The N.E.B. thus avoids a sudden transition to the singular, but by so doing misses the sense of bewilderment expressed in this abrupt return to thought of betrayal. The sheer horror of treachery is that it shatters trust and without trust human intercourse becomes a matter of uncertainty and fear. The *promised word* loses its sacredness, *speech* becomes mere flattery and *words* are simply a screen to hide treacherous swords drawn ready to kill.

35

22f. Though friends fail him, God is trustworthy. He will sustain the faithful and bring judgement on the oppressors.

22. It has sometimes been thought that these words would have been uttered by a priest, but they could equally represent the sufferer exhorting himself to renewed trust. *your fortunes:* the Hebrew reads 'what he has given you' or 'your burden', the Septuagint and 1 Pet. 5: 7 have 'your cares', and other alternatives are found in the versions, but nothing that corresponds with the N.E.B. reading. *never let the righteous be shaken:* contrast Ps. 1: 5.

23. *Cast them:* or 'Thou shalt cast them', expressing the same final assurance as the rest of the verse. *the pit of destruction:* Sheol, the place of the dead. The later notion of the everlasting fires of judgement and hell is not to be found here, though Sheol does mean eternal separation from God and all his joys (Ps. 6: 5). *but I will put my trust in thee:* presumably expecting a fate very different from those he curses. Most scholars would argue that he seeks no more than deliverance from oppression, a restoration of peace and the prolongation of his life, but this concluding contrast between himself and his persecutors could imply that his hope extends beyond the grave, that, like the author of Ps. 49: 15 or 73: 24 (see comment), he looks for ultimate redemption from Sheol and the eternal enjoyment of God's life-giving presence. ✳

IN GOD I TRUST

56

1 Be gracious to me, O God, for the enemy persecute me, my assailants harass me all day long.

2 All the day long my watchful foes persecute me; countless are those who assail me.

3 Appear on high[a] in my day of fear;

[a] Appear on high: *prob. rdg.; Heb.* Height.

I put my trust in thee.
With God to help me I will shout defiance,   4
in God I trust and shall not be afraid;
what can mortal men do to me?
All day long abuse of me is their only theme,   5
    all their thoughts are hostile.
In malice they are on the look-out, and watch for me,   6
    they dog my footsteps;
but, while they lie in wait for me,
it is they who will not*a* escape.   7
O God, in thy anger bring ruin on the nations.

Enter my lament in thy book,*b*   8
store every tear in thy flask.*c*
Then my enemies will turn back   9
    on the day when I call upon thee;*d*
for this I know, that God is on my side,
with God to help me I will shout defiance.*e*   10
In God I trust and shall not be afraid;   11
what can man do to me?
I have bound myself with vows to thee, O God,   12
and will redeem them with due thank-offerings;
for thou hast rescued me from death*f*   13
to walk in thy presence, in the light of life.

[a] it is . . . not: *prob. rdg.; Heb.* for iniquity.
[b] Enter . . . book: *prob. rdg.; Heb. obscure.*
[c] *Prob. rdg.; Heb. adds* is it not in thy book?
[d] Enter . . . thee: *or* Thou hast entered my lament in thy book, my tears are put in thy flask. Then my enemies turned back, when I called upon thee.
[e] *Prob. rdg.; Heb. adds* With the LORD to help me I will shout defiance.
[f] *Prob. rdg.; Heb. adds* is it not my feet from stumbling (*cp. Ps. 116: 8*).

✶ The Hebrew text of this psalm has suffered a great deal in transmission, as is clearly shown by the number of footnotes in the N.E.B. The result has been a vast array of conjectural emendations and an equally confusing divergence of opinion about the psalm's interpretation. Nor is the problem a modern one only. The Septuagint and Targum have titles that clearly suggest use by the community living in exile from Jerusalem, whereas the Hebrew, by ascribing it to David 'when the Philistines took him in Gath' (1 Sam. 21: 10 – 22: 1), implies individual use in time of harassment. The psalm is arranged in two parts. Prayer for help amid persecution dominates the first section (verses 1–7) and confident anticipation of deliverance the second (verses 8–13), but the refrain repeated in both gives the whole composition the flavour of a confession of trust in the face of danger (verses 4, 10–11).

1–4. He prays for help and declares his trust in God.

1. *Be gracious:* an unconditional appeal for help (cp. Ps. 51: 1). *the enemy persecute me:* literally 'men trample on me'.

2. The repetition of words and phrases from verse 1 emphasizes the urgency of his situation.

3. *Appear on high:* the Hebrew reading, 'Height' (N.E.B. footnote), has been variously treated as a divine title, 'O thou most High' (Authorized Version), or as an adverb, 'proudly' (Revised Standard Version), qualifying 'assail' in verse 2. The N.E.B. has not only altered the word, but has removed it to verse 3. *trust* in God is the perfect antidote to *fear* (Ps. 27: 1; John 14: 1), but it may call for a deliberate act of will in the teeth of rising panic.

4. This verse, repeated as a refrain in verses 10–11 (cp. also Ps. 118: 6 and Heb. 13: 6), expands on the faith that undergirds verse 3 and its thought is well illustrated in the teaching of Jesus in Matt. 10: 28. *I will shout defiance:* based on a small emendation; the Hebrew reads 'I will praise his word', presumably referring to God's promise to protect his people, the revealed word on which man's *trust* must rest. *mortal men:* literally 'flesh' (verse 11 reads 'man', *'ādām*), that is, man as a

perishable and frail creature in contrast to God who is eternal and almighty (cp. Isa. 31: 3).

5–7. From the height of faith his thoughts return to his enemies and he prays for judgement.

5. *All day long:* repeated here for the third time (verses 1, 2). The worst part of his plight is the unrelenting pressure. *abuse of me is their only theme:* assuming a quite unnecessary emendation. The Hebrew makes perfectly good sense: 'they twist my words', that is, they distort and pervert everything he says in an attempt to rouse others to anger against him.

6. Once more the N.E.B. differs from the older translations because of its emendations, but it has not greatly altered the sense of the Hebrew which likens the enemy to men lurking unseen in ambush, ever watchful and ready to pounce (cp. Ps. 59: 3).

7. Emendation can hardly be avoided in the first half of this verse, but some rendering like the Revised Standard Version's 'recompense them for their crime' suits the parallelism better. Reference to *the nations* has suggested to some that the psalm is either a prayer of the community or of the king on behalf of his nation in time of war, but it is perhaps best to retain the individual interpretation. Since the sufferer's hope rests in God's promise to his people (verse 4 in the Hebrew), his own prayer for judgement is a call for the vindication of those promises which have national and universal implications (cp. Ps. 7: 6–9).

8–11. He renews his appeal for help and reaffirms his trust in God.

8. The double metaphor of recording and storing emphasizes his desire that everything about his plight be noted and taken into account when judgement is passed (verse 9). *Enter my lament in thy book:* this may equally be treated as a statement of confidence (N.E.B. footnote: 'Thou hast entered . . .'), but either translation assumes a virtual rewriting of the Hebrew and makes the third component of the verse (N.E.B. footnote: 'is it not in thy book?') superfluous. The Hebrew,

which certainly reads 'you have taken account of my wanderings', may be somehow related to the psalm-title, for it was as a wanderer and fugitive that David went to Gath. *every tear:* a token of distress rather than, as some commentators suggest, of contrition or intimate love. The relegated third line could be a scribal comment stressing the confidence that God does not forget the needs of the faithful.

9. *will turn back:* will suffer a reversal of their fortunes. The reference is more correctly to the future than to the past (N.E.B. footnote). His suffering is not ended, but he rests assured and can say *I know* because his trust is in God and in the promise of his word (see on verse 4).

10f. See verse 4. There is no good reason why the second half of verse 10 should be relegated to the footnotes. Repetition for emphasis is a notable feature of this psalm (see on verses 2, 4, 5).

12f. He confidently looks forward to the time when he will present his thank-offering.

12. *vows:* promises made to God in time of suffering (cp. Ps. 66: 13f.). *thank-offerings:* the Hebrew word can mean either sacrifices or songs of gratitude, but the purpose in offering each is the same.

13. *thou hast rescued:* a statement of faith anticipating deliverance (cp. Ps. 55: 18). *death:* the antithesis of *life* and the negation of all that God's *presence* means. The realm of death is Sheol, a place of gloom (Ps. 88: 12), and in sickness or distress its shadow falls over the sufferer who may then know something of the fear of its grasp. Into this darkness God's healing or deliverance comes like *light*, like 'the sun of righteousness' that rises 'with healing in his wings' (Mal. 4: 2). Though the psalmist's words refer to this present existence, they contain overtones of hope for ultimate delivery from the power of death (cp. Ps. 55: 23). 'is it not my feet from stumbling' (N.E.B. footnote): though the syntax is awkward, it need not be assumed that this phrase is imported from the almost identical Ps. 116: 8. It is required here in

the Hebrew to complete the metrical and parallel structure
of the verse. ✲

LET THY GLORY SHINE OVER ALL THE EARTH

57

Be gracious to me, O God, be gracious;   1
for I have made thee my refuge.
I will take refuge in the shadow of thy wings
    until the storms are past.
I will call upon God Most High,   2
on God who fulfils his purpose for me.
He will send his truth and his love that never fails,   3
he will send from heaven and save me.
God himself will frustrate my persecutors;
for I lie down among lions, man-eaters,   4
    whose teeth are spears and arrows
    and whose tongues are sharp swords.
Show thyself, O God, high above the heavens;   5
    let thy glory shine over all the earth.
Men have prepared a net to catch me as I walk,   6
    but I bow my head to escape from it;
they have dug a pit in my path
    but have fallen into it themselves.

My heart is steadfast, O God,   7[a]
    my heart is steadfast.
I will sing and raise a psalm;
    awake, my spirit,   8
awake, lute and harp,

[a] *Verses 7–11: cp. Ps. 108: 1–5.*

I will awake at dawn of day.[a]

9   I will confess thee, O Lord, among the peoples,
       among the nations I will raise a psalm to thee,

10   for thy unfailing love is wide as the heavens
       and thy truth reaches to the skies.

11   Show thyself, O God, high above the heavens;
       let thy glory shine over all the earth.

✶ The title in the Hebrew ascribes this psalm to David, 'when he fled from Saul, in the cave', presumably referring to 1 Sam. 22 or 24, and inviting the worshipper to see the same power of God that sustained David in his time of trouble at work in his own personal crisis. Like several others, this psalm is suitable for use in a night vigil (see p. 14, section C). It falls into two parts, each ending with a refrain (verses 5, 11): in the first the battle with the powers of darkness is almost over and the psalmist's plea for protection is suffused with confidence; in the second his song surges in praise and anticipation as he waits for the coming of the dawn and his God. It is not without reason that this psalm is regularly used in the Christian Church on Easter morning. It is impossible to tell when it was written, but it is probably older than Ps. 108 where the opening verses 1–5 are identical with Ps. 57: 7–11.

1–4. He appeals for protection, confident that God will save him.

1. *I will take refuge*: probably in the temple, as in some of the other vigil psalms (Pss. 5: 7; 27: 4). *in the shadow of thy wings*: a metaphor suggesting comfort and security (see on Ps. 17: 8).

2. The title *Most High* ('*elyōn*, see on Ps. 7: 17) calls to mind the pre-Israelite god of Jerusalem who was 'creator of heaven and earth' (Gen. 14: 19, 22), and its use here is most appropriate since the psalmist looks for the assertion of God's

[a] at dawn of day: *or* the dawn.

universal sovereignty (verses 5, 11). The parallel description of
him as the one *who fulfils his purpose for me* indicates a confident
appropriation of God's sovereignty to his own situation.

3. Firm in the faith that God is in sovereign control, he proclaims his belief that his salvation is at hand. God's *truth* and
his love that never fails, portrayed as angels of mercy (cp. Ps.
43: 3) sent out as it were to do battle with the persecutors,
represent the promises of God's covenant which form the
basis of his hope (see on Pss. 51: 1; 54: 5).

4. The pictures are intentionally grotesque. Wild animals
in the psalms are a symbol of ferocity and cruelty (cp. Ps. 22:
12f.), but here they are demonic creatures, man-eating lions
with *spears*, *arrows* and *swords* for teeth and tongues. They also
move on a supernatural plane, for they are the persecutors
from whom God's angels (verse 3) are to rescue the psalmist.
He is unable to fight them; he can only *lie down* helplessly and
wait for God's salvation. The imagery is well suited to a night
vigil setting (cp. on Ps. 5: 9).

5. The refrain calls on God to assert his universal sovereignty
(see verse 2). Most appropriately God's *glory* at his appearing is
likened to the brilliance of the rising sun (cp. Ps. 19: 1).

6–10. He sees the enemies enmeshed in their own traps and
calls on his God with a heart full of praise.

6. Despite the N.E.B.'s division, this verse does not belong
to the first part of the psalm. It acts as a transition verse and as
a preface to the psalm of praise that follows. The mood has
changed. The vigil is approaching its conclusion and the
psalmist has escaped. The wickedness of the enemies has proved
self-destructive, for they are now trapped and defeated (cp.
Ps. 7: 15). It is typical of the fluidity of psalm imagery that
they were beasts in verse 4 and are now depicted as huntsmen
(cp. Ps. 17: 11f.).

7. *My heart is steadfast*: his fear has vanished and he is filled
with new confidence as dawn approaches. His gaze is fixed on
God alone and his whole attention is now given to singing
God's praise.

8. *my spirit:* literally 'my glory', the God-given faculty of praise (see on Ps. 30: 12). Offerings of praise and thanksgiving were frequently accompanied by stringed instruments such as the *lute and harp* (cp. Ps. 150: 3). The correct translation of the third line is 'I will awake the dawn' (cp. N.E.B. footnote) and its background is mythological. Dawn was sometimes conceived as a winged goddess (Ps. 139: 9 – for these references see the Revised Standard Version or the Authorized Version; the N.E.B. generally removes the anthropomorphisms) with a womb (Ps. 110: 3) and beautiful eyelids (Job 3: 9), the mother of the Day Star, Venus (Isa. 14: 12). In Greek myth she spent her nights asleep in the ocean bed and had to be wakened by another goddess. But in the present setting the personification is no more than poetic. Dawn is the symbol of the expected coming of God that will end the night of watching and bring restored joy. The psalmist's three exclamations in this verse express his mounting excitement as that hour approaches.

9. *among the peoples, among the nations:* in his overflowing joy he wishes the whole world could hear the praises of his God, a wish that is picked up by Paul as expressive of what he sees fulfilled in Christ (Rom. 15: 9).

10. Cp. Ps. 36: 5. God's loving faithfulness had been his only real source of hope during his hours of spiritual darkness (verses 3f.).

11. Concluding refrain; see verse 5. ✷

THERE IS A GOD THAT JUDGES

58

1 Answer, you rulers:[a] are your judgements just?
  Do you decide impartially between man and man?
2 Never! Your hearts devise all kinds of wickedness
  and survey the violence that you have done on earth.

[a] *Or* you gods.

Wicked men, from birth they have taken to   3
    devious ways;
liars, no sooner born than they go astray,
venomous with the venom of serpents,   4
of the deaf asp which stops its ears
and will not listen to the sound of the charmer,   5
    however skilful his spells may be.

O God, break the teeth in their mouths.   6
Break, O LORD, the jaws of the unbelievers.[a]
May they melt, may they vanish like water,   7
may they wither like trodden grass,[b]
    like an abortive birth which melts away   8
    or a still-born child which never sees[c] the sun!
All unawares, may they be rooted up like[d] a thorn-bush, 9
    like weeds which a man angrily[e] clears away!

The righteous shall rejoice that he has seen vengeance   10
    done
    and shall wash his feet in the blood of the wicked,
        and men shall say,   11
'There is after all a reward for the righteous;
after all, there is a God that judges on earth.'

✻ There are a number of psalms dealing with the injustice of
life, but they tend to tackle the problem in different ways (see
p. 14, section E and vol. I, p. 230); this one calls down God's curse
on the wicked. In form it is similar to Ps. 52: both open with an

[a] the jaws of the unbelievers: *or* the lions' fangs.
[b] like trodden grass: *prob. rdg.; Heb. obscure.*
[c] sees: *prob. rdg.; Heb.* they see.
[d] may they be rooted up like: *prob. rdg.; Heb.* your pots.
[e] angrily: *prob. rdg.; Heb.* like anger.

indignant accusation, continue with a description of the wicked and a call for vengeance, and end with an assurance of vindication and rejoicing for the righteous. The curse is as vital a part of God's covenant as the blessing (Deut. 28; 30: 15–20) and any prayer for intervention must countenance the operation of both. It is because this psalm is concerned almost exclusively with the wicked that it lays greater stress on the curse. The language is strikingly vehement, but that only helps to warn against man's tendency to underestimate the viciousness of evil. This psalm cannot be dated.

1f. The psalmist, standing before the throne of God like a prosecutor in a law-court, accuses the wicked of perverting justice.

1. *you rulers:* or, as N.E.B. footnote, 'you gods'. The belief is sometimes found that God is surrounded by divine beings whose function is to do his bidding and to see that his will is obeyed on earth (1 Kings 22: 19–22; Job 1: 6), but these could also be held responsible for the wrongs of mankind (Ps. 82). However, the psalm itself may more fittingly apply to earth's human rulers, in which case the title 'you gods' is one full of sarcasm (cp. Ps. 52: 1); that is, they lord it like gods over the righteous, but their injustice is far from godlike.

2. The corruption of justice was a common problem in ancient Israel (Exod. 23: 1–3, 6–8; Amos 5: 12), and it did not result simply from carelessness or accidental oversight. It was the symptom of a deliberate ruthlessness emanating from hearts that had become deeply distorted by sin (cp. Ps. 36: 1). In derisive contrast with God who 'saw all that he had made, and it was very good' (Gen. 1: 31), these self-appointed 'gods' can only look upon the havoc they have wreaked *on earth*.

3–5. The psalmist's portrait of the wicked has an aura of utter evil.

3. The faithful man can also say, 'In iniquity I was brought to birth' (Ps. 51: 5), but he prays for cleansing and a new heart (Ps. 51: 7–12), whereas the wicked man allows evil to become his second nature.

4f. As the *deaf asp* resists *the sound of the charmer* and remains dangerous, so the wicked man resists the call of God and continues to inflict deadly harm with his *venom* (his lies, verse 3).

6–9. God's judgement on evil is that it must be rendered harmless, indeed utterly annihilated, lest it continue to do damage. Thus the psalmist now invokes God's curse on the wicked who have shown themselves to be so incurably corrupt.

6. *unbelievers*: the older translation 'young lions' (see also on Ps. 35: 17) fits the context better, for breaking the teeth of a wild animal was one way of rendering it harmless (cp. Ps. 3: 7). The lion metaphor also supplies a suitable image of ferocity to supplement the picture of stealth and poison in verses 4–5.

7. *vanish like water*: winter rains soak the land and fill the wadis, but by summer the wadis are empty and the earth is dry. The second half of the verse has suffered badly in transmission and the Hebrew yields no good sense. The N.E.B. adopts an interpretation favoured by most scholars.

8. *like an abortive birth ... or a still-born child*: like people that are as though they had never existed (cp. Job 3: 16; Eccles. 6: 3–5). So may the wicked vanish!

9. By emendation the N.E.B. has offered a reasonable interpretation of a very difficult Hebrew sentence. The ungodly man is *like a thorn-bush* or *weeds* that must be rooted up and destroyed (cp. Ps. 52: 5), quite unlike the loyal servant of God who is compared elsewhere to a tree firmly rooted in fertile soil (Pss. 1: 3; 52: 8).

10f. The psalm closes on a note of confident anticipation.

10. The language of this verse may at first seem utterly spiteful, but what other can *The righteous* do than *rejoice* on the day that God vindicates their faith (see also on Ps. 52: 6)? *vengeance* is not an expression of human spite, but an act of God; it is his intervention to restore the justice that *the wicked* have corrupted in their desire to usurp his place and act like

gods themselves (verse 1). *wash his feet in the blood of:* this is a metaphor from the field of battle depicting God's victorious troops wading through the blood of the slain. But the warfare in this psalm is spiritual, not physical.

11. *reward:* literally 'fruit'; the harvest of righteousness is assured, but *the righteous* must be patient (cp. Gal. 6: 7–10). ✳

GOD IS MY STRONG TOWER

59

1   Rescue me from my enemies, O my God,
      be my tower of strength against all who assail me,
2   rescue me from these evildoers,
        deliver me from men of blood.

3   Savage men lie in wait for me,
      they lie in ambush ready to attack me;
      for no fault or guilt of mine, O LORD,
4–5 innocent as I am,[a] they run to take post against me.
    But thou, LORD God of Hosts, Israel's God,
      do thou bestir thyself at my call, and look:
      awake, and punish all the nations.
      Have no mercy on villains and traitors,
6   who run wild at nightfall like dogs,
      snarling and prowling round the city,
15[b] wandering to and fro in search of food,
      and howling if they are not satisfied.

7   From their mouths comes a stream of nonsense;
      'But who will hear?' they murmur.[c]

8 But thou, O LORD, dost laugh at them,

[a] as I am: *prob. rdg., cp. Targ.; Heb. om.*
[b] *Verse transposed.*
[c] they murmur: *so Symm.; Heb. om.*

and deride all the nations.

O my*a* strength,*b* to thee I turn in the night-watches;   9
for thou,*c* O God, art my strong tower.

My God, in his true love, shall be my champion;   10
with God's help, I shall gloat over my watchful foes.

Wilt thou not kill them, lest my people forget?   11
Scatter them by thy might and bring them to ruin.

Deliver them,*d* O Lord, to be destroyed   12
by their own sinful words;

let what they have spoken entrap them in their pride.

Let them be cut off for their cursing and falsehood;
bring them to an end in thy wrath,   13
and they will be no more;

then they will know that God is ruler in Jacob,
even to earth's farthest limits.*ef*

But I will sing of thy strength,   16
and celebrate thy love when morning comes;
for thou hast been my strong tower
and a sure retreat in days of trouble.

O thou my strength, I will raise a psalm to thee;   17
for thou, O God, art*g* my strong tower.*h*

✴ In the Hebrew this psalm falls into two parts, a plea for deliverance (verses 1–5) and a prayer for God to assert his

[a] my: *so Sept.; Heb.* his.
[b] *Or* refuge.
[c] thou: *so Pesh.; Heb. om.*
[d] Deliver them: *prob. rdg.; Heb.* Our shield.
[e] *Prob. rdg.; Heb. adds* (14) who run wild at nightfall like dogs, snarling and prowling round the city (*cp. verse 6*).
[f] *Verse 15 transposed to follow verse 6.*
[g] thou . . . art: *so Pesh.; Heb.* God is.
[h] *So many MSS.; others add* God of my unfailing love.

victory over his enemies (verses 10–13), and each section is followed by variant forms of a refrain (verses 6–9, 14–17). The N.E.B. has altered the structure by omitting verse 14 and transposing verse 15 to follow verse 6, thus making the psalm a continuous unit without a refrain. This rearrangement is completely arbitrary, but fortunately the theme of the psalm is not affected by it. The Hebrew also has a title ascribing the psalm to David 'when Saul sent men to watch his house in order to kill him'. Hence the worshipper, who would have found this psalm suitable for use as a vigil prayer for release from the hostile forces of darkness (see p. 14, section C), is invited to compare his situation with David's on the night when Saul's men besieged him in his home (1 Sam. 19: 11–18). The psalm itself offers little clue about its date.

1–8. He prays for deliverance, pleading his own innocence, and calls on God to punish his vicious enemies.

1. *be my tower of strength:* literally 'set me on high', that is beyond reach of my foes, but as in verses 9, 17, God himself is this inaccessible place.

1f. The parallelism suggests that *enemies, all who assail me, evildoers* and *men of blood* are poetic synonyms describing the same foe. The terms clearly indicate their malicious and murderous intention and the four-fold plea emphasizes the urgency of the psalmist's need (cp. Ps. 5: 1f.).

3. The idea of a sinister enemy lurking unseen in the darkness, like Saul's men in 1 Sam. 19: 11, aptly suggests the terrors of the night that threaten the worshipper.

3f. *for no fault or guilt of mine . . . innocent as I am:* these synonymous expressions lay no claim to sinless perfection, but make the protestation that the enemies' action is in no way provoked. *post:* attacking positions.

4f. The epithet *LORD God of Hosts* reminds that God has the power to defend (cp. Ps. 46: 7), and the title *Israel's God* recalls his covenant obligation to intervene on behalf of his people. *bestir thyself . . . awake:* a metaphorical summons to action that would be very apt in a night vigil setting (see on

Ps. 17: 15). *all the nations*: this must be metaphorical, like the descriptions of the enemies as men in ambush (verse 3), as *villains and traitors* (verse 5), as wild dogs (verses 6, 15), as scoffers (verse 7) and as proud liars (verse 12). Whoever added the title to this psalm must have known that David was not beset by foreign nations in 1 Sam. 19: 11, but he was prepared to accept a comparison between the attack on the king and an assault on Israel by hostile nations. The psalmist has appealed to the national god, *Israel's God*, and thus naturally depicts the assailants as national enemies (cp. Ps. 7: 8). The metaphor may also suggest the magnitude of the threat to the worshipper.

6, 15. The N.E.B. omits verse 14, presumably on the grounds that it unnecessarily duplicates verse 6, and is consequently obliged to transpose verse 15. It would, however, seem better to retain the arrangement of verses in the Hebrew text and find a refrain which occurs in two different forms. The use of variant refrains in Hebrew poetry is not unusual (cp. on Pss. 49: 20; 62: 5f.). The comparison with *snarling* and *howling* wild *dogs* that haunt the rubbish dumps and hungrily prowl the streets scavenging for food vividly illustrates the devilish nature of the psalmist's fear. His enemies are creatures of the dark; their inhuman activity begins *at nightfall*.

7. *'But who will hear?'*: cp. the sarcastic 'Where is your God?' in Ps. 42: 3. The figure has changed again, for the enemies are now men who scoff at the psalmist's faith, their taunt implying that God is unconcerned, or perhaps even not there at all (cp. Ps. 14: 1). The translation of the first half of this verse depends on emendation, but the Hebrew may be literally rendered 'They slaver with their mouths, swords are in their lips'. This would complete the description of the wild dogs and further illustrate their mythological nature (cp. Ps. 57: 4).

8. *But thou, O LORD:* we are jolted out of the psalmist's nightmarish world with this sudden reminder of God's overseeing and omnipotent presence. The very human image of God's scorn emphasizes the impotence of the enemies (cp.

Pss. 2: 4; 37: 13) and is a source of encouragement to the sufferer's faith.

9-17. He calls on God to activate his covenant promises by bringing judgement on his enemies before the eyes of the world. Then he will raise his morning hymn.

9. This verse marks the turning-point in the psalm. With slight variation it is used to close the psalm and its description of God as a *strong tower* recalls the opening plea (verse 1). When the sufferer turns his gaze from the turbulence around him and fixes his eyes on God, then he finds renewed strength which enables him to look beyond the encompassing darkness to the coming light of God (verse 16).

10. As so often in the psalms, the sole basis of the worshipper's hope is God's *true love*, his faithfulness to his promise to protect his loyal servants (see on Ps. 51: 1). This allusion to the covenant shows that the invocation of wrath on the enemies that follows here, and is also found in other vigil psalms, is not so much a spiteful plea for vengeance as a prayer that God will vindicate his righteousness by executing judgement and acting upon his promises to bless the faithful and punish the wicked (cp. Exod. 20: 5f.).

11. *Wilt thou not kill them*: the Hebrew reads 'Do not kill them', implying that before their final destruction (verse 13) they will serve God's purpose by suffering publicly as an object lesson to others (cp. Exod. 9: 16). By turning the command into a question the N.E.B. gives the impression that the psalmist seeks their speedy extermination lest they lead astray the faithful.

12. *Deliver them*: the Hebrew reads 'Our Shield' as a title of God (cp. Ps. 33: 20). The belief that sin can be self-destructive is expressed several times in the psalms (e.g. Pss. 7: 15; 57: 6), but this is not a principle that operates of itself, for ultimately God has to let the process begin. *pride* is rebellion, for it exalts self instead of God and finds expression in the mockery of faith and in the claim that God does not care (verse 7; cp. Ps. 10: 4).

13. This verse opens in Hebrew with an impassioned cry for action: 'Consume in wrath, consume'. The tone in the N.E.B. is gentle by comparison. The purpose in the execution of judgement is in the end that men everywhere will know that God's purpose is not thwarted, that he is faithful to his promises, that he has sovereign authority over both his covenanted people and those who molest them (the 'nations' of verses 5, 8).

14, 15. See on verse 6.

16. The dominant theme of this psalm is that God is the psalmist's *strength* or his *strong tower* (verses 1, 9, 17); in God he finds *a sure retreat*. The language is clearly spiritual, but it well becomes a setting in the temple where the worshipper has sought sanctuary for his vigil (cp. Ps. 57: 1). *morning:* the expected hour of salvation when 'the sun of righteousness shall rise with healing in his wings' (Mal. 4: 2) bringing the vigil to its joyous conclusion, and thus an occasion for songs of praise.

17. See verse 9; the night of waiting now gives way to the morning of song. The N.E.B. omits the closing words of the Hebrew psalm, 'the God who shows me unfailing love', even though they aptly recall the very hope on which the psalmist's trust is founded (verse 10). *

DELIVER THOSE THAT ARE DEAR

60

O God, thou hast cast us off and broken us;   1
thou hast been angry and rebuked us cruelly.

Thou hast made the land quake and torn it open;   2
it gives way and crumbles into pieces.

Thou hast made thy people drunk with a bitter   3
    draught,
thou hast given us wine that makes us stagger.

4   But thou hast given a warning to those who fear thee,
       to make their escape before the sentence falls.[a]

5[b]   Deliver those that are dear to thee;
       save them with thy right hand, and answer.
6   God has spoken from his sanctuary:[c]
       'I will go up now and measure out Shechem;
       I will divide the valley of Succoth into plots;
7   Gilead and Manasseh are mine;
       Ephraim is my helmet,[d] Judah my sceptre;
8   Moab is my wash-bowl, I fling my shoes at Edom;
       Philistia is the target of my anger.'

9   Who can bring me to the fortified city,
       who can guide[e] me to Edom,
10   since thou, O God, hast abandoned us
       and goest not forth[f] with our armies?
11   Grant us help against the enemy,
       for deliverance by man is a vain hope.
12   With God's help we shall do valiantly,
       and God himself will tread our enemies under foot.

✴ The title in the Hebrew ascribes this psalm to David 'when he was at war with Aram-naharaim and Aram-zobah, and Joab marched back to destroy twelve thousand Edomites in the Valley of Salt' (Jerusalem Bible). The allusion can only be to the episode recorded in 2 Sam. 8: 13f., though the number of the slain is rather higher there. It must be assumed that Edom

[a] *Lit.* before truth.
[b] *Verses 5–12: cp. Ps. 108: 6–13.*
[c] from his sanctuary: *or* in his holiness.
[d] my helmet: *lit.* the refuge of my head.
[e] *So Sept.; Heb.* has guided.
[f] *So Pesh.; Heb. adds* O God.

had taken advantage of David's absence during his campaigns into Syria (2 Sam. 8: 3–12) and inflicted serious harm on Judah, thus occasioning the despatch of Joab's battalion and the dedication of this psalm. In view of the specific reference to Edom in verse 9, this could be the original setting of the psalm, though its inclusion in the psalter shows that it continued to be used in later times, thus implying a wider application as a prayer for help in times of military upheaval. Hence its context is closely similar to that of Ps. 44, with which it also shares much in tone and language, although there is no anguished cry or attempted self-justification as in Ps. 44: 17–22. Despite the opening expostulations (verses 1–4), a calmer mood prevails and attention is focused on a divine promise of victory (verses 5–8) that provides a basis for prayer and confidence (verses 9–12). See the comments on Ps. 108 for discussion of the re-use of verses 5–12 in that psalm.

1–4. The psalmist laments the plight of God's people.

1. The repeated *thou hast* in this and the following verses is reminiscent of the series in Ps. 44: 9–14, though the mood is now more disconcerted than indignant. On this occasion affliction is recognized as an expression of God's displeasure, though for what reasons is not stated. There is, however, a sense of shock at the harshness of God's rebuke and an unwillingness to accept it as final. *and rebuked us cruelly*: the Hebrew is more commonly represented in translation as a cry for help, 'restore us', or 'turn to us again'.

2. The language is metaphorical. The disarray of the nation is as though the land had been torn apart by an earthquake. *it gives way . . . .*: this translation depends on a slight emendation. The Hebrew again offers a prayer for help: 'mend its rifts, for it continues to totter'.

3. 'The cup of his wrath' is a well-known metaphor for God's judgement (cp. Isa. 51: 17, 22). Here the image of the nation staggering under judgement as in a drunken stupor, the mockery of all onlookers, is fitting to portray the disarray of a people reeling under the shock of invasion or defeat. *drunk*

with a bitter draught: these words introduce another emendation, for the Hebrew reads 'experience (literally 'see') hard things'.

4. The signal for retreat is given, thus completing the tale of woe in verses 1–4. But that signal also betokens God's continuing concern for *those who fear* him. A note of hope has now entered the psalm. *before the sentence falls:* the Hebrew contains a unique word of uncertain meaning. The rendering 'before truth' (N.E.B. footnote, cp. the Authorized Version) makes little sense in the context. Many of the ancient versions read 'before the bow' which would be in keeping with the psalm's general military setting.

5–8. Hope is strengthened by recalling an oracle promising Israel possession of Canaan and supremacy over her neighbours.

5. God's anger is formidable (verse 1), but not final, for his people remain *dear* to him (literally 'thy beloved'; cp. Isa. 5: 1). It is with faith in his abiding love that they offer this prayer for deliverance, their 'fear' (verse 4) being the reverential counterpart to his love, rather than terror in the face of his wrath (cp. Ps. 33: 18).

6. What follows may be an oracle from the sacred traditions of the sanctuary, one that was rehearsed periodically at festivals, but it could equally be a poetic recasting of the ancient promise that Israel would occupy the land. The alternative translation, 'in his holiness' (N.E.B. footnote) implies the utter dependability of his word (cp. Ps. 89: 35). Succoth and Shechem, on either side of the Jordan, were the first places where Jacob halted and settled on his return to Canaan (Gen. 33: 17f.). Hence they represent the whole land, both east and west, promised as an inheritance to his descendants.

7. *Gilead* and *Manasseh* stand for Israel's holdings in Transjordan, *Ephraim* and *Judah* for the western territory. God is here likened to a mighty warrior. Ephraim, as the most powerful tribe, is his *helmet*; Judah, with its strong tradition of Davidic kingship, is his *sceptre* (cp. Gen. 49: 10).

8. The neighbouring nations are allotted menial status, but they are not discarded as useless, for they too must serve God. The picture is of the warrior returning home, calling for his *wash-bowl*, flinging his *shoes* into a corner and shouting at his slave. *my anger:* an interpretative paraphrase, not represented in the Hebrew.

9–12. The final plea for help is also a confession that a humbling lesson has been learned. The people have been brought to see that no one but God can *help against the enemy*. Without him they lost their battles and without him they know they can obtain no *deliverance*. But now they have learned to trust God again, there is every reason for confidence, for he remains the warrior-king who has promised to lead them to victory over their enemies.

9. *the fortified city:* the inaccessibility of some Edomite cities, e.g. Petra, is well known (cp. Obad. 3). On the historical setting, see pp. 54f., but in later usage *Edom* would typify any comparable aggressor. *me:* the change to singular suggests the likelihood that this psalm was normally recited by the king or some other leader of worship on behalf of the people (cp. on Ps. 44: 4).

10. *goest not forth . . .:* cp. Ps. 44: 9.

11. *deliverance by man is a vain hope:* see on Ps. 44: 3.

12. *tread our enemies under foot:* like a goring ox (cp. Ps. 44: 5). ✶

I WILL MAKE MY HOME WITH GOD

61

Hear my cry, O God, listen to my prayer.   1
From the end of the earth I call to thee with fainting   2
    heart;
  lift me up[a] and set me upon a rock.

[a] lift me up: *prob. rdg., cp. Sept.; Heb. obscure.*

3 For thou hast been my shelter,
       a tower for refuge from the enemy.
4 In thy tent will I make my home for ever
       and find my shelter under the cover of thy wings.
5 For thou, O God, hast heard my vows
       and granted the wish*a* of all who revere thy name.

6 To the king's life add length of days,
       year upon year for many generations;
7   may he dwell in God's presence for ever,
       may true and constant love preserve*b* him.

8 So will I ever sing psalms in honour of thy name
       as I fulfil my vows day after day.

✶ The reference to 'the end of the earth' in verse 2 and the
prayer for the king in verses 6–7 have often been taken to
indicate that this is the psalm of an exile yearning for his
homeland, but the distance is probably spiritual rather than
geographical, for the 'home' he seeks for himself and his king
is God's 'tent' (verse 4), the place of his protecting 'presence'
(verse 7). The prayer for the king clearly indicates that the
psalm was written before the exile.

1–5. He seeks refuge and security with God.

1. *Hear . . . listen:* it is not just a sympathetic ear he wants,
but active intervention (verse 2).

2. *the end of the earth:* any place far removed from the
temple, possibly even the edge of the underworld. But the use
is metaphorical, spatial distance symbolizing remoteness from
God, as in Ps. 42: 6 or Ps. 139: 7–10. *with fainting heart:* joy,
courage and physical strength weaken as the sense of separation from God grows (see on Ps. 22: 14f.). *lift me up and set me*

[a] *Prob. rdg.; Heb.* the inheritance.
[b] *So some MSS.; others add an unintelligible word.*

upon a rock: this translation partly follows the Septuagint; the Hebrew reads 'lead me to the rock that is higher than I'. *a rock:* the figure of a strong, safe refuge, like Mount Zion, the rock on which the temple stands (cp. Ps. 125: 1); but in the poetic imagery of the psalms this rock is also God himself (Ps. 18: 2).

3. Though in his suffering he has lost his knowledge of God's nearness, yet his past experience encourages confidence. *the enemy* may here be any agency, whether human, demonic or psychological, that disturbs his relationship with God (cp. on Ps. 5: 3).

4. Because he has known God's care in times gone by, he now determines to commit himself entirely to his custody and *find . . . shelter* in his presence. *In thy tent:* possibly an allusion to the temple, as in Ps. 15: 1, or perhaps a symbol of the hospitality and protection God extends to those who make their home with him (cp. Ps. 23: 5f.). *the cover of thy wings:* another image of intimate care and protection (cp. Ps. 17: 8).

5. As he recalls past mercies and commits himself to God, so his confidence grows and he knows that God has heard. *vows:* promises made in time of trouble (Ps. 66: 13f.). *the wish:* better as the Hebrew, 'the inheritance' (N.E.B. footnote), a term used of Israel's possession of the land, but here a metaphor of the spiritual heritage and blessing that awaits the faithful *who revere thy name* (see on Ps. 37: 3).

6f. Inspired by his new assurance, he prays for God's blessing on the king. The transition may seem abrupt, but the psalmist offers this prayer in recognition that his own security is intimately bound up with his membership of the covenant community and with the welfare of its head, the Davidic king, who is both the mediator of God's promises to his people and also God's representative among them responsible for maintaining peace and justice in Israel (cp. Ps. 72).

6. This is more than an elaborate 'Long live the king!' The psalmist is thinking of God's promise to David (cp. 2 Sam. 7: 8–16) that his sons would reign after him 'for ever'. Hence

the prayer that *the king's life* be prolonged *for many generations*
is as much a prayer for the dynasty as for the ruling monarch.

7. *may he dwell in God's presence for ever:* this translation
brings out the correspondence with verse 4, but there is an
even closer correspondence with 2 Sam. 7: 16 if *dwell* is re-
translated 'be enthroned' (so the Revised Standard Version).
His prayer is that the promise to David may be upheld so that
the nation may know the security of living under God's care.
true and constant love: literally 'truth and constant love', common poetic synonyms for God's faithfulness to his promised
word (cp. Pss. 25: 10; 57: 3).

8. In the full assurance of faith he looks forward to a life
filled with joyous praise. God's *name* (cp. verse 5) is God himself as he has been revealed to men.   ✳

GOD IS MY TOWER OF STRENGTH

62

1 Truly my heart waits silently for God;
    my deliverance comes from him.
2 In truth he is my rock of deliverance,
    my tower of strength, so that I stand unshaken.
3   How long will you assail a man with your threats,
    all battering on a leaning wall?
4 In truth men plan to topple him from his height,
    and stamp on the fallen stones.[a]
  With their lips they bless him, the hypocrites,
    but revile him in their hearts.
5 Truly my heart waits silently for God;
    my hope of deliverance comes from him.
6 In truth he is my rock of deliverance,
    my tower of strength, so that I am unshaken.

[a] the fallen stones: *transposed from end of verse 3.*

My deliverance and my honour depend upon God, 7
God who is my rock of refuge and my shelter.
Trust always in God, my people, 8
pour out your hearts before him;
 God is our shelter.

In very truth men are a puff of wind, 9
 all men are faithless;
put them in the balance and they can only rise,
 all of them lighter than wind.

Put no trust in extortion, 10
 do not be proud of stolen goods;
though wealth breeds wealth, set not your heart on it.
One thing God has spoken, 11
 two things I have learnt:
'Power belongs to God'
and 'True love, O Lord, is thine'; 12
thou dost requite a man for his deeds.

✻ The main characteristic of this psalm is its note of confidence. Knowing the 'deliverance' of God, the worshipper rests unafraid of human hostility (verses 1–4), and knowing the 'hope' that God inspires, he urges others to trust him too (verses 5–8). His message, that man, even in all his material wealth, has no security and is powerless before God (verses 9–12), is reminiscent of other psalms that are addressed to men rather than God (cp. Pss. 1, 37, 49). Dating this psalm is largely a matter of conjecture.

1–4. The psalmist confronts his enemies with the futility of their malicious invectives. Verses 1f contain a refrain that recurs with variants in verses 5f.

1. *Truly* or 'In truth' or 'In very truth' is repeated six

times sounding the psalm's note of assurance and emphasizing
the contrast between human transience (verse 9) and the permanence of God (verses 2, 6). *waits silently:* unlike his enemies
whose feverish activity expresses basic insecurity (verses 3f),
the psalmist has a positive hope and an experience of peace
that result from the knowledge that his *deliverance* or salvation
is with God (cp. Ps. 37: 7).

2. The titles portray divine strength, faithfulness and
stability (see on Ps. 18: 2). Hence the man who makes God his
trust can say *I stand unshaken*, very much in contrast to man
without God whose life is no more than 'a puff of wind'
(verse 9; cp. Matt. 7: 24–7).

3. The *threats* the psalmist fears most are the hypocritical
show of friendship (verse 4) and the glitter of wealth (verse 10)
that insidiously allure men from faith in God. He compares
this danger to the incessant *battering* of enemy siege-engines on
the weakest part of a city's defences, where the wall is already
leaning as if to fall.

4. *his height:* the defensive 'rock' or strong 'tower' on
which he has taken his stance (verse 2), that is, his faith in God.
topple . . . fallen stones: continuing the metaphor of verse 3.
hypocrites: the purpose of their smooth talk is not so much to
ingratiate themselves as to mask their treachery (cp. Ps. 12: 2).

5–8. He calls the faithful to renewed trust in God.

5f. Cp. verses 1f. The N.E.B. translation smooths over
some minor differences between the two versions of the
refrain, but it retains the important variant: 'deliverance' is
now replaced by *hope of deliverance*, or better just 'hope'. Not
only does he rejoice in past or present deliverance, but the
assurance he finds in God enables him to look forward with
hope and to encourage others to do the same. The purposeful
introduction of variants to refrains in Hebrew poetry is not
uncommon (cp. on Ps. 49: 20).

7. Knowledge of deliverance directed the psalmist's
thoughts to his enemies (verses 1–4), but the assurance of hope
turns his mind entirely to God and so he reiterates his con-

fession of faith. *my honour:* or 'my glory'; the word contains the double notion of dignity and happiness.

8. Cp. Phil. 4: 6: 'have no anxiety, but in everything make your requests known to God in prayer'. The appeal to *Trust always in God* must also be compared with the warning against trust in material possessions in verse 10. *pour out your hearts:* cp. Ps. 42: 4.

9–12. He warns against materialism and reasserts the power and the faithfulness of God.

9. *In very truth:* contrast verses 2, 6 which speak of God's permanence. *faithless:* better 'deceptive', literally 'a lie'; though they appear to have great security and importance, in reality they are ephemeral, *a puff of wind* (cp. Ps. 39: 5), and weightless *in the balance*, mere nothings.

10. *Put no trust:* the negative counterpart of verse 8. *wealth breeds wealth:* hence the temptation to *set...your heart on it* and even to obtain it by *extortion* or theft. The psalmist's warning is about trust in, not use of, material possessions (cp. 1 Tim. 6: 17–19).

11. *One . . . two:* this kind of formula is a fairly common poetic device in which the greater numeral is the significant one (cp. Prov. 30: 18, 21, 29). Here the implication is that the number of essential things to be *learnt* about God is very small and may be reduced to just two (cp. Mark 12: 29–31). Firstly, God does not only make promises of blessing and protection, he also has the power to fulfil them.

12. Secondly, God is true to these promises, for in his *True love* he is faithful to his covenant with his people (see on Ps. 51: 1). Therefore he will *requite a man for his deeds* (cp. Rom. 2: 6; Rev. 2: 23; 22: 12) and those whose deeds express their trust in him will never have anything to fear; they will surely know him as their 'tower of strength' (verse 6). ✻

MY HEART THIRSTS FOR GOD
63

1 O God, thou art my God, I seek thee early
     with a heart that thirsts for thee
     and a body wasted with longing for thee,
  like a dry and thirsty land that has no water.

2 So longing, I come before thee in the sanctuary
     to look upon thy power and glory.

3 Thy true love is better than life;
     therefore I will sing thy praises.

4 And so I bless thee all my life
     and in thy name lift my hands in prayer.

5 I am satisfied as with a rich and sumptuous feast
     and wake the echoes with thy praise.

6 When I call thee to mind upon my bed
     and think on thee in the watches of the night,

7 remembering how thou hast been my help
     and that I am safe in the shadow of thy wings,

8 then I humbly follow thee with all my heart,
     and thy right hand is my support.

9 Those who seek my life, bent on evil,
     shall sink into the depths of the earth;

10 they shall be given over to the sword;
     they shall be carrion for jackals.

11 The king shall rejoice in God,
     and whoever swears by God's name shall exult;
     the voice of falsehood shall be silenced.

✻ This psalm expresses a rich variety of religious sentiments.
It passes rapidly through expressions of longing (verses 1–2),

praise (verses 3–5), confidence (verses 6–8) and judgement (verses 9–10) to a prayer that mentions the king (verse 11), but this sequence is unusual and raises problems about determining the psalm's setting in worship. There are, however, some indications that it would be suitable for use in a night vigil (see especially verses 1 and 6), and its theme is similar to that already seen in other vigil psalms (e.g. Ps. 27), namely the soul's longing for God's nearness and its confident hope of satisfaction. The Hebrew text has a title that ascribes the psalm to David 'when he was in the Wilderness of Judah', thus inviting the worshipper to compare his plight with David's either when he fled from Saul (1 Sam. 23: 14; 24: 1) or from Absalom (2 Sam. 15: 23). The reference to the king in verse 11 certainly suggests that it was composed before the exile.

1f. The psalmist seeks God's presence in the temple.

1. *I seek thee early:* literally 'I seek thee at dawn.' Daybreak, bringing light and warmth to the earth, is an apt symbol of hope for relief from oppression and the joy of spiritual satisfaction (cp. on Pss. 5: 3; 17: 15). The psalmist's need is indeed spiritual. It is no physical disease that causes his body to waste, but the thirst of his *heart*, his *longing* for God (cp. Ps. 42: 2). Thirst and water continue to be used as symbols of spiritual longing and satisfaction in the New Testament (cp. John 4: 14; Rev. 22: 17).

2. *in the sanctuary:* see on verse 6 and cp. Pss. 5: 7; 27: 4f. *come before . . . look upon:* both Hebrew verbs could be translated 'look upon'. They are used elsewhere in connection with prophetic visions and here express the psalmist's hope that the dawning will bring the vision of God that is to restore his joy (cp. Ps. 17: 15). It has been suggested that the phrase *power and glory* cloaks an allusion to the Ark in the sanctuary, but it more probably refers to the experience of God's presence for which the psalmist's heart thirsts (cp. on Ps. 57: 5).

3–5. With complete faith in God's love he offers praise in anticipation of blessing.

3. *true love:* the faithfulness of God to bless his covenant people (see on Ps. 51: 1). In the Old Testament *life* is normally represented as the greatest of all blessings, but the psalmist realizes that communion with God is worth even more (cp. Ps. 27: 4; Phil. 1: 21).

4. By faith he has already entered into the joy of God's presence and so begins to *bless* or praise him. The style is that of hymns and thanksgiving psalms, characteristic of which is the exuberant vow of praise *all my life. lift my hands:* a traditional attitude of prayer expressing both adoration (Ps. 134: 2) and expectant supplication (Ps. 28: 2). *in thy name:* in recognition that the power of God revealed in history is still operative in the worshipper's life.

5. The N.E.B. offers a paraphrase rather than a translation of this verse. The satisfaction of knowing God's nearness is compared with being a guest at a banquet, feasting on the choicest foods (cp. Ps. 23: 5; Luke 14: 7–24). The man who has found this joy cannot but sing God's praise (cp. Ps. 22: 26).

6–8. During the night he meditates on God's protection and support.

6. *upon my bed:* the setting is the sanctuary, not a private bedroom (verse 2). It has therefore been held that this psalm was used at evening as the worshipper prepared to sleep at the sanctuary in expectation of a dream-vision, like Solomon's in the shrine at Gibeon (1 Kings 3: 4–15). But the psalmist hopes for his encounter at dawn (verse 1) and expects to spend the long hours of darkness, *the watches of the night,* in meditation (*think:* the verb is better translated 'meditate', as in Ps. 1: 2; so also the Revised Standard Version). The bed was then probably just a rug or mattress that the psalmist had brought for his own comfort.

7. *I am safe:* this translation depends on emendation. It suitably expresses the notion of security that is also conveyed by the phrase *in the shadow of thy wings* (cp. Ps. 57: 1), though it lacks the positive vitality of the Hebrew 'I sing praises' (cp.

verse 3). The temple setting itself doubtless helps to engender a sense of safety and confidence.

8. This is almost a definition in personalized language of the *ḥesed* relationship between God and his people in the covenant (verse 3), sometimes summed up in the words 'I will be your God and you shall be my people' (Jer. 7: 23). God's *right hand* is a symbol of his power (cp. Ps. 17: 7).

9–11. He stands firm in his faith that God will give judgement in favour of his loyal servants.

9. This is the first mention of enemies and since his problem is the loss of spiritual *life* or vitality (verses 1–2), they probably represent everything, human or otherwise, that separates him from God (see on Ps. 5: 3). Their fate is to return to their natural home in *the depths of the earth*, to Sheol, the source and destiny of all enervating and death-bearing forces.

10. God's victory will leave the spiritual battleground strewn with corpses, left unburied like *carrion for jackals*.

11. *The king shall rejoice in God:* some commentators regard this as intrusive, some think it indicates that the psalmist was the king, and some believe that it is a prayer for the king. But *The king . . . and whoever swears by God's name* is probably a comprehensive phrase denoting the whole community of the faithful with the king as its head, that is, in contrast with the opposing community picturesquely labelled *the voice of falsehood* (literally 'the mouth of liars'). The whole verse thus expresses the psalmist's confidence in God's faithfulness to vindicate his promises to his people and it is in the context of this hope that his expectation of personal fulfilment lies (see on verses 3, 8). ✲

67

KEEP ME SAFE FROM THE SECRET PLOTS OF
THE WICKED

64

1 Hear me, O God, hear my lament;
   keep me safe from the threats*a* of the enemy.
2   Hide me from the factions of the wicked,
       from the turbulent mob of evildoers,
3   who sharpen their tongues like swords
      and wing their cruel words like arrows,*b*
4   to shoot down the innocent from cover,
      shooting suddenly, themselves unseen.
5 They boldly*c* hide their snares,
   sure that none will see them;
6 they hatch their secret plans*d* with skill and cunning,
   with evil*e* purpose and deep design.
7   But God with his arrow shoots them down,
      and sudden is their overthrow.

8   They may repeat their wicked tales,*f*
       but their mischievous tongues*g* are their undoing.
       All who see their fate take fright at it,
9   every man is afraid;
         'This is God's work', they declare;
         they learn their lesson from what he has done.

[a] *Lit.* scares.
[b] and wing . . . arrows: *prob. rdg.; Heb.* they tread their arrow a cruel
word.   [c] *See first note on verse 8.*
[d] their secret plans: *prob. rdg.; Heb. unintelligible.*
[e] evil: *prob. rdg.; Heb.* man.
[f] They . . . tales: *transposed from after* boldly *in verse 5.*
[g] their mischievous tongues: *prob. rdg.; Heb.* against them their
tongues.

The righteous rejoice and seek refuge in the LORD   10
   and all the upright exult.

* Protection against slander and malicious intrigue is the psalmist's whole desire. His calumniators may think themselves safe in their stealth, but he knows that nothing is hidden from God and their cunning and mischief will ultimately be their own undoing. The text of this psalm is badly damaged and presents many translation problems. Its date is unknown.

1–4. He appeals for protection from enemies who expertly camouflage their treachery.

1. The N.E.B. fails sufficiently to capture the mood of fearful horror expressed in the Hebrew: 'preserve my life from the enemy's terror'. He feels more than threatened; he is alarmed.

2. *Hide me:* 'shelter me', as in the phrase 'hide me in the shadow of thy wings' (Ps. 17: 8). *factions:* this rendering suits the parallelism, but the Authorized Version's 'secret counsel' captures the image of calculated scheming seen later in verse 6. *the wicked:* the ungodly, as opposed to the 'righteous' of verse 10. The Hebrew word used here suggests deliberate intention to cause hurt.

3. Having likened his slanderers to a plotting faction, he now compares their words with weapons used by insurgents. Some scholars have seen here a cloaked allusion to the casting of spells, but the tongue can be a cruel enough weapon without recourse to magic. 'they tread' (N.E.B. footnote): the archer puts his foot on the bow, not the arrow, to bend it.

4. Like any subversive movement, they fight *unseen* from the shadows, attacking *suddenly* and unexpectedly *from cover*. They are the faceless enemy that cannot be encountered in open conflict; no one can tell with whom the slanderous rumours started.

5–7. Though they feel safe in their secrecy, God knows their deeds and will reward them accordingly.

5. *their snares:* further instruments of subterfuge. Metaphors drawn from hunting are frequently used of enemy activity in the psalms (cp. Ps. 7: 15). *none will see them:* they would conceal their purposes from others by native cunning, but they would worry little about trying to hide them from God, for they doubtless believe he has no active care for this world (Ps. 10: 13).

6. This verse seems to be textually corrupt, and it is difficult to avoid some emendation. The Hebrew could be interpreted as an utterance of delight by the wicked as they approve their apparent success in concealing their conspiracy: 'Who can search out our crimes? We have thought out a cunningly conceived plot.' (Revised Standard Version.) But the N.E.B. translation presents a terrifying picture of human malice and intellect conniving together to *hatch . . . secret plans* too brutal and subtle for any man to withstand.

7. God's recompense matches the crime precisely. *with his arrow* he *shoots* down the ungodly, just as they do to the sufferer, and his action is equally *sudden* (cp. verses 3–4). The theme of this and the following verses is that sin has a boomerang effect, that it rebounds on the head of its perpetrators.

8–10. The consequence of God's judgement is that the faithful will rejoice and all who see it will learn to fear God.

8. There are problems in this verse that suggest a need for textual emendations, but the importation of a line from verse 5 is quite unnecessary. The main point appears to be that it is the very weapons they used against others, their own sharp tongues (verse 3), that prove to be the *undoing* of the wicked.

9. *every man:* not the whole of mankind, but all who see or hear of his case. Divine vindication is a public act. *is afraid:* this is a wholesome fear or reverence of God, unlike the 'fear' inspired by the wicked (see on verse 1).

10. *The righteous rejoice:* or 'Let the righteous rejoice.' Though the psalmist still awaits his final deliverance, the vision of judgement has strengthened his faith to the extent that he can once more begin to *rejoice* and can summon others

to share in his joy. *The righteous;* those who have a right
relationship with God, the faithful. ✳

GOD GIVES BLESSING IN ABUNDANCE

65

We owe thee praise, O God, in Zion;   1–2
thou hearest prayer, vows shall be paid to thee.
All men shall lay their guilt before thee: 3
     our sins are too heavy for us;[a]
     only thou canst blot them out.
Happy is the man of thy choice, whom thou dost bring   4
     to dwell in thy courts;
   let us enjoy the blessing of thy house,
     thy holy temple.
   By deeds of terror answer us with victory,   5
     O God of our deliverance,
   in whom men trust from the ends of the earth
     and far-off seas;
     thou art girded with strength,   6
and by thy might dost fix the mountains in their place,
dost calm the rage of the seas and their raging waves.[b]   7
     The dwellers at the ends of the earth   8
     hold thy signs in awe;
thou makest morning and evening sing aloud in triumph.

Thou dost visit the earth and give it abundance,   9
     as often as thou dost enrich it
   with the waters of heaven, brimming in their
     channels,

     [a] *So Sept.; Heb.* me.
     [b] *Prob. rdg.; Heb. adds* and tumult of people.

providing rain[a] for men.
For this is thy provision for it,

10 watering its furrows, levelling its ridges,
softening it with showers and blessing its growth.

11   Thou dost crown the year with thy good gifts
and the palm-trees drip with sweet juice;

12   the pastures in the wild are rich with blessing
and the hills wreathed in happiness,

13   the meadows are clothed with sheep
and the valleys mantled in corn,
      so that they shout, they break into song.

﹡ In this hymn the congregation offers praise to God for his generous mercy towards those who would enter his presence (verses 1–4), for the sense of worship and joy that his creation inspires (verses 5–8) and for the rich abundance with which he provides for the earth (verses 9–13). The concluding section suggests that the psalm would have been suitable for use when the winter rains had softened the soil and clothed the earth with verdure, perhaps in connection with the offering of the first sheaf at Passover time (Lev. 23: 10–14). But the opening verses show clearly that it also had a much wider significance for the life and worship of the people. The date of composition is uncertain.

1–4. Praise to God who hears, forgives and blesses all who come to him.

1f. These verses point to a festival setting or some special occasion when the people assembled in the temple on Mt Zion to give thanks in fulfilment of *vows* made in times of hardship (cp. Ps. 66: 13f.). The psalm would be particularly appropriate after a season of drought (cp. verses 9–13) when *prayer* for relief would certainly have been offered, but in less dramatic

[a] *Or* corn.

circumstances the *praise* would relate to the answering of regular, yearly prayers for prosperity, or even to the granting of other more spiritual blessings. *We owe thee praise:* as in the versions; the Hebrew reads 'praise is silence for thee', suggesting submissive and trusting reverence (cp. Ps. 62: 1, 5).

3. *All men:* literally 'all flesh'; in the context this refers primarily to Israel or to all whose prayer has been heard, but faith must also look forward to a time when all mankind will acknowledge the grace and power of God (cp. Ps. 22: 27) who alone is able to *blot out...sins* and relieve the burden of *guilt* that becomes *too heavy* for human shoulders to bear.

4. *Happy is the man of thy choice:* these words must apply to all God's people, for a similar benediction is pronounced over the whole nation in Ps. 33: 12 and the privilege of dwelling in God's *courts* is extended to all the faithful in Ps. 15. The immediate setting here is the Jerusalem temple, but the worshipper's thoughts are lifted to God and to *the blessing* of dwelling in his presence all the days of his life (cp. Ps. 23: 6).

5–8. Praise to God who inspires all men and creation with wonder and joy.

5. *By deeds of terror answer us:* this prayer sits most awkwardly in the context and the Hebrew is perhaps better represented, as in most other English translations, by a further ascription of praise in keeping with the mood of the psalm as a whole: 'Thou dost answer us in acts that fill us with awe.' *victory:* literally 'righteousness'; God's saving interventions must always be expressions of his divine, moral character. *in whom men trust:* that is, unconsciously at present, for few know him to be their provider and sustainer, but as in verse 3, the hope of ultimate open acknowledgement is also implied.

6f. *girded with strength:* like a warrior equipped for battle. The enemies are *the seas and their raging waves*, symbols of turbulence and disorder (cp. Ps. 93: 3), sometimes personified in the creation stories of the ancient world as a monstrous many-headed sea-serpent (cp. Ps. 74: 13f.). Though the earth is constantly threatened by these raging waters, God is

73

eminently able to maintain *calm* in his universe (and amongst its tumultuous people, N.E.B. footnote), for his *might* created it. It was he who fixed the very *mountains*, those tokens of complete solidity and permanence.

8. *signs:* not simply the heavenly bodies as in Gen. 1: 14, but anything that shows God's power and tells of his glory to all mankind, as far as *the ends of the earth* (cp. Ps. 19: 4). The triumph song of *morning and evening* is the hymn of praise that reflects God's majesty and splendour through all creation (see more fully on Ps. 19: 1–4).

9–13. Praise to God who with rich bounty stirs the earth to life and song.

9f. *the waters of heaven:* literally 'the stream of God'. God is likened to a master-gardener (cp. Ps. 1: 3) supplying water for the earth from his own store (see on Ps. 33: 7), and conducting it in streams along *brimming* irrigation *channels* (cp. Job 38: 25) to the *furrows* and *ridges* of the fields. The autumn rains soften the hard, baked soil, preparing it for ploughing and cultivation; the spring rains provide the *growth*. *rain:* the translators must have thought this rendering required by parallelism and context, for the Hebrew reads 'corn' (as N.E.B. footnote).

11. When the rains have been plentiful, the farmer can watch his crops maturing and feel sure that God is going to *crown the year* with an abundant harvest. *the palm-trees:* the more familiar translation is 'thy cart-tracks', suggesting the picture of a richly laden harvester's waggon overflowing with produce.

12f. *the pastures in the wild*, usually drab and unfit for cultivation, are garlanded with rich greenery, while sheep and corn cover the hills and valleys like a festive robe. The very earth is alive with happiness and song, sharing in the festival praise of the worshipping congregation. ✻

74

COME AND SEE WHAT GOD HAS DONE

66

Acclaim our God, all men on earth;   1
   let psalms declare the glory of his name,   2
   make glorious his praise.
Say unto God, 'How fearful are thy works!   3
Thy foes cower before the greatness of thy strength.

  All men on earth fall prostrate in thy presence,   4
and sing to thee, sing psalms in honour of thy name.'

  Come and see all that God has done,   5
   tremendous in his dealings with mankind.

  He turned the waters into dry land   6
so that his people*a* passed through the sea*b* on foot;
there did we rejoice in him.*c*

  He rules for ever by his power,   7
his eye rests on the nations;
let no rebel rise in defiance.

  Bless our God, all nations;   8
   let his praise be heard far and near.
He set us in the land of the living;   9
he keeps our feet from stumbling.

  For thou, O God, hast put us to the proof   10
   and refined us like silver.

  Thou hast caught us in a net,   11
thou hast bound our bodies fast;
thou hast let men ride over our heads.   12

[a] his people: *Heb*. they.
[b] *Lit*. river.
[c] there . . . him: *or* where we see this, we will rejoice in him.

We went through fire and water,
   but thou hast brought us out into liberty.[a]

13 I will bring sacrifices into thy temple
      and fulfil my vows to thee,
14   vows which I made with my own lips
        and swore with my own mouth when in distress.
15   I will offer thee fat beasts as sacrifices
        and burn rams as a savoury offering;
      I will make ready oxen and he-goats.

16 Come, listen, all who fear God,
      and I will tell you all that he has done for me;
17   I lifted up my voice in prayer,
        his high praise was on my lips.[b]
18   If I had cherished evil thoughts,
        the Lord would not have heard me;
19   but in truth God has heard
        and given heed to my prayer.
20   Blessed is God
      who has not withdrawn his love and care from me.

☆ The most striking peculiarity of this psalm is the abrupt
change from 'we'/'us' in verses 1–12 to 'I'/'me' in verses
13–20. Amongst a wide variety of explanations are suggestions that the psalm is composite, or that it was written for use
by the king speaking on behalf of both his people and himself,
or that it is a thanksgiving liturgy in which a worshipper
comes forward to dedicate his offering at the end of a congregational hymn of praise. However, there is no good reason
why this whole psalm could not also be used by any individual
as he celebrates some personal deliverance: as he prepares to

[a] *So Sept.; Heb.* moisture.
[b] on my lips: *lit.* under my tongue.

present his offering (verses 13–15), he calls on the assembled congregation, indeed on all men (verse 1), to share his joy by giving thanks for God's greater acts in the history of his people (verses 1–12) and bears testimony before them to his own experience of God's loving action (verses 16–20). Perhaps the best comment on this psalm is Ps. 22: 22–31, where many of the same themes are to be found. The date of composition cannot be determined.

1–7. He summons all men to praise God and acknowledge his majestic power, seen especially in his historic dealings with Israel (cp. Ps. 22: 27f.).

1. *all men on earth:* literally 'all the earth' (so also verse 4). This is the exuberant invitation of an elated worshipper; in his rapture of praise he would have the whole earth join in his song.

2. *the glory of his name:* the splendour of his revealed majesty. God's *name* is God himself or his presence as known by men. *declare:* to God and to men; *praise*, as it were, reflects God's splendour back to God himself, but also outwards to other people (cp. Ps. 96: 1–3).

3. *How fearful:* the action of God strikes terror in the heart of his enemies, but inspires wonder and praise in the faithful (see Ps. 65: 5). *thy works:* the psalmist thinks especially of the exodus (verse 6), but also of many other occasions of deliverance (verse 12).

4. Cp. verses 1–2. In a moment of deep ecstasy the psalmist grasps this vision of universal praise. But it represents the consummation of all religious hope which can be realized now only in spiritual foretaste. Hence the tenses are more commonly rendered in the future in the older translations.

5. *Come and see:* probably a general invitation to learn of God's works rather than to watch them enacted in a cultic drama (cp. Ps. 46: 8). *tremendous:* the same Hebrew word is translated 'fearful' in verse 3.

6. *waters . . . sea:* literally 'sea . . . river'. The two words are commonly used as synonyms in Canaanite poetry. Thus the N.E.B. considers that the allusion is simply to the crossing of

the Red Sea (Exod. 14: 21 – 15: 21), but the psalmist may also have been thinking of the similar crossing of the River Jordan (Josh. 3: 9 – 4: 24). Both events are fundamental in the story of God's saving acts (cp. Ps. 114: 3, 5), the former concluding the escape from slavery, the latter inaugurating the occupation of the promised land. *there did we rejoice:* the verb could equally be a future, hence the paraphrase in the N.E.B. footnote, 'where we see this', that is, every time these events are re-hearsed anew.

7. God's sovereignty is eternal and unchanging. He rules now by the same power he manifested at the Red Sea and the Jordan and will continue to do so *for ever. his eye rests:* he is the world's watchman, the vigilant governor of *the nations.* Note the contrast with verse 6: God's acts in history bring joy to the faithful, but stand as a warning to the rebel (see also on verse 3).

8–12. He calls his own people to praise, reminding them of God's continuing providence (cp. Ps. 22: 23).

8. *all nations:* rather 'peoples'; there is no 'all' in the Hebrew. Though it is sometimes synonymous with 'nations' (cp. Ps. 67: 3), this word usually denotes a religious group and here probably refers to those in Israel and outside who acknowledge the LORD. Certainly this section no longer speaks of God's 'fearfulness' or the right attitude of the nations; it is concerned solely with his care for Israel.

9. *in the land of the living:* literally 'among the living' or 'in life'; that is, in well-being. This meaning is required by the parallelism, for *feet . . . stumbling* is a figure of misfortune (cp. Ps. 121: 3).

10. The story of God's dealings with Israel is one of constant review and purification. But Israel is precious to him and his processes of scrutiny and judgement are as careful and thorough as those of a silversmith refining his valuable metals. The same metaphor is also used of his dealings with individuals (cp. Ps. 26: 2).

11. The process of purification is not explained, though the

graphic metaphors generally suggest punishment by foreign oppression. But the figures are largely conventional and cannot be tied to any particular events in history.

12. *men ride over our heads:* a picture of defeated soldiers flung to the ground and mercilessly trampled by enemy horses (cp. Isa. 51: 23). *fire and water:* symbols of extreme danger. *liberty:* not escape from meaningless suffering, but the final goal of a process of purification wrought by God himself. Where God is acknowledged king, no suffering is meaningless (cp. Rom. 5: 3–5). 'moisture' (N.E.B. footnote): the Hebrew is more usually rendered 'saturation' or 'abundance', the allusion being to the luxuriance of the promised land.

13–15. The psalmist now prepares to present his own thank-offering in fulfilment of vows made in his hour of distress (cp. Ps. 22: 25f.).

15. The quantity of the sacrifices listed here is more than any but a king or some extremely wealthy person could possibly afford. But this is poetry and it is unlikely that it should be so literally interpreted. The parallel structure of the verse shows that the poet is simply describing the same kind of sacrifice in three different ways. (According to Lev. 22: 18f. the votive offering may be 'a male without defect, of cattle, sheep, or goats'.) Nevertheless, his imagined offerings are lavish, and this is perhaps because he is trying to express his desire to give beyond his best, knowing that even that would be an offering far too small to repay God's kindnesses.

16–20. He concludes by giving testimony to the way God has answered his prayers (cp. Ps. 22: 24).

16. *all who fear God:* those who stand in awe and reverence before him, the faithful. The invitation is addressed first and foremost to the congregation present, but doubtless the wider appeal of verses 1 and 8 are still in mind.

17. *prayer* for help coupled with *praise* anticipating the action of God in faith is a common feature in the psalms (Pss. 13, 22), as also in the teaching of the New Testament (Phil. 4: 4–6; 1 Thess. 5: 16–18).

18. To be effective, prayer must also be offered in utter sincerity (Ps. 17: 1; 1 John 3: 21f.).

19. *has heard:* and answered; when God hears, he does not simply listen, he responds in action.

20. *his love and care:* literally 'my prayer and his love'. That is, he blesses God because he has not rejected his prayer and also because he has faithfully maintained his promised love (see on Ps. 51: 1) towards him. These are fitting words to end a psalm that began with praise for the loving care shown by God in his sovereign dealings with his people, for in them the psalmist acknowledges that he personally enjoys the same privileges only because he is a member of this faithful community. Hence his invitation to others who would share in these blessings is 'Come, acclaim him also as your king, and praise him' (verses 1–7). ✶

GOD GRANT US HIS BLESSING

67

1 God be gracious to us and bless us,
   God make his face shine upon us,

2 that his*a* ways may be known on earth
   and his*a* saving power among all the nations.

3 Let the peoples praise thee, O God;
   let all peoples praise thee.

4 Let all nations rejoice and shout in triumph;
   for thou dost judge the peoples with justice
   and guidest the nations of the earth.

5 Let the peoples praise thee, O God;
   let all peoples praise thee.

6 The earth has given its increase
   and God, our God, will bless us.

[a] *So Pesh.; Heb.* thy.

God grant us his blessing, 7
that all the ends of the earth may fear him.

✻ It is usually held, on the basis of verse 6*a*, that this is a harvest thanksgiving hymn, but there is a great deal more in it
than thankfulness for a good crop. It is much rather the prayer
of a congregation or an individual that God will bless his
people with the bounteousness of his presence, for which the
fruits of the earth are but an illustration, and thus make his
goodness known to all men. The psalm has a well-balanced
structure: it opens and closes with prayers for blessings that
will lead to world-wide conversion (verses 1–2, 7), while the
middle section falls into two parallel parts, each a call to
universal praise (verses 3–4*a*, 5) followed by the motives for
praise, firstly, God's just, world-wide rule and secondly, his
bounty (verses 4*b*–*c*, 6). The allusion to the earth's increase
need not, therefore, limit its usefulness to the season of harvest.
The psalm provides no clues about its date of composition.

1. These opening words are taken from the priestly blessing of
Num. 6: 24–6 and are a prayer for the knowledge of God's vital
and personal presence (*his face*) which brings blessings beyond
measure, certainly beyond the joy of harvest (Ps. 4: 6f.). *make
his face shine:* that is, with the radiance of delight and approval.

2. God's blessing is not granted for selfish enjoyment, but to
reveal *his ways . . . on earth*, so that others, ultimately *all the
nations*, will see his glory and themselves desire to enter his
presence and serve him; cp. the promise to Abraham in Gen.
12: 1–3.

3. The word translated *peoples* usually denotes a religious
group (see on Ps. 66: 8), but here is synonymous with 'nations'.
Behind such a vision of the nations worshipping the God of
Israel lies the belief that he is ultimately supreme in the world.

4. *rejoice:* free joy is the essence of true worship (cp. Ps. 32:
11). No compulsion is laid on the nations; they rejoice as they
see the *justice* of God's rule, that it is without tyranny or

partiality, and as they see that he guides them like a loving shepherd (the same Hebrew verb is used in Ps. 23: 2).

5. See verse 3.

6. It is perhaps best to see here, not thanksgiving for a particular harvest just completed, though the psalm would certainly be appropriate to such an occasion, but a general reference to the continuing bounty of God as the living illustration of his just rule and shepherd-like care (verse 4), or of that blessing on Israel which will convert the nations (verses 1–2). *will bless:* that is, will continue to bless as he has done; or it may be preferable to translate 'is blessing', on analogy with the parallel verse 4 where the same Hebrew tenses are rendered by the English present.

7. A résumé of the opening prayer. *all the ends of the earth:* the whole earth to its furthest bounds; the Israelites believed the earth to be like a flat disc suspended in a cosmic sea (see on Ps. 24: 2). *fear:* stand in awe and reverence before; 'the fear of the LORD' is virtually a synonym for true religion (cp. Pss. 33: 8; 34: 9). *

GOD ARISES IN VICTORY

68

* Probably no other psalm presents as many problems of interpretation as this one. The Hebrew text abounds with words that are either corrupt or unique in the Old Testament, the style changes abruptly several times, and there are many awkward, sudden shifts in thought. In consequence there exists a great variety of theories about the psalm's origin and use, some of which imply that it is not properly a psalm at all. For example, it has been described as a random collection of poetic fragments and even as an index-catalogue of the first lines of about thirty different psalms. Some scholars believe it to be a collection of short songs written and arranged to accompany the different actions in some festival drama that is

unfortunately lost to history. But there are also many who would argue for its unity as a hymn in two parts reviewing the past and future of the people of God, bracketed by introductory and concluding calls to praise (verses 1–6, 32–5). The first section (verses 7–18) surveys Israel's history from the exodus to the conquest of Jerusalem, interpreting it as God's triumphant march from Mt Sinai to Mt Zion; the second (verses 19–31) looks forward to the final victory of God and the establishment of his universal kingdom, to the day when Israel will rejoice, the nations will be subdued and peace will reign on earth. Several scholars believe this to be one of the earlier psalms in the Psalter, but opinion is divided on this matter. ✶

God arises and his enemies are scattered;   1
   those who hate him flee before him,
   driven away like smoke in the wind;   2
   like wax melting at the fire,
   the wicked perish at the presence of God.
But the righteous are joyful, they exult before God,   3
     they are jubilant and shout for joy.

Sing the praises of God, raise a psalm to his name,   4
   extol him who rides over the desert plains.*a*
Be joyful*b* and exult before him,
   father of the fatherless, the widow's champion –   5
     God in his holy dwelling-place.
God gives the friendless a home   6
   and brings out the prisoner safe and sound;
but rebels must live in the scorching desert.

   O God, when thou didst go forth before thy people,   7
     marching across the wilderness,

[a] over the desert plains: *or* on the plains.
[b] Be joyful: *prob. rdg.; Heb.* In the LORD is his name.

8 earth trembled, the very heavens quaked
before God the lord of Sinai, before God the God of
      Israel.

9   Of thy bounty, O God, thou dost refresh with rain
      thy own land in its weariness,
      the land which thou thyself didst provide,
10   where thy own people made their home,
which thou, O God, in thy goodness providest for the
      poor.

11–13 The Lord proclaims good news:[a]
'Kings with their armies have fled headlong.'
O mighty host, will you linger among the sheepfolds
      while the women in your tents divide the spoil –
an image of a dove, its wings sheathed in silver
      and its pinions in yellow gold –
14   while the Almighty scatters kings far and wide
      like snowflakes falling on Zalmon?

15   The hill of Bashan is a hill of God indeed,
      a hill of many peaks is Bashan's hill.
16 But, O hill of many peaks, why gaze in envy
at the hill where the LORD delights to dwell,
where the LORD himself will live for ever?
17   Twice ten thousand were God's chariots, thousands
      upon thousands,[b]
when the Lord came in holiness from Sinai.[c]
18 Thou didst go up to thy lofty home with captives in
      thy train,

[a] proclaims good news: *or* gives the word, women bearing good news.
[b] thousands upon thousands: *mng. of Heb. phrase uncertain.*
[c] came . . . from Sinai: *prob. rdg.; Heb. obscure.*

having received tribute from men;
in the presence of the LORD God no rebel could live.[a]

✻ 1–6. Introductory call to praise. God's action brings judgement, but to the faithful that means blessing and joy.

1. These opening words are a variation on the prayer of Moses when the Ark began its journey in the wilderness (Num. 10: 35). It may be, as some believe, that this psalm was composed to accompany a ritual procession with the Ark in Jerusalem (see also on verses 24–7), but the psalmist's thoughts dwell more on God himself, or his 'presence' (verse 2), of which the Ark was a symbol. *his enemies:* that is *those who hate him* or 'the wicked' (verse 2), those who are not of the community of 'the righteous' (verse 3), his faithful people.

2. *driven away like smoke in the wind:* a picture of that which has no real worth or permanence and must disappear without trace (cp. Pss. 1: 4; 37: 20).

3. On the surpassing joy of the faithful in God's 'presence', see especially 4: 6–8.

4. The middle portion of this verse admits of more than one translation. *extol:* or 'build up a highway' (cp. Isa. 57: 14; 62: 10); literally 'lift up', with no object expressed. The context may suggest praise, or equally a summons to the faithful, like that in Isa. 40: 3, to 'clear a highway across the desert for our God'. *who rides over the desert plains:* or 'who rides upon the clouds' (Revised Standard Version). In Canaanite literature Baal is sometimes named 'the cloud-rider' and the picture of God as a heavenly charioteer does appear in verse 33 (cp. Pss. 18: 10; 104: 3), but the N.E.B.'s translation coheres better with the theme of God's wilderness journey in verses 1 and 7–8. *Be joyful:* this reading depends on an emendation; but by regarding the particle translated 'In' in the N.E.B. footnote as an indicator of emphasis, it is also possible to render the Hebrew 'his name is none other than the LORD'.

[a] in the presence . . . live: *so Pesh.; Heb. unintelligible.*

5. *the fatherless, the widow:* typical examples of the weak and 'friendless' (verse 6) who ultimately can look to none but God for protection (cp. Ps. 10: 14). *his holy dwelling-place:* the temple on Mt Zion is an earthly representation of God's heavenly abode (see on Ps. 11: 4) and probably both are in mind here (cp. verses 16, 34–5).

6. This verse contains a clear allusion to the exodus. God brought out a *friendless* people held *prisoner* in Egypt and sought to give them *a home* (see verse 10). But the wilderness generation proved to be a race of *rebels* and therefore spent their lives *in the scorching desert*, being refused entry to the promised land (Num. 14: 26–35; Ps. 95: 8–11). Here is a statement of God's dealings with his own people, not with mankind in general.

7–18. God's triumphant march from Sinai to Zion.

7. God leads his people out *across the wilderness* like a military commander *marching* in triumph at the head of his army. Verses 7–8 are a most appropriate adaptation of Judg. 5: 4f., lines from the victory hymn of Deborah celebrating God's help in battle against the Canaanites.

8. *God the lord of Sinai:* a very likely rendering of an obscure Hebrew construction. Older translations suggest a reference to the earthquake that accompanied God's appearance on Mt Sinai, according to the Hebrew text of Exod. 19: 18. The divine titles in this verse describe the relationship between God and Israel established at Mt Sinai; they do not limit his activity to one place or nation.

9f. The scene now moves to Canaan, God's *own land* which in his goodness he had prepared as a home for his *own people*. Though it knew *weariness* in the dry summer seasons, unlike Egypt or the wilderness it was a land of abundant rain (cp. Ps. 65: 9f.). *the poor:* the humble faithful who know that they are not self-sufficient and realize their need for God (cp. on Ps. 40: 17).

11–13. The psalmist now recalls the battles in the time of the judges by which possession of the land was secured, his language once more recalling the song of Deborah. The cry of triumph is raised and the poet, excitedly reliving the scene, urges the host of Israel to follow up its victory and not *linger among the* peaceful *sheepfolds* (cp. Judg. 5: 16) while *the women* share out rich *spoil* of war (cp. Judg. 5: 30) which includes objects like this richly plated *image of a dove*. The translation of these verses actually presents many problems, some of which the N.E.B. has resolved by emendation and re-arrangement of the text. The *mighty host* in the Hebrew is in fact a company of 'women bearing good news' (N.E.B. footnote), possibly wives greeting their battle-stained husbands with joyous triumph-songs (cp. 1 Sam. 18: 6f.). Again, the *dove* of silver and gold is attached to *the sheepfolds* in the Hebrew, perhaps emphasizing the picture of pastoral peace and wealth that awaits Israel in Canaan.

14. *like snowflakes:* a picture of pell-mell flight. *Zalmon:* the name means 'dark', 'shady' and may refer to any wooded height; there was a hill near Shechem known by this name (Judg. 9: 48), but no battle is known to have been fought there.

15–18. The poet's thoughts turn to Mt Zion, the final resting-place for the Ark (2 Sam. 6), God's chosen abode at the end of his journey from Sinai.

15. *a hill of many peaks:* probably Mt Hermon to the north of Bashan which itself is not actually a mountain but a rich plateau region in northern Transjordan (cp. Ps. 22: 12). *a hill of God:* a hill worthy to be the abode of God, or simply 'a mighty hill'.

16. The stately northern mountains are represented as looking *in envy* on the insignificant little hill of Zion. *where the LORD delights to dwell:* see verse 5.

17. God is depicted as entering Zion in triumph at the head of a vast army. *God's chariots:* probably his heavenly host (2 Kings 6: 17), but the psalmist doubtless also has the host of Israel in mind (cp. verse 24). *in holiness:* surrounded by an aura of glorious splendour and divine majesty (see on Ps. 29: 2).

18. The triumph scene continues: the conqueror comes bringing war-prisoners in his train and bearing tribute from the defeated, presumably the kings of Canaan. This verse is cited by Paul in Eph. 4: 8 in connection with the gifts of the Spirit, but reading 'he gave gifts to men' (so also the Targum and Peshitta). ✳

19   Blessed is the Lord:
    he carries us day by day,
        God our salvation.
20 Our God is a God who saves us,
    in the LORD God's hand lies escape from death.[a]
21 God himself will smite[b] the head of his enemies,
      those proud sinners with their flowing locks.
22 The Lord says, 'I will return from the Dragon,[c]
      I will return from the depths of the sea,
23 that you may dabble your feet in blood,
      while the tongues of your dogs are eager[d] for it.'

24   Thy procession, O God, comes into view,
    the procession of my God and King into the
          sanctuary:
25 at its head the singers, next come minstrels,
      girls among them playing on tambourines.
26   In the great concourse they bless God,
    all Israel assembled[e] bless the LORD.
27 There is the little tribe of Benjamin leading them,

[a] in the LORD God's hand ... death: *or* death is expelled by the LORD God.
[b] will smite: *or* smites.   [c] the Dragon: *or* Bashan.
[d] are eager: *prob. rdg.; Heb.* from enemies.
[e] assembled: *prob. rdg.; Heb. obscure.*

there the company of Judah's princes,
the princes of Zebulun and of Naphtali.

O God, in virtue of thy power*ᵃ* –   28
that godlike power which has acted for us –
command kings to bring gifts to thee   29
    for the honour of thy temple in Jerusalem.
Rebuke those wild beasts of the reeds, that herd of bulls,   30
    the bull-calf warriors of the nations;*ᵇ*
scatter these nations which revel in war;
    make them bring tribute*ᶜ* from Egypt,   31
    precious stones and silver from Pathros;*ᵈ*
let Nubia stretch out*ᵉ* her hands to God.

All you kingdoms of the world, sing praises to God,   32
    sing psalms to the Lord,
to him who rides on the heavens, the ancient heavens.   33
Hark! he speaks in the mighty thunder.
Ascribe all might to God, Israel's High God,   34
    Israel's pride and might throned in the skies.
    Terrible is God as he comes from his*ᶠ* sanctuary;   35
    he is Israel's own God,
who gives to his*ᵍ* people might and abundant power.

        Blessed be God.

✼ 19–31. The final victory of God.
    19. *day by day:* the story of God's past acts of salvation and
the hope of his future intervention are only of real value if they

[*a*] O God . . . power: *prob. rdg.; Heb.* Your God your power.
[*b*] *See second note on verse 31.*   [*c*] *Mng. of Heb. word uncertain.*
[*d*] precious . . . Pathros: *prob. rdg., transposed from verse 30 and slightly
altered.*   [*e*] stretch out: *prob. rdg.; Heb. obscure.*
[*f*] his: *so Sept.; Heb.* thy.   [*g*] his: *so Sept.; Heb. om.*

relate directly to man's present experience of God (cp. Deut. 5: 2–5). It is because they offer encouragement to faith, comfort in distress and incitement to obedience and praise that the psalms so often dwell upon them at length. *he carries us:* for a comparable metaphor, see Ps. 28: 9.

20. *death* is more than the termination of earthly existence; it is the antithesis of all that God is and gives. Its power is felt in sickness, despair or whatever weakens the life-principle in man. But *God's hand* is stronger. He delivers the faithful from death's grasp in this life and restores them to an enjoyment of his presence that not even the grave can destroy. *escape* is thus from the stranglehold of death and consequent separation from God (cp. Ps. 88: 5), not from the natural process of dying (see also on Pss. 6: 5; 49: 15).

21. *his enemies:* all that militate against God, including the minions of death (verse 20; cp. Ps. 73: 19) and the Dragon (verse 22). *smite the head:* cp. Ps. 74: 13, 'thou didst . . . break the sea-serpent's heads'. *flowing locks:* not merely a sign of pride; the warrior's hair was left uncut in wartime as a token of personal consecration (cp. Judg. 5: 2, N.E.B. footnote).

22. *the sea:* the repository of all earth's turbulence, sometimes personified as a monstrous *Dragon* which God conquers at creation (cp. Ps. 74: 13f.). The sea still rages and is daily defeated (Ps. 93: 3f.), but God's final conquest and victor's return lie in the future at the end of time. The traditional translation (N.E.B. footnote) suggests a return, perhaps a gathering-in of God's people to Mt Zion (verses 24–7), from earth's furthest extremities, 'Bashan' here being representative of the highest heights as opposed to *the depths of the sea.*

23. This is the scene of a battle-field when the fighting has ended, but as in Ps. 58: 10, the picture is metaphorical, for the setting is God's cosmic and final war against proud sinners, death and the Dragon.

24. *Thy procession:* the final victory march of God's people from his battle with the sea. It is possible that the psalmist's picture contains reflections of some festival ritual with the

Ark (see on verse 1), but the following verses suggest that his pattern is first and foremost the triumphal procession of Israel from the Red Sea (verse 7) to *the sanctuary* in Zion (verse 17).

25. *girls . . . playing on tambourines:* so also the women led the victory song at the sea in Exod. 15: 20 (cp. on verses 11–13).

26f. *all Israel:* only four tribes are named, two each of the southernmost and of the northernmost, but these must represent all twelve. *the princes:* not simply tribal representatives in a formal procession, but leaders of the whole tribes marching together as of old. *Benjamin leading them:* possibly because Saul, the first king, came from Benjamin or because Jerusalem was theoretically within its borders (Josh. 18: 16).

28. The celebration of victory passes naturally into prayer for its universal consummation. *which has acted for us:* that is in the exodus and settlement.

29. This prayer corresponds with the triumph scene in verse 18.

30. The various animal figures present a general image of warlike strength, even brutality, and are not to be identified with any particular nations (cp. Pss. 22: 12f.; 57: 4).

31. *Egypt . . . Pathros . . . Nubia:* that is, Lower and Upper Egypt and Ethiopia respectively, representing together the most venerable and also the most remote and exotic of the ancient nations. *stretch out her hands:* with gifts, or perhaps as a token of submission and worship (cp. Ps. 63: 4).

32–5. Concluding call to praise.

32. *sing praises . . . :* cp. verse 4; the original invitation that was addressed to Israel (see on verse 6) is now extended to *All you kingdoms of the world*, in keeping with the psalm's triumphant climax in the tribute of the nations.

33. *who rides on the heavens:* see on verse 4. *he speaks in the mighty thunder:* cp. Ps. 29.

34. *High God:* reading Hebrew ʿal as an abbreviation for ʿelyōn, a title for God used elsewhere in the psalms (see Ps. 57: 2). But ʿal is also the ordinary preposition meaning 'upon',

'over', hence the more widely accepted interpretation of this
verse: '*Ascribe all might to God*, whose *pride* is over *Israel* (to
protect his people) and whose *might* is *in the skies* (supreme in
the universe).' Indeed God's favour towards Israel and his
supremacy in the world are the main themes of this psalm.

35. *Terrible:* inspiring awe and reverence among the faithful, but terror among his enemies (cp. Ps. 66: 3). *his sanctuary:*
as in verses 5 and 16, both the Jerusalem temple and God's
heavenly abode are probably in mind. ✷

REPROACH IN GOD'S SERVICE HAS BROKEN
MY HEART

69

✷ This is the cry of one sunk in misery and beset by many
foes (verses 1–6) who scorn him for his devotion to God
(verses 7–12). He calls to God for help (verses 13–18) and,
bemoaning his condition (verses 19–21), calls down a curse on
his persecutors (verses 22–8). Then, as in the similar Ps. 22, his
theme turns to praise (verses 29–31) and he calls on the faithful
to join in his song (verses 32–6). His greatest burden is the sense
of dereliction: he is spurned by his fellows, even by his own
family (verses 8, 12), he has lost his awareness of God's
presence (verses 16–17) and the very friends to whom he turns
for comfort have only bitterness to offer (verses 20f.). His
situation is remarkably similar to that in which Jeremiah
found himself and there are some correspondences with the
prophet's use of language. The early church also noted the
close similarity in the persecution and sufferings of Jesus Christ,
for no psalm apart from Ps. 22 is more frequently cited in the
New Testament. Its traditional use by Christians on Good
Friday is thus most fitting. The closing verses 35f. suggest that
the psalm was composed during the exile, or else that it was
expanded by an editor during the exile. ✷

Save me, O God;   1
for the waters have risen up to my neck.
I sink in muddy depths and have no foothold;   2
I am swept into deep water, and the flood carries me
    away.
I am wearied with crying out, my throat is sore,   3
my eyes grow dim as I wait for God to help me.
Those who hate me without reason   4
are more than the hairs of my head;
they outnumber my hairs, those who accuse me falsely.
How can I give back what I have not stolen?
O God, thou knowest how foolish I am,   5
and my guilty deeds are not hidden from thee.
Let none of those who look to thee be shamed on my   6
    account,
O Lord GOD of Hosts;
let none who seek thee be humbled through my fault,
O God of Israel.
For in thy service I have suffered reproach;   7
I dare not show my face for shame.
I have become a stranger to my brothers,   8
an alien to my own mother's sons;
bitter enemies of thy temple tear me in pieces;[a]   9
those who reproach thee reproach me.
I have broken[b] my spirit with fasting,   10
only to lay myself open to many reproaches.
I have made sackcloth my clothing   11
and have become a byword among them.
Those who sit by the town gate talk about me;   12

[a] bitter . . . pieces: *or* zeal for thy temple has eaten me up (*cp. John 2: 17*).   [b] *So Scroll; Heb.* I wept.

drunkards sing songs about me[a] in their cups.

13   But I lift up this prayer to thee, O LORD:
      accept me[b] now in thy great love,
      answer me with thy sure deliverance, O God.

14   Rescue me from the mire, do not let me sink;
      let me be rescued from the muddy depths,[c]

15   so that no flood may carry me away,
          no abyss swallow me up,
          no deep close over me.

16 Answer me, O LORD, in the goodness of thy unfailing
          love,
      turn towards me in thy great affection.

17   I am thy servant, do not hide thy face from me.
      Make haste to answer me, for I am in distress.

18   Come near to me and redeem me;
          ransom me, for I have many enemies.

✻ 1–6. The psalmist appeals to God for rescue.

1f. He likens himself to a drowning man, but *the waters*
signify the sinister power of earth's harmful and death-bearing
forces (cp. Ps. 71: 20). They are the *muddy depths* of Sheol, the
place of the dead, elsewhere characterized as a land of 'mire'
and 'clay' (Ps. 40: 2); they are also the *deep water* or *the flood*
of the cosmic subterranean ocean, the repository of turbulence
and destruction (see on Ps. 24: 2). The psalmist's picture
of himself floundering in this flood of calamity conveys
the notion of weakness, terror, complete helplessness and
the urgency of his situation (cp. Jer. 38: 22; Jonah 2:
2–6).

[a] sing . . . me: *so Sept.; Heb.* songs.   [b] *Prob. rdg.; Heb.* acceptance.
[c] from . . . depths: *prob. rdg.; Heb.* from my haters and from the
depths.

3. He is completely exhausted by the strain of prolonged prayer with no answer. *my eyes grow dim:* grief has sapped his vitality and taken the sparkle from his eye (cp. Ps. 6: 7).

4. *hate me without reason:* applied to Jesus' enemies in John 15: 25 (but see also Ps. 35: 17). It is not only the number of the foes that distresses him, but the groundlessness of their enmity. He knows that he is not faultless (verse 5), but he is convinced that their accusations are false and unprovoked. *more than the hairs of my head:* a poetic hyperbole (cp. Ps. 40: 12). *How can I give back what I have not stolen?:* probably a popular proverb applicable to any situation of injured innocence.

5. By admitting his sins he commits himself to God's mercy, but his confession is not an admission that the accusations of his enemies are justified (see verse 4). *how foolish I am:* all sin, whether inadvertent or deliberate, is essentially foolishness (Ps. 107: 17).

6. His salvation will be a cause of rejoicing among the faithful (verse 32), but if he is abandoned, they must be discouraged and face the contempt of the world. Suitably the divine titles express his confidence in God, firstly that he has the power to intervene because he is sovereign over the *Hosts* of the universe (Ps. 24: 10), and secondly that he has promised to do so to protect his covenant people, *Israel.*

7–12. The faithful are bound to be discouraged if he is abandoned, for it is in God's service that he suffers reproach.

7. Cp. Jer. 15: 15: 'see what reproaches I endure for thy sake'.

8. Even his nearest relations treat him as a stranger, a very serious matter in a society where the bonds of kinship and life in the family unit are fundamental. The picture is one of complete forsakenness (see further verses 16–21).

9. *bitter enemies of thy temple tear me in pieces:* this rendering offers a good parallel to the rest of the verse, but the older translation, represented in the footnotes and reinforced in John 2: 17, makes perfectly good sense, especially in conjunction with verses 10*a* and 11*a*. To the majority of worshippers

'zeal for' the temple would mean devoted love for God's house (see Ps. 26: 8), perhaps even a desire to see it purged of abuses (John 2: 17), but to someone living after the fall of Jerusalem (verses 35f.) it would be a consuming desire to see it rebuilt. *those who reproach thee reproach me:* the faithful servant feels the bitterness of blasphemy against God as if it were directed personally against himself. These words are applied to Jesus in Rom. 15: 3.

1of. His *fasting* and *sackcloth* must express sorrow for his sins (verse 5; cp. Ps. 30: 11) or the intensity of his prayer (verse 3; cp. Ps. 35: 13). But there is no answer, only further *reproaches* and he becomes *a byword*, or object of scorn, among his people.

12. *by the town gate:* the civic centre where men in ancient Israel met to transact business, to hold court or simply to exchange gossip. He is the talk of the town, an object of bawdy ridicule.

13–18. He renews his prayer for deliverance.

13. *accept me now:* a translation based on conjectural emendation; the Hebrew reads 'at an acceptable time', implying a recognition that deliverance must come when God wills it, not necessarily immediately, as the N.E.B. would have it. God's *great love* or faithfulness (see on Ps. 51: 1) is his sole basis for hope (cp. verse 16). He certainly cannot plead his own merit (verses 5f.). *sure deliverance:* or 'salvation', that is release from suffering, victory over his enemies and vindication of his faith (see on Ps. 3: 2).

14f. He takes up the metaphors of verses 1f. Though the terminology is slightly different, the allusions are the same. *from the muddy depths:* a conjectural reading, but reference to 'my haters' in the Hebrew jars at this point (see the N.E.B. footnote). *close over me:* literally 'close its mouth over me', depicting the *deep* as a gross, devouring monster and conjuring an image of nightmarish terror.

16f. *Answer me:* not simply with words, but with 'deliverance'. The most intolerable aspect of his suffering is that he has incessantly cried out to God, even till his throat grew sore with his crying (verse 3), but has received no answer. This sense of dereliction is not simply something that adds to his sorrow. It is more unbearable than all the reproaches and pain he endures. Hence the climax of his prayer is his appeal *turn towards me*, or 'look at me', *do not hide thy face from me*, 'Come near to me' (verse 18). When God hides his face, he expresses displeasure, but when he turns to the worshipper, he makes his face shine upon him in blessing (Num. 6: 25). *I am thy servant:* he pleads his own faithfulness and dedication as a motive for God to act in his faithfulness or *unfailing love* (*ḥesed*, see verse 13); this is a direct appeal to the covenant relationship that exists between God and his people.

18. *Come near:* bring help and make your presence felt (see verses 16f.). *redeem me:* 'do your duty by me'. The redeemer is one who makes himself responsible for restoring the property or honour of another, usually a kinsman (cp. Ps. 19: 14), but here the verb and its parallel, *ransom*, are used figuratively of God's deliverance according to the obligation he has laid on himself in the covenant. ✶

Thou knowest what reproaches I bear,	19
all my anguish is seen by thee.	
Reproach has broken my heart,	20
my shame and my dishonour*a* are past hope;	
I looked for consolation and received none,	
for comfort and did not find any.	
They put poison in my food	21
and gave me vinegar when I was thirsty.	
May their own table be a snare to them	22
and their sacred feasts lure them to their ruin;	
may their eyes be darkened so that they do not see,	23
let a continual ague shake their loins.	

[a] my shame and my dishonour: *transposed from after* reproaches *in verse 19.*

24   Pour out thine indignation upon them
            and let thy burning anger overtake them.
25   May their settlements be desolate,
            and no one living in their tents;
26   for they pursue him whom thou hast struck down
      and multiply*a* the torments of those*b* whom thou hast
            wounded.
27   Give them the punishment their sin deserves;*c*
            exclude them from thy righteous mercy;
28   let them be blotted out from the book of life
            and not be enrolled among the righteous.

* 19–21. Forsaken by God, he finds no consolation amongst men, only inhuman enmity.

19. *Thou knowest . . . seen by thee:* cp. verse 5. Jeremiah used similar language in his appeals to God (Jer. 12: 3; 15: 15).

20. Cp. Jer. 23: 9. The removal of *my shame and my dishonour* from verse 20 to this point improves the poetic structure, but is otherwise unsupported.

21. What his contemporaries offered him in answer to his cries for 'comfort' was 'Reproach' or scorn (verse 20). Unlike, God who welcomes the needy to a sumptuous table (Ps. 23: 5) they act like treacherous and insulting hosts. The *vinegar*, a sour, undrinkable wine, here offered in metaphor, was to be offered in reality to Jesus (Matt. 27: 48), according to John 19: 28f. as a prophetic fulfilment of this verse.

22–8. He prays for retribution. God's covenant with his people, which is the psalmist's ground for hope (verses 13, 16), is a promise of blessing to the faithful, but it equally implies curse for the ungodly. God has set two ways before men; one is a way that prospers, but the other is doomed (1: 3, 6). The

[a] *So Sept.; Heb.* and recount.
[b] *Or, with one MS.,* him.
[c] Give them . . . deserves: *or* Add punishment to punishment.

present invocation of wrath is therefore a plea for vindication through the activation of the covenant promises that undergird the whole of Israel's faith. Nevertheless, the language is particularly vehement. This, of course, emphasizes the extremity of his distress, and probably more vividly than anything else in the psalm, but it makes a stark contrast to the prayer of Jesus in his extremity: 'Father, forgive them' (Luke 23: 34).

22. Deprive them of food and fellowship. *their own table:* on which they set 'poison' and 'vinegar' before their guests (verse 21), a symbol of their deceit, not unlike *their sacred feasts* at God's table that outwardly betoken a love for God and the brethren when there is none to be found in their hearts.

23. Deprive them of their faculties and strength. *their eyes:* probably representative of all the senses, including the power of mental and spiritual discernment. *loins:* the source of human strength and vigour. Verses 22f. are quoted in Rom. 11: 9f.

24. Deprive them of all divine pity. *indignation* and *burning anger overtake them:* in contrast with the goodness and love unfailing that follow the faithful (Ps. 23: 6).

25. Deprive them of their homes and families. *settlements . . . tents:* terms drawn from nomadic culture, but used here to include any kind of dwelling-place. This verse is cited in Acts 1: 20.

26. *pursue:* or 'persecute'. The psalmist is prepared to accept whatever punishment or suffering God requires him to bear, but his persecutors seek to *multiply* his *torments* without cause (verse 4) or because he is acting in God's service (verse 7). *those whom:* his problem is one shared by others of the faithful. Obedient service of God inevitably evokes the scorn of the world.

27. Deprive them of forgiveness and mercy; that is, presumably, if they remain unrepentant. This is probably the most terrifying of the curses, especially if the harsher translation given in the N.E.B. footnote is adopted; but it is not without parallel in the teaching of Jesus (cp. Matt. 6: 15).

28. Deprive them of acceptance in your presence. *the book of*

life: containing a list of all the names of *the righteous* or the faithful (Dan. 12: 1). The metaphor probably derives from the civilian practice of keeping registers of citizens and directs attention to the privileges that citizenship brings. These are summed up in the one word, *life*, which denotes the vitality and joy experienced in fellowship with God who is 'the fountain of life' (Ps. 36: 9). To *be blotted out from* this book is to be denied these privileges. The imprecation, like the others that precede it, relates firstly to man's earthly existence, but the finality of divine judgement has eternal implications as the New Testament writers realized (cp. Luke 10: 20). *

29   But by thy saving power, O God, lift me high
         above my pain and my distress,
30   then I will praise God's name in song
         and glorify him with thanksgiving;
31 that will please the LORD more than the offering of a
         bull,
         a young bull with horn and cloven hoof.

32   See and rejoice,*ᵃ* you humble folk,
         take heart, you seekers after God;
33   for the LORD listens to the poor
         and does not despise those bound to his service.*ᵇ*
34   Let sky and earth praise him,
         the seas and all that move in them,
35–36   for God will deliver Zion
         and rebuild the cities of Judah.
         His servants' children shall inherit them;
         they shall dwell there in their own possession
         and all who love his name shall live in them.

[a] and rejoice: *prob. rdg., cp. Pesh.; Heb.* let them rejoice.
[b] those . . . service: *lit.* his prisoners.

✶ 29–31. In contrast with the fate awaiting his foes, he looks forward to deliverance and so his song turns to praise.

29. His final prayer for help, but it is equally possible to render as an expression of confidence: 'thy saving power will lift me high . . .'

30. *then:* the addition of this word, not represented in the Hebrew, introduces the erroneous notion that he intends to reserve his praise for a *thanksgiving* after his restoration. But in verses 32 and 34 he invites others to join his song forthwith in the full assurance that God will act. The transition to praise is a common feature in the psalmists' prayers for help and is best regarded as an act of faith or an expression of trust in the midst of suffering (see on Ps. 13: 5).

31. There is an intentional word-play in the Hebrew: a 'song' (*shīr*) expressing 'thanksgiving' *will please the LORD more than the offering of a* costly *bull* (*shōr*). The psalmist does not thereby repudiate all sacrifice, but declares his conviction that no ritual action can express the same true depth of worship as heart-felt praise (cp. Pss. 40: 6f.; 51: 16f.). *with horn and cloven hoof:* that is, fully grown and ritually acceptable for sacrifice according to the Mosaic priestly regulations (Lev. 11: 3–8).

32–6. Convinced of ultimate victory he invites the faithful and the whole world to join in his song of praise.

32. *See and rejoice:* his confidence and praise must inspire others to *take heart*, but their sharing in his song will equally strengthen his faith and increase his joy in his suffering. *seekers after God:* to enter God's presence, to feel his face shine in blessing (verses 16f.), is the 'one thing' the faithful seek (Ps. 27: 4, 8).

33. When *the LORD* listens he answers and acts to bring deliverance (verses 16f.). *the poor:* the godly who do not have the material wherewithal to withstand the reproaches of society (see on Ps. 9: 12) that must be endured by *those bound to* God's *service* (cp. verse 7).

34. The whole world is invited to praise God because

whenever he intervenes to establish righteousness, he shows himself to be judge and ruler of the universe (cp. Ps. 96: 11–13).

35f. These verses appear to reflect conditions after the destruction of Jerusalem in 587 B.C., when the temple on Mount Zion was in ruins, *the cities of Judah* lay desolate and *His servants' children* in exile longed for the day they could return and *dwell there in their own possession*. It is possible to spiritualize and think of the persecuted worshippers yearning for a day when their brokenness (verse 20) and dereliction (verses 16–18) will be no more, but it is unlikely that such interpretation represents the psalmist's original intention. If the whole psalm was not first composed during the exile, then it is probable that these verses were added to adapt it for use by the community living under the new conditions that prevailed at that time. ✶

HASTEN TO HELP ME, O LORD

70

1ᵃ   Show me favour,ᵇ O God, and save me;
       hasten to help me, O LORD.

2   Let all who seek my life be brought to shame and
           dismay,
       let all who love to hurt me shrink back disgraced;

3   let those who cry 'Hurrah!' at my downfallᶜ
       turn back at the shame they incur,

4   but let all who seek thee
       be jubilant and rejoice in thee,
       and let those who long for thy saving help ever cry,
       'All glory to God!'

5   But I am poor and needy;
       O God, hasten to my aid.

[a] *Verses 1–5: cp. Ps. 40: 13–17.*
[b] Show me favour: *prob. rdg., cp. Ps. 40: 13; Heb. om.*
[c] at my downfall: *so Sept.; Heb. om.*

Thou art my help, my salvation;
  O LORD, make no delay.

☆ This urgent appeal for speedy rescue from the malice of
oppressors is identical with Ps. 40: 13–17, apart from some
small variations, such as the substitution of the title 'God' for
'the LORD' in verses 1 and 4 (see pp. 4f.). It is usually thought
that Ps. 70 predates Ps. 40, but no precise dates can be given.
The Hebrew text has a title, found also in Ps. 38, 'to bring to
remembrance', that is to set the situation before God and ask
for his help.

  1. *Show me favour:* these words are not in the Hebrew, but
are imported from Ps. 40: 13. They are required by the sense,
the metre and the parallelism. *hasten:* because the need is
urgent. *O LORD:* presumably this title has been retained for
the sake of poetic variation (cp. verse 5).

  2. As in Pss. 35: 4, 26; 71: 13, which are variants of this
verse, those who seek his *life* and his *hurt* are probably being
compared with defeated warriors shrinking back in dismay
and disgrace. Verses 2–4 show many points of contact with
Ps. 35: 25–7.

  3. As in Ps. 35: 21, 25, this picture of perverted glee at his
misfortunes is probably intended to convey an impression of
the psalmist's own feelings of terror rather than describe
anything his enemies actually do or say. *turn back:* like a routed
army (see verse 2); Ps. 40: 15 reads 'be horrified', but the two
verbs could very easily be confused in Hebrew.

  4. Cp. Ps. 35: 27. Just as his vindication must bring shame
to his persecutors and silence their spiteful jeers (verse 3), so it
will give the faithful cause to *be jubilant and rejoice*. A new and
happier sound will be heard, an unending cry of praise: '*All
glory to God!*', a cry not unlike the song of heaven itself
(Isa. 6: 3; Rev. 5: 13). *who seek thee:* perhaps in the temple, but
more probably in spiritual experience, as the parallel *who long
for* (literally 'love') *thy saving help* implies.

5. *I am poor and needy:* though a godly man, he recognizes that he lacks the physical, material and spiritual strength to stand alone against the buffeting of the world; he knows his continuing need of God (see also on Ps. 9: 12; cp. Matt. 5: 3). But he makes his final appeal in the strong assurance that God is veritably his *help* and *salvation. hasten to my aid:* this offers a better parallel to *make no delay* than the variant 'think of me' in Ps. 40: 17 and it stresses again in conclusion the urgency of the psalmist's need (see verse 1). *O God . . . O LORD:* the use of the two titles is probably for the sake of poetic variation, but it is not clear why they should differ from those in Ps. 40: 17 where the sequence is 'O Lord (Master) . . . O my God'. ✳

GOD IS MY HOPE ALL MY LIFE LONG

71

1   In thee, O LORD, I have taken refuge;
      never let me be put to shame.

2   As thou art righteous rescue me and save my life;
      hear me and set me free,

3   be a rock of refuge for me,
      where I may ever find safety at thy call;
      for thou art my towering crag and stronghold.

4   O God, keep my life safe from the wicked,
         from the clutches of unjust and cruel men.

5   Thou art my hope, O Lord,
      my trust, O LORD, since boyhood.

6   From birth I have leaned upon thee,
      my protector since I left*a* my mother's womb.*b*

7   To many I seem a solemn warning;
      but I have thee for my strong refuge.

[a] my . . . left: *or* who didst bring me out from.
[b] *See note on verse 15.*

My mouth shall be full of thy praises,   8
    I shall tell of thy splendour all day long.
Do not cast me off when old age comes,   9
    nor forsake me when my strength fails,
when my enemies' rancour bursts upon me[a]   10
and those who watch me whisper together,
saying, 'God has forsaken him;   11
after him! seize him; no one will rescue him.'
O God, do not stand aloof from me;   12
O my God, hasten to my help.
Let all my traducers be shamed and dishonoured,[b]   13
let all who seek my hurt be covered with scorn.[c]
But I will wait in continual hope,   14
I will praise thee again and yet again;
    all day long thy righteousness,   15
    thy saving acts, shall be upon my lips.
Thou shalt ever be the theme of my praise,[d]
although I have not the skill of a poet.
I will begin with a tale of great deeds, O Lord GOD,   16
and sing of thy righteousness, thine alone.
O God, thou hast taught me from boyhood,   17
all my life I have proclaimed thy marvellous works;
and now that I am old and my hairs are grey,   18
    forsake me not, O God,
when I extol thy mighty arm to future generations,
thy power and righteousness, O God, to highest heaven;   19
    for thou hast done great things.

[a] enemies' . . . me: *prob. rdg.; Heb.* enemies say of me.
[b] *So many MSS.; others* and waste away.
[c] *So Pesh.; Heb. adds* and dishonour.
[d] *Line transposed from verse 6.*

Who is like thee, O God?

20 Thou hast made me pass through bitter and deep distress,
    yet dost revive me once again
  and lift me again from earth's watery depths.

21 Restore me to honour, turn and comfort me,

22   then I will praise thee on the lute
      for thy faithfulness, O God;
    I will sing psalms to thee with the harp,
      thou Holy One of Israel;

23   songs of joy shall be on my lips;
    I will sing thee psalms, because thou hast redeemed me.

24 All day long my tongue shall tell of thy righteousness;
    shame and disgrace await those who seek my hurt.

✻ Like Ps. 31, which has almost identical opening verses, this psalm makes much use of stereotyped language. Its many reminiscences of other psalms, especially Pss. 22, 35, 40, suggest that it post-dates these, but its date of composition is impossible to determine. The psalmist's prayers for present deliverance and protection (verses 1-4, 12f., 21) and his pleadings that God will never forsake him (verses 9-11, 18) clearly indicate that the psalm was composed for use in times of distress, but it is permeated and dominated by his expressions of trust, hope and even praise (verses 1-3, 5-8, 14-24). Quite clearly the one thing he dreads most is lest God should abandon him (verses 9-12, 18), but he knows from his own and his people's past experience (verses 5f., 17) that God is a sure refuge and strength in whom he may rely in hope all his days. The comfort and encouragement transmitted through its expression of utter faith in the midst of suffering make it a fitting choice for use by any in sickness or distress.

1-4. The psalmist expresses his confidence in God as he prays for help and protection.

1–3. The N.E.B. translation obscures the close linguistic correspondences with Ps. 31: 1–3*a*. There are some minor differences, but they do not alter the meaning of these verses. *As thou art righteous:* herein lies the psalmist's sure basis for hope, that God is true to his promises and will protect his faithful people. This psalm makes repeated reference to God's 'righteousness' (verses 15, 16, 19, 24).

4. The parallelism implies that the *unjust and cruel men* are identical with *the wicked*, the enemies of God who refuse to walk in his ways (Ps. 1: 1).

5–8. Whatever others might think, he knows that his hope and strength lie with God.

5f. Cp. Ps. 22: 9f. *hope* in the psalms is not wishful straining after some future utopia, but an attitude of *trust* in God that results from personal surrender, as the psalmist himself attests when he says *I have leaned upon thee*. It is this hope that brings the strength and courage that enable him to wait expectantly for the operation of God's righteousness (verses 14f.; cp. Pss. 27: 14; 31: 24). Furthermore, his hope has been tested and proved in past experience and he can remember no occasion when God has failed him *since boyhood*, indeed since *birth*. *my protector:* the meaning of the Hebrew word is disputed, but the parallelism supports this translation.

7. *a solemn warning:* a public example of the way God punishes; the majority (*many*) in ancient Israel looked on suffering as a sign of divine disfavour (see on Ps. 31: 11). But there were also those who, knowing this theology to be inadequate, found peace, often after a heart-rending search for truth, in the personal experience of God's presence (see pp. 119f. and vol. 1, p. 170). Amongst these is the author of Ps. 71. Despite the *many*, he could say *I have thee for my strong refuge*.

8. *I shall tell:* not at some future date after complete healing has taken place, but now, even in the midst of suffering, because 'Thou art my hope' (verse 5; cp. Ps. 42: 5). God's *splendour* is the radiant 'glory' of his presence (Ps. 29: 1f.).

9–13. Having found strength in God's presence, he prays

that he will never be forsaken and that deliverance will come quickly.

9. There is no need to think, as some commentators do, that the psalmist is an old man (see verse 18). He is simply looking down the years ahead to *old age*, just as he has already looked back to his youth (verses 5f.), and is praying that the close fellowship with God he has hitherto enjoyed will not be lost for the rest of his life, especially when his own *strength fails*. To the faithful the feeling of forsakenness is a far greater cause of anguish than any physical torment (cp. Ps. 69: 16f.).

10. The enfolding of God's love means security, hope and strength (verses 5–8), but his withdrawal leaves the sufferer unprotected against the *rancour*, the hostile gaze and the malicious whispering of a world that now assumes an almost nightmarish quality (cp. Ps. 31: 13).

11. The image of haunting terror is intensified with these words which represent the psalmist's own feelings rather than anything the enemies might say.

12. Cp. Pss. 22: 11; 40: 13. This is perhaps the most spontaneous prayer in the psalm. It expresses no deep theology, but is a simple cry from the psalmist's heart, reflecting the 'sudden alarm' (Ps. 31: 22) felt when he turns his thoughts upon his environment. Whilst his mind was fixed on God he knew courage and hope.

13. Cp. Pss. 35: 4, 26; 40: 14. He prays that his *traducers* (better 'adversaries'), who would bring disgrace upon him, may find their enmity return upon their own head and cover them with shame, dishonour and *scorn*, the garments of defeat and humiliation.

14f. As his thoughts return to God, new words of hope and praise are on his lips.

14. *But I*: these abrupt and emphatic words show, not that the psalmist is contrasting his own future with that of his enemies, but that he has made a deliberate decision to spurn his gloomy thoughts and *wait* expectantly *in continual hope*. *praise* follows naturally, since his hope is focused on God (verse 5).

15. God's *saving acts* are the outworking of his *righteousness* (verse 2) in history and in the life of the faithful. *Thou shalt ever . . .:* there is no manuscript support for the transposition of these words from verse 6 where they fit equally well. *I have not the skill of a poet:* or 'for their number is past my knowledge' (Revised Standard Version). The precise meaning of the Hebrew is uncertain, but the implication is that the psalmist can find no words adequate to sing either the praise of God (N.E.B.) or his saving acts (Revised Standard Version).

16–20. As he thinks upon the works of God and past mercies in his own life, so he sings praises and prays again that he will never be forsaken.

16. *great deeds:* a synonym for 'saving acts' (verse 15) or 'marvellous works' (verse 17; cp. on Ps. 9: 1) referring to the great salvation events of Israel's history, though more recent acts of deliverance in the life of the psalmist or his immediate forebears may also be in mind.

17. It is not clear exactly what has been *taught.* It could be the story of God's *marvellous works* (see verse 16), or how to give praise (verse 15), or the discipline of faith through suffering that produces endurance and hope (verse 20; cp. Rom. 5: 3–5), or perhaps a combination of all three, for tradition, worship and faith together constitute a fairly comprehensive picture of man's knowledge of and relationship with God.

18. *now that I am old:* better translated 'when I am old', for the Hebrew does not suggest that the psalm was composed for the exclusive use of old men. The worshipper is portrayed looking ahead 'to old age' (so literally) and praying, exactly as in verse 9, that God will *forsake* him *not* at the end of his days. God's *mighty arm* is a symbol of the divine power (cp. Ps. 37: 17) that has protected (verse 20) and guided (verse 17) the psalmist throughout his life.

19. *to highest heaven:* that is, beyond the limits of human understanding (see Ps. 36: 5). Before the incomparable magnitude of God he can only cry in wonder *Who is like thee?*

(cp. Ps. 35: 10). And yet in words of praise he reaches out with his heart into this divine infinity beyond the borders of the mind.

20. *distress* as well as 'honour' (verse 21) come from God, for it is through suffering that man learns to have the kind of hope in which the psalmist rejoices (verses 5, 14; cp. Rom. 5: 3–5). *earth's watery depths:* the primordial waters undergirding the earth, the mysterious sphere of destruction and death (see on Pss. 24: 2; 42: 7). In suffering he is, as it were, sinking into the waters of death, but God can *lift* him up and *revive* him, for his presence is life.

21–4. With a final appeal for restoration, he gives thanks and praise for the victory that is all but won.

21. *honour:* the Hebrew word is used almost exclusively of God's 'greatness'. The psalmist thinks of his personal dignity deriving from God, in much the same way as he finds his strength, protection, hope and trust in the divine presence (verses 3, 5). Some versions actually suggest the reading 'your honour'.

22. *then:* better 'indeed'. The N.E.B. implies that worship is conditional upon restoration, but the text affirms that *praise* is already offered in hope and trust in God (verses 8, 14) and the very utterance of verses 22–4 is in itself a song of praise, even amid suffering. *Holy One of Israel:* this title is found frequently in Isaiah, but seldom elsewhere (cp. Pss. 78: 41; 89: 18). Here it reminds of God's *faithfulness* and 'righteousness' (verse 24), that because of his holiness he cannot be untrue to his covenant with his people (see on Ps. 22: 3).

23. *because thou hast redeemed me:* since he trusts in God's faithfulness, he knows his restoration to be assured, so much so that he feels it has virtually taken place already. This is the reason why this psalm, which is a prayer for deliverance, is so full of hope and praise.

24. Cp. verses 13, 15. *

ENDOW THE KING WITH THY OWN JUSTICE

72

O God, endow the king with thy own justice,   1
    and give thy righteousness to a king's son,
  that he may judge thy people rightly   2
    and deal out justice to the poor and suffering.
May hills and mountains afford thy people   3
    peace and prosperity in righteousness.
      He shall give judgement for the suffering   4
      and help those of the people that are needy;
      he shall crush the oppressor.
      He shall live as long*a* as the sun endures,   5
      long as the moon, age after age.
He shall be like rain falling on early crops,   6
    like showers watering*b* the earth.
In his days righteousness*c* shall flourish,   7
prosperity abound until the moon is no more.
May he hold sway from sea to sea,   8
from the River to the ends of the earth.
Ethiopians shall crouch low before him;   9
his enemies shall lick the dust.
The kings of Tarshish and the islands shall bring gifts,   10
the kings of Sheba and Seba shall present their tribute,
  and all kings shall pay him homage,   11
    all nations shall serve him.
For he shall rescue the needy from their rich oppressors,   12
  the distressed who have no protector.

     [*a*] He . . . long: *so Sept.; Heb.* They shall fear thee.
     [*b*] like showers watering: *prob. rdg.; Heb. unintelligible.*
     [*c*] *So some MSS.; others* a righteous man.

13   May he have pity on the needy and the poor,
         deliver the poor from death;
14   may he redeem them from oppression and violence
         and may their blood be precious in his eyes.

15   May the king live long
      and receive gifts of gold*a* from Sheba;
      prayer be made for him continually,
         blessings be his all the day long.
16   May there be abundance of corn in the land,
         growing in plenty to the tops of the hills;
      may the crops flourish like Lebanon,
         and the sheaves*b* be numberless as blades of grass.
17   Long may the king's name endure,
         may it live for ever*c* like the sun;
      so shall all peoples*d* pray to be blessed as he was,
         all nations tell of his happiness.

18 Blessed be the LORD God, the God of Israel,
      who alone does marvellous things;
19 blessed be his glorious name for ever,
      and may his glory fill all the earth.
                  Amen, Amen.

20 Here end the prayers of David son of Jesse.

✻ This psalm is a prayer that the king might have a long and
prosperous reign. It may have been used at the time of a king's
coronation and accession to the throne, and it may have been
used more frequently, possibly at an annual commemoration

         [a] Or frankincense.
         [b] the sheaves: prob. rdg.; Heb. from a city.
         [c] live for ever: so Sept.; Heb. unintelligible.
         [d] all peoples: prob. rdg., cp. Sept.; Heb. om.

of God's covenant with the house of David (see Ps. 132) or an annual reaffirmation of God's kingship in the world (see Ps. 93). The Hebrew title of the psalm ascribes it to Solomon, while verse 20 includes it with the 'prayers of David' (see p. 5). We can say that it is not impossible that either David or Solomon composed it; but we know little about the compilation of the Psalter, and it is also possible that the psalm was connected by later tradition with the time of Solomon because of the similarity of verses 10f., 15, to 1 Kings 10: 25, and then included with one of the 'Davidic' collections of psalms (Pss. 51–72; see p. 5).

There has been some discussion about which king, if any, served as the model for the psalm. The reigns of Solomon or Hezekiah were suggested by older commentators, while more recently, attention has been drawn to texts from Israel's neighbours in the ancient Near East which contain wishes for the king's prosperity. For example, in an Egyptian text expressing joy at the accession of Ramses IV (about 1164–1157 B.C.) we read:

> 'They who were hungry are sated and gay;
>> they who were thirsty are drunken.
> They who were naked are clothed in fine linen;
>> they who were dirty are clad in white.
> They who were in prison are set free;
>> they who were fettered are in joy.
> The troublemakers in this land have become peaceful.'

(J. B. Pritchard, *Ancient Near Eastern Texts*, p. 379.)

However, even if the psalm has something in common with other 'royal' texts of the ancient world, this does not detract from its picture of the hoped-for rule. There is much to be said for the view that while the psalm contains some conventional language, it is ultimately a description of the rule of God (see verse 1), as it should be exercised by his earthly representative. In Jewish and Christian interpretation the psalm was understood messianically, in terms of the future king who would establish God's rule in the world. Although it is never referred

to in the New Testament, the psalm inspired the hymn 'Hail
to the Lord's Anointed'.

1–7. These verses present a general problem of interpretation, since the Hebrew verbs strictly understood make verses
2–7 statements, dependent on verse 1. The sense is that if God
endows the king with the necessary gifts (verse 1) then what is
described in verses 2–7 will follow. Verse 8 then begins a
prayer for the extension of the king's dominion. The N.E.B.
takes verse 3 as a prayer, but its connection with verses 4–7 is
then not clear. The Revised Standard Version adopts a different
approach and makes verses 2–7 a prayer in each case: e.g. 'May
he judge . . .', 'Let the mountains bear prosperity . . .', 'May he
defend the cause . . .'. The present commentary regards verses
2–7 as statements dependent upon verse 1.

1f. *justice . . . righteousness:* qualities of insight, fairness and
strength such that when the king administers justice, this will
approximate as closely as possible to God's will. *deal out justice
to the poor and suffering:* cp. Ps. 82: 3f.

3. It is not clear what the N.E.B. translation of this difficult
verse can mean. Some translators delete *in* before *righteousness,*
giving the sense 'may the mountains bring peace, and the hills
righteousness to the people'. This could mean either that if the
whole realm (symbolized by 'mountains' and 'hills') is justly
governed, there will be peace and justice for the people; or it
may imply a 'sympathy' on the part of the natural order with
the king's rule, so that even mountains and hills somehow
express peace and justice (cp. Ps. 85: 10–12). It is, however,
possible to exaggerate the Hebrew view of the 'sympathy'
between the created order and social justice. A more straightforward interpretation is to regard the verse in the light of Lev.
26: 3–6: 'If you conform to my statutes . . . I will give you rain
at the proper time.' The Hebrew can then be rendered
'because of righteousness, the hills and mountains will bring
prosperity to the people'; cp. also Ps. 121: 7. In verse 16 the
prayer is that the corn should grow to the tops of the mountains
(N.E.B. 'hills'). *peace and prosperity:* a double translation of the

single Hebrew word *shālōm* to bring out its full meaning.

5. *He shall live:* the Hebrew 'They shall fear thee' (see the
N.E.B. footnote) is addressed to God. In the N.E.B. the
statement that the king will live *as long as the sun endures* is
either a hyperbole typical of court style, or refers to the dynasty
of David (Ps. 89: 36f.).

6. This verse is best understood in terms of 2 Sam. 23: 3f.
'He who rules men in justice . . . is like . . . a morning that is
cloudless after rain and makes the grass sparkle from the earth.'
The effect of the king's rule upon his people will be like the
effect of rain revitalizing the ground.

7. *righteousness:* Hebrew 'a righteous man' (N.E.B. footnote) would mean that there was full opportunity for the
practice of virtue. The N.E.B. rendering would include both
the upholding of right by the king and the practice of virtue by
the people.

8–14. The prayer for the geographical extension of the
realm is not primarily a desire for territorial expansion or the
acquisition of material wealth. It is a prayer that God's justice
exercised by the king (verses 12–14) will become a world-wide
justice desired by the nations.

8. *sea to sea:* probably from the Mediterranean sea in the
west to the Persian Gulf in the east. Like the second half of the
verse, where *the River* means the Euphrates, the verse helps to
indicate the whole of the then-known world from an Israelite
standpoint. Cp. also the imagery of Ps. 89: 25.

9. *Ethiopians:* Hebrew 'those who inhabit the desert'. Many
commentators emend the text to 'his foes'. *lick the dust:* bow
before him to the ground, in submission.

10. *Tarshish:* usually identified with a part of Spain. *the
islands:* probably another term for the far west. *Sheba and Seba:*
probably references to South Arabia, the area of modern
Yemen.

12. *For he shall rescue:* although the Hebrew word rendered
For is taken by some in the sense of 'surely', it is best to make
verses 8–11 dependent on the *For* of verse 12. It will not be by

force of arms, but by the recognition of his justice, that the king will get universal homage. Cp. Ps. 82: 3f.

14. *redeem:* Hebrew verb *gā'al* meaning 'act as their kinsman, to maintain their rights'. See on Ps. 19: 14. *their blood:* their life.

15–17. These verses repeat and sum up much of what has already been said.

15. *live long:* Hebrew 'may he live', an exclamation similar to the longer phrase 'Long live the king!' (e.g. 1 Sam. 10: 24). *prayer be made:* prayer for his well-being and prosperity.

16. *abundance of corn:* see the interpretation of verse 3, in terms of Lev. 26: 3–6. *like Lebanon:* either Lebanon is thought to symbolize the best fertile land, or the wish is that the crops will grow as tall and strong as do cedars in Lebanon. *the sheaves:* if the Hebrew 'from a city' is correct (see the N.E.B. footnote) this is a prayer for an increase of population, asking that the men of the city shall be as *numberless as blades of grass*.

17. *may it live for ever:* the Hebrew may be connected with a noun meaning 'offspring' with the sense 'may his name have issue', i.e. may his dynasty endure; but the Hebrew is very difficult.

18f. These verses are often described as doxologies similar to those found at 41: 13; 89: 52 and 106: 48 which close books 1, 3 and 4 of the Psalter. It is possible that, originally, they were added specifically to this psalm, either to include a reference to God's *marvellous things* (including his deeds in history) or to refer the psalm more closely to God, after the exile. They may have served as the model for the other doxologies, although the latter are much shorter. If we regard the verses as part of the psalm as a whole, they are a positive reminder that we should 'Put no faith in princes' (Ps. 146: 3). For no human ruler, however just and wise, can ultimately overcome the limitations of human frailty; and that is why this psalm has for so long been seen as a description of one who, while human, has transcended human limitations.

20. Because other 'Davidic' psalms are found later in the

Psalter, this verse originally probably concluded an independent collection of 'David' psalms. The 'doxology' of verses 18f.
may already have been attached to the psalm before this verse
was added. ✼

BOOK 3

GOD IS MY POSSESSION FOR EVER

73

How good God is to the upright!^a   1
   How good to those who are pure in heart!

My feet had almost slipped,   2
   my foothold had all but given way,
because the boasts of sinners roused my envy   3
   when I saw how they prosper.
No pain, no suffering is theirs;   4
   they are sleek and sound in limb;
they are not plunged in trouble as other men are,   5
   nor do they suffer the torments of mortal men.
Therefore pride is their collar of jewels   6
   and violence the robe that wraps them round.
Their eyes gleam through folds of fat;   7
   while vain fancies pass through their minds.
Their talk is all sneers and malice;   8
   scornfully they spread their calumnies.
Their slanders reach up to heaven,   9
   while their tongues ply to and fro on earth.
And so my^b people follow their lead^c   10

[a] How . . . upright: *prob. rdg.; Heb.* How good it is to Israel!
[b] *So Sept.; Heb.* his.
[c] their lead: *prob. rdg.; Heb.* hither.

and find nothing to blame in them,^a

11 even though they say, 'What does God know? –
The Most High neither knows nor cares.'

12 So wicked men talk, yet still they prosper,
and rogues^b amass great wealth.

13 So it was all in vain that I kept my heart pure
and washed my hands in innocence.

14 For all day long I suffer torment
and am punished every morning.

15 Yet had I let myself talk on in this fashion,
I should have betrayed the family of God.^c

16 So I set myself to think this out
but I found it too hard for me,

17 until I went into God's sacred courts;
there I saw clearly what their end would be.

18 How often thou dost set them on slippery ground
and drive them headlong into ruin!

19 Then in a moment how dreadful their end,
cut off root and branch by death with all its terrors,

20 like a dream when a man rouses himself, O Lord,
like images in sleep which are dismissed on waking!

21 When my heart was embittered
I felt the pangs of envy,

22 I would not understand, so brutish was I,
I was a mere beast in thy sight, O God.

23 Yet I am always with thee,
thou holdest my right hand;

[a] and find . . . in them: *prob. rdg.; Heb. obscure.*
[b] yet . . . rogues: *prob. rdg.; Heb.* those at ease for ever.
[c] the family of God: *lit.* thy family.

thou dost guide me by thy counsel   24
and afterwards wilt receive me with glory.^a
Whom have I in heaven but thee?^b   25
And having thee,^c I desire nothing else on earth.
Though heart and body fail,^d   26
yet God is my possession for ever.
They who are far from thee are lost;   27
thou dost destroy all who wantonly forsake thee.
But my chief good is to be near thee, O God;   28
I have chosen thee, Lord GOD, to be my refuge.^e

☆ With this psalm we reach one of the high points of Old
Testament faith. The problem of the unfairness of life is the
theme of several psalms already discussed, all of which have
some community of thought and expression with Ps. 73 (see
p. 14, section E). The continuing prosperity of the ungodly is
always a stumbling-block to man's faith in a righteous
God, but the psalmists constantly reassert the faithfulness and
justice of God (e.g. Pss. 9: 7f.; 11: 5) and present the godly life
as one that offers stability and permanence in his presence (Pss.
1: 3; 37: 11; 52: 8). It is thus inevitable that they should
occasionally speak of a future with God more glorious than
deathly existence in the gloom of Sheol (verse 24, cp. Ps. 49:
15). However, these glimmerings of hope in an after-life
cannot rest on logical reasoning of the human mind, as the
psalmist himself realizes (verse 16); they must depend on the
insight of faith, or divine revelation (verse 17; cp. Ps. 49: 4).
Reason can lead to loss of faith (verse 2), disillusionment (verse
13) and mental torment (verse 16), and it takes a vision of God

[a] and afterwards . . . glory: or, *with slight change of text*, and dost lead
me along the path of honour.
[b] but thee: *so Targ.; Heb. om.*
[c] *Or* And compared with thee.
[d] *So one MS.; others add* the rock of my heart.
[e] *Prob. rdg.; Heb. adds* to tell all thy works.

(verse 17) to restore understanding (verse 22), confidence (verse 23) and hope (verse 24). Job went through the same kind of mental anguish as the psalmist, and his statement after his encounter with God could equally have been made by the man who wrote Ps. 73: 'I knew of thee then only by report, but now I see thee with my own eyes' (Job 42: 5). Man's deepest needs will never be supplied by a theology or an explanation, but only by entry into the presence of God himself and there he will find a reality so great that it demands his wholehearted repentance (verses 21f.) and total commitment (verses 25, 28). The old problems are not answered; they simply recede before the vision of the glory of God. It is only proper that this psalm should be in the form of a testimony, for it speaks of deeply personal matters of faith rather than universal concepts of philosophy. Its date is uncertain, though many scholars think it was written after the exile.

1. In this opening ascription of praise the psalmist expresses his conclusions from the insight granted him. The vision of God or entry into his presence is promised to the *pure in heart* in both Testaments (Ps. 24: 3–5; Matt. 5: 8), and this is precisely the *good* that he experienced. *the upright:* this rendering suits the parallelism, but the Hebrew reads 'Israel' (N.E.B. footnote), which may also be apt if interpreted in a religious rather than a political or geographical sense: 'God's faithful people'.

2–12. The psalmist tells how his faith was undermined when he considered the prosperity of the wicked.

2. He had *almost* lost his *foothold* on God's 'path' (cp. Ps. 17: 5), that is, he had almost lost his faith.

3. One of the things his experience taught him was that it was his own *envy*, rather than the apparent inequality of life, that had led him to question God's justice and caused the erosion of his faith. The sinner boasts in his own strength instead of in God (Ps. 49: 6).

4. The following characterization of the ungodly as arrogant and malicious yet carefree and prosperous (cp. Pss. 10: 2–11; 36: 1–4) is true to life, but it is a portrait painted by

one whose eyes are full of bitterness and envy (verse 21). There is a greater pathos in the language he uses after verse 17.

5. It is because of their wealth that they escape the toil and so also the suffering which is the lot of ordinary folk.

6. Their *pride* is like a *collar* (literally 'chain') worn as a badge of office (cp. Gen. 41: 42) and *violence* has become as much part of them as their own clothing.

7. Their *vain fancies* are their arrogant and mischievous thoughts, and it is these that cause their eyes to *gleam*.

8. *Their talk* is a complete contrast with the speech of the man whom God receives into his presence (Ps. 15: 1–3).

9. The Hebrew is much more picturesque: 'they set their mouth to the heavens', like some gross mythological monster with its jaws gaping wide to receive its prey, and 'their tongue struts through the earth', like an insolent and overweening mischief-maker.

10. Dazzled by their prosperity and haughty manner, many *follow their lead*, currying favour with them and even approving of their evil ways. The Hebrew is most obscure: 'therefore his people return hither and waters of fullness are drained by them'. Perhaps this is a metaphor describing how the crowd look to them and imbibe their teaching with a sense of satisfaction.

11. The speakers are the 'wicked' (so verse 12), not their deluded admirers. There is 'no place for God' (Ps. 10: 4) in their self-sufficient lives and so they choose to believe that he is unconcerned and indeed irrelevant (Pss. 36: 1; 53: 1). The use of the title *The Most High* reminds that it is against the supreme ruler of the universe they blaspheme (see on Ps. 57: 2).

12. This is precisely the problem. Despite even their blasphemy, *they prosper*.

13–17. The psalmist tells of his despondency and mental confusion before he went into the presence of God.

13. *all in vain:* his temptation to reject belief in the purposefulness of a way of life based on faith in a just God contrasts sharply with his ultimate realization that God is unspeakably

'good to those who are pure in heart' (verse 1). *washed my hands in innocence:* a metaphorical expression derived from priestly purification rituals (see on Ps. 26: 6), here synonymous with *kept my heart pure.*

14. If the only apparent reward of faith is suffering, it is but natural that doubts should arise, especially when the theological system encourages the godly to expect material blessing.

15. The psalmist's temptation was to *talk* and argue in the same way as the wicked, but he realized that this could disturb the faith of his brothers in *the family of God* to which he himself belonged. No man is an island.

17. The psalmist gives no details of what happened, and individual worshippers will relate the psalm to their own personal experience of God. The change, however, is remarkable. The man who was hitherto so deeply troubled could now say *I saw clearly* and emerge from his encounter with an astounding certainty of God's providential care (verses 23–8). By revelation and faith he has obtained an insight and assurance that his own reason could not supply (verse 16). *God's sacred courts:* the temple buildings, or, if used metaphorically, the spiritual meeting-point between God and the psalmist.

18–20. The apparent stability of the wicked is illusory; their real fate is terrible.

18. They are not trouble-free, as the psalmist had formerly thought (verses 3–5), but basically insecure, as though standing *on slippery ground. drive them headlong:* cp. the picture of Death herding the wicked into Sheol in Ps. 49: 14.

19. *in a moment . . . root and branch:* so insecure is their way of life that *their end* is both sudden and total. *terrors* may be, as in Job 18: 14, the demonic attendants of Death, their king.

20. *like a dream* that flits *on waking*, their lives are completely transitory and of no consequence. Cp. Ps. 1: 4 which uses a different simile.

21–8. With inspired certainty and conviction, and yet in

humility and penitence, the psalmist tells of his own new relationship with God.

21f. When man meets God the truth of self-realization dawns and he sees that the real trouble lies not in the organization of the universe, but in his own selfishness and *envy*. Horrified to find that in the bitterness of his protest against life he had virtually lowered himself to the level of *a mere beast*, he must cry with Job, 'I melt away; I repent in dust and ashes' (Job 42: 6).

23. *holdest my right hand:* to support and protect (cp. Ps. 63: 8). The certainty of faith that came in his vision was of God's unfailing care and it is this that enabled him to sing 'How good God is' (verse 1). The mood of these opening words returns to the psalm at this point.

24. Some scholars have thought that this verse, far from saying anything about life after death, simply reasserts the traditional view (see on verse 14) that God will ultimately lead the faithful through to victory in this life, and it is to emphasize this kind of conclusion that the emended reading in the N.E.B. footnote has been proposed. It is significant that the ambiguity should exist, for it shows that the psalmist's primary interest lies elsewhere (see verse 25). He tells of a very personal insight of faith and the problem arises when we try to find here a doctrinal statement rather than the inner conviction of the heart. However, when he expresses this conviction in the words 'God is my possession for ever' (verse 26), it is almost impossible to comprehend how that 'for ever' could end in the murk of Sheol in isolation from God (cp. Ps. 6: 5; 88: 5). Already he knows the guiding of God's *counsel* (possibly a reference to the insight granted in verse 17) and this is for him, as it were, 'a pledge' (2 Cor. 5: 5) of greater *glory* yet to come. The reality of his experience is so strong that he speaks with absolute certainty: 'I am always with thee' (verse 23). He has glimpsed eternity and there he is with God. The wicked can have no such assurance for their *afterwards* is oblivion (verses 18–20, 27). See further on Ps. 49: 15.

25. This cry of praise expresses the heart of the psalmist's gospel, that knowledge of God's nearness is worth more than everything that life can offer. His former troubles cease to have any real significance in God's presence.

26. No matter how much he may suffer, the psalmist has a *possession* (see on Ps. 16: 5f.) of infinite value, unlike the wealth of the wicked that counts for nothing before God (Ps. 49: 7; cp. Matt. 6: 19–21).

27. Since 'the fountain of life' is with God (Ps. 36: 9), to *forsake* him is to draw near to death. Sheol is the inevitable destiny of the wicked.

28. *my chief good:* re-echoing his opening words the psalmist sums up and restates the truth he has learned about the infinite value of knowing God's presence (cp. verses 24f.). No longer is he tempted to follow the wicked, for he has chosen God *to be my refuge.* 'to tell all thy works' (N.E.B. footnote): finally he dedicates himself to the task of bearing testimony to all God has taught him, for when God grants new insight, it is for the upbuilding of his people, not for private enjoyment. Here is an echo of the sense of community responsibility found in verse 15. This clause offers a significant climax to the psalm and should not have been relegated to a footnote. ✶

FORGET NOT FOR EVER THE SUFFERINGS OF THY SERVANTS

74

1 Why hast thou cast us off, O God? Is it for ever?
 Why art thou so stern, so angry with the sheep of thy
  flock?
2   Remember the assembly of thy people,
   taken long since for thy own,[a]
 and Mount Zion, which was thy home.

[a] *Prob. rdg.; Heb. adds* thou didst redeem the tribe of thy possession.

Now at last[a] restore what was ruined beyond repair,   3
the wreck that the foe has made of thy sanctuary.

The shouts of thy enemies filled the holy place,[b]   4
they planted their standards there as tokens of victory.
They brought it crashing down,[c]   5
     like woodmen plying their axes in the forest;
they ripped[d] the carvings clean out,   6
they smashed them with hatchet and pick.
They set fire to thy sanctuary,   7
tore down and polluted the shrine sacred to thy name.
They said to themselves, 'We will sweep them away',[e]   8
and all over the land they burnt God's holy places.[f]

We cannot see what lies before us,[g] we have no prophet 9
     now;
we have no one who knows how long this is to last.
How long, O God, will the enemy taunt thee?   10
Will the adversary pour scorn on thy name for ever?
Why dost thou hold back thy hand,   11
why keep thy right hand within thy bosom?

But thou, O God, thou king from of old,   12
     thou mighty conqueror all the world over,
by thy power thou didst cleave the sea-monster in two 13
and break the sea-serpent's heads above the waters;
thou didst crush Leviathan's many heads   14

[a] Now at last: *prob. rdg.; Heb.* Thy steps.
[b] the holy place: *or* thy meeting place.
[c] They . . . down: *prob. rdg.; Heb. unintelligible.*
[d] they ripped: *so Sept.; Heb.* and now.
[e] We . . . away: *so Pesh.; Heb.* their offspring.
[f] holy places: *or* meeting places.
[g] what . . . us: *prob. rdg.; Heb.* our signs.

and throw him to the sharks[a] for food.

15 Thou didst open channels for spring and torrent;
   thou didst dry up rivers never known to fail.

16 The day is thine, and the night is thine also,
   thou didst ordain the light of moon and sun;

17   thou hast fixed all the regions of the earth;
   summer and winter, thou didst create them both.

18 Remember, O LORD, the taunts of the enemy,
   the scorn a savage nation pours on thy name.

19 Cast not to the beasts the soul that confesses thee;[b]
   forget not for ever the sufferings of thy servants.

20 Look upon thy creatures:[c] they are filled with hatred,
   and earth is the haunt of violence.

21   Let not the oppressed be shamed and turned away;
   let the poor and the downtrodden praise thy name.

22 Rise up, O God, maintain thy own cause;
   remember how brutal men taunt thee all day long.

23   Ignore no longer the cries of thy assailants,
   the mounting clamour of those who defy thee.

✻ In much the same vein as Ps. 44, God's people pray for
deliverance from extreme national distress. The description of
the havoc wrought in the sanctuary (verses 3–8) seems particularly appropriate to the state of Jerusalem after its destruction
by the Babylonians in 587 B.C. (see also Ps. 79). The psalm may
therefore have first been used on special days of fasting and
lamentation at services held on the ruined temple site (cp. Jer.
41: 4f.; Zech. 7: 3–5). Its inclusion in the Psalter indicates its
continued use in Israel after the exile, thus suggesting a wider
application to more general conditions of suffering and oppres-

[a] to the sharks: *prob. rdg.*; *Heb.* to a people, desert-dwellers.
[b] that confesses thee: *so Sept.*; *Heb.* of thy turtle-dove.
[c] thy creatures: *prob. rdg.*; *Heb.* the covenant, because.

126

sion that were reminiscent of the hardships of the Babylonian oppression, and perhaps even seen as a recurrence of these.

1–3. A cry of dereliction and a prayer for help.

1. *Why*: a cry of anguish, rather than a plea for an explanation (cp. Ps. 22: 1). In the depths of their misery, God's people can see no end to their suffering, but their faith assures them that it is his love, not his anger, that is *for ever* (cp. Ps. 106: 1 and often) and that they, as *the sheep of thy flock* (cp. Pss. 79: 13; 100: 3), can expect their shepherd to care for them.

2. Israel has good reason to expect God's care, for she is *the assembly* or community of his choice and her worship is centred on *Mount Zion*, the place of his choice. That God's choice is an expression of his love and not without cost to himself is emphasized in the Hebrew by the parallel verbs *taken* (literally 'purchased') and 'thou didst redeem' (N.E.B. footnote; see further on Ps. 69: 18).

3. The N.E.B. translators have virtually rewritten the Hebrew of the first line of this verse, but it remains an appeal to God to intervene. *beyond repair*: the word used in the Hebrew re-echoes the cry in verse 1, 'Is it for ever?'

4–8. A picture of the destruction and desecration of the temple.

4. The blasphemous *shouts of thy enemies* replace the praises of the faithful and shatter the reverent silence of the sanctuary. *tokens of victory*: literally 'signs', and so possibly idolatrous emblems replacing the symbols of Israel's faith.

5f. *like woodmen . . .*: the simile may have been suggested by a memory of the wood-panelling and tree-carvings on the inner walls of the temple (1 Kings 6: 16, 29), but the psalmist doubtless also had the destruction and removal of all its decorative objects in mind (2 Kings 25: 13–17).

7. *They set fire . . .*: see 2 Kings 25: 9. *the shrine sacred to thy name*: literally 'the dwelling-place of thy name' (cp. Deut. 12: 11; 1 Kings 8: 29). God's *name* is here a symbol of his presence, like his 'glory' in the comparable expression in Ps. 26: 8.

8. *holy places:* literally 'meeting places' (N.E.B. footnote), and therefore sometimes taken to refer to synagogues (so the Authorized Version). There were probably synagogues in Israel by the time of the Maccabees when the temple was defiled and idols erected throughout the land in 167 B.C. (1 Macc. 1: 54), but it is unlikely that the psalm is to be dated so late. If the psalm was composed during the exile, the allusion can hardly be to local sanctuaries, despite the fact that the singular of this word is used of the temple in verse 4, for these had been abolished by King Josiah in 622 B.C. (2 Kings 23: 8). However, it seems that local worship of every kind did not cease and some priests continued to minister in the rural areas (2 Kings 23: 9).

9–11. The psalmist renews his protest at God's continued inactivity.

9. *we have no prophet now:* by the Maccabaean era the voice of prophecy had fallen silent (1 Macc. 9: 27), but a similar cry to this was also heard during the exile when prophets like Ezekiel were very active (Lam. 2: 9). The point of the complaint seems to be that *no one* can prophesy *how long this is to last.*

10. The questioning style re-echoes the mood of verses 1–3 where the psalmist pleaded God's care for his people, but now he pleads that God should have a care for his own reputation and honour (*name*).

11. *Why:* see verse 1. *hold back thy hand:* restrain thy power.

12–17. Despite present distress, God has the power to intervene and conquer; to this creation itself attests.

12. *But thou, O God, thou king:* the Hebrew reads as a statement of confidence, 'God is my king.' The introduction of the pronoun 'my' suggests the possibility that the speaker is a leader of the community (cp. Ps. 44: 4). *thou mighty conqueror:* literally 'working salvation', which suggests vindication of faith and release from suffering as well as victory over enemies (see on Ps. 3: 2).

13. In ancient times the story of creation was sometimes

told as a battle in which the creator subdues the turbulent sea personified as a monstrous serpent. He cleaves its carcass in two, raising one half to form the sky and lowering the other to form the earth.

'He split her like a shellfish into two parts:
Half of her he set up and ceiled it as sky.'
(J. B. Pritchard, *Ancient Near Eastern Texts*, p. 67.)

A more refined doctrine of creation was to evolve in Israel (Gen. 1: 1 – 2: 4), but the old mythological pictures reappear in the psalms as poetical symbols of the continuing conflict between God and earth's destructive forces, especially as embodied in the enemies of Israel (cp. Pss. 46: 2f.; 65: 6f.).

14. *Leviathan:* the sea-serpent subdued at creation (verse 13; cp. Ps. 68: 22), like the Leviathan of Canaanite mythology which was a seven-headed sea-monster slain by Baal. In Ps. 104: 26 this raging dragon of the deep has become no more than God's 'plaything'. *sharks:* an emended reading, literally 'the slippery ones of the sea'; the Hebrew actually reads 'a people, desert-dwellers' (N.E.B. footnote), which could be interpreted as 'beasts of the wilderness'.

15. God harnessed the turbulent waters to the service of the earth, directing them through springs and along *torrent*-beds. *dry up rivers:* possibly an allusion to the crossing of the Red Sea (Exod. 14: 21–31) or the Jordan (Josh. 3: 15–17).

16f. Having created, God ordains the regular passage of day and night and the cycle of the seasons, he establishes the harmonious movements of the luminaries and the fixed contours of the earth (Gen. 1: 9f., 14–18); as king of his creation (verse 12), he has issued decrees imposing order in his kingdom.

18–23. Encouraged by contemplation of God's power, the psalmist turns again to prayer.

18. *Remember:* cp. verse 2 where the plea was to save his people; here it is to save his own reputation (see also verses 10 and 22).

19. *the soul that confesses thee . . . thy servants:* the psalmist

pleads the people's basic fidelity as a motive for God to act, not as a complaint that their suffering is unmerited (contrast Ps. 44). He has already accepted what has happened as an expression of God's anger (verse 1), but his prayer is that it may be *not for ever* (cp. verses 1, 10). 'thy turtle-dove' (N.E.B. footnote): a portrait of Israel as a defenceless people.

20. *thy creatures:* adopting a widely accepted emendation. The Hebrew reads 'Have regard for the covenant; for the dark places of the land are full of the habitations of violence.' Such an appeal to God's promises would be an apt counterpart to the plea of faithfulness in the preceding verse.

22. *Rise up, O God:* a call to battle (see on Ps. 44: 26). *thy own cause:* Israel's cause is also God's, for they are the people he himself has chosen (verse 2), and so it is not only their well-being, but God's honour that is at stake. This theme has been sounded several times in the psalm already and is finally re-echoed in the words *remember . . . taunt thee* which repeat the cry of verses 10 and 18. *

GOD IS JUDGE

75

1 We give thee thanks, O God, we give thee thanks;
   thy name is brought very near to us
   in the story of thy wonderful deeds.

2 I seize the appointed time
   and then I judge mankind with justice.

3 When the earth rocks, with all who live on it,
   I make its pillars firm.

4 To the boastful I say, 'Boast no more',
   and to the wicked, 'Do not toss your proud horns:

5 toss not your horns against high heaven
   nor speak arrogantly against your Creator.'

6 No power from the east nor from the west,

no power from the wilderness, can raise a man up.
    For God is judge;   7
he puts one man down and raises up another.

    The LORD holds a cup in his hand,   8
and the wine foams in it, hot with spice;
he offers it to every man[a] for drink,
and all the wicked on earth must drain it to the dregs.
    But I will glorify him for ever;   9
I will sing praises to the God of Jacob.

    I will break off the horns of the wicked,   10
but the horns of the righteous shall be lifted high.

✶ It is possible to interpret this psalm in two different ways. It could be a composition for liturgical use: the congregation first gives thanks (verse 1), and God, perhaps through a prophet, responds with words of assurance (verses 2–3); then follows an address, possibly delivered by a priest, warning the people of God's judgement (verses 4–8) and concluding in praise (verse 9); and finally God speaks again (verse 10). Alternatively, it may be read as the praise-filled conversation of the soul who, gratefully acknowledging his share in Israel's heritage (verse 1), recites and so reappropriates the promises of God (verses 2–3). Strengthened thus by his praise and God's word, he reminds all who would hear, but particularly himself, of God's power and man's weakness (verses 4–8). And so he turns again to praise (verse 9), recalling finally the promise in God's word (verse 10). Neither interpretation affects the theme or the theology of the psalm. The date of writing cannot be determined.

    1. The hymn of thanks. *thy name:* God himself as known to man, here virtually a synonym for 'thy presence'. Though God is always *very near*, the faithful can lose their awareness of his presence. But then the knowledge of his nearness may be

[a] every man: *so Sept.; Heb.* from this.

restored or intensified as they contemplate his *wonderful deeds* (see on Ps. 71: 16f.), his great redemptive miracles and acts of deliverance in their nation's history or their own lives (cp. Ps. 22: 1–5).

2f. God speaks. Man may think he is inactive and far from 'near', but he is in control and is only waiting for the right moment to act.

2. The allusion is probably to historical acts of divine intervention rather than to the last judgement, for the next verse implies the continuation of history. *the appointed time:* though 'the destined hour' is not known by men, 'it will come . . . it will not fail' (Hab. 2: 3). These words speak assurance to the faithful.

3. Behind all earth's terrors and disasters God is still active establishing and maintaining order. *its pillars:* the natural and the moral worlds are both likened to a building supported by pillars or by foundations (Job 9: 6; Pss. 11: 3; 82: 5).

4–9. The psalmist speaks. Some commentators would continue the speech of God to verse 5, but verses 4–8 cohere well as a unit contrasting the futile arrogance of puny men with the irresistible power of the universal judge.

4. *the boastful:* those who pride themselves in their own strength and self-sufficiency and not in God (cp. Ps. 52: 1 and contrast Ps. 34: 2). *toss your proud horns:* like a defiant wild ox (Ps. 92: 10).

5. *against your Creator:* introducing a slight emendation; the Hebrew reads 'with a (stiff, proud) neck', but the Septuagint has 'against God'.

6. *the wilderness:* probably the wilderness of Sinai, hence the south. It is unlikely that there is special significance in the absence of any allusion to the north. The message is clear: it is futile to look for human help from whatever quarter, for man's only real hope lies in God.

7. His judgement is not arbitrary; it is the proud and wicked that he *puts . . . down,* the humble and righteous that he *raises up* (verse 10; cp. Ps. 147: 6; Luke 1: 51–3).

8. *a cup:* a common figure of God's judgement (cp. Pss. 11: 6; 60: 3). *every man* must taste something of God's wrath, but *the wicked . . . must drain it to the dregs* (cp. Isa. 51: 17) and receive the full measure of punishment due to them.

9. Though wrath awaits the wicked, the faithful can already sing God's praises knowing that their lot is to enter the joy of God's presence and *glorify him for ever. God of Jacob:* Israel's God; the title reminds the worshipper that he is heir to God's promises to his people (cp. Ps. 24: 6).

10. God speaks again reasserting the theme of his judgement (see on verse 7), thus offering final strength and encouragement to the faithful. *the righteous:* those who have a right relationship with God (see on Ps. 1: 5). ✳

WHO CAN STAND IN THY PRESENCE WHEN THOU ART ANGRY?

76

In Judah God is known,   1
his name is great in Israel;
his tent is pitched in Salem,   2
in Zion his battle-quarters are set up.*ᵃ*
He has broken the flashing arrows,   3
shield and sword and weapons of war.

Thou art terrible,*ᵇ* O Lord, and mighty: 4
men that lust for plunder stand aghast,   5
the boldest swoon away,
and the strongest cannot lift a hand.
At thy rebuke, O God of Jacob,   6
rider and horse fall senseless.
Terrible art thou, O Lord;   7

[a] are set up: *prob. rdg.; Heb.* thither (*at beginning of verse 3*).
[b] terrible: *so Theod.; Heb.* illuminated.

who can stand in thy presence when thou art angry?

8   Thou didst give sentence out of heaven;
     the earth was afraid and kept silence.

9   O God, at thy rising*^a* in judgement
     to deliver all humble men on the earth,

10   for all her fury Edom shall confess thee,
     and the remnant left in Hamath shall dance in
          worship.

11 Make vows to the LORD your God, and pay them duly;
     let the peoples all around him bring their tribute;*^b*

12   for he breaks the spirit of princes,
     he is the terror of the kings on earth.

✣ This psalm describes the power of God, using the metaphor
of a mighty warrior. The metaphor probably recalls those
events of Israel's history in which God was believed to have
delivered his people in time of war. The divine warrior is also
a judge, whose sentence is not only just, but who will bring
even rebellious men and nations to rejoice in his kingship.

1. *known:* renowned, rather than merely known about.

2. *tent . . . battle-quarters:* the reference is to the temple in
Jerusalem, which is described as God's headquarters for battle.
Salem: this abbreviated or ancient poetic name for Jerusalem is
found only here in the psalms (cp. also Gen. 14: 18). It may
have suggested 'peace' and 'wholeness' to the Hebrew.
Although God is described as a warrior, his aim is to establish
peace in the whole world.

3. *flashing arrows:* arrows which travel so fast that they look
like lightning (and see further on Ps. 78: 48).

4. *Thou art terrible:* in favour of the N.E.B. (see footnote),
the motif of God being terrible recurs at verses 7 and 12.

[a] O God . . . rising: *prob. rdg.; Heb.* When God rises.
[b] *Prob. rdg.; Heb. adds* for the terror (*cp. verse 12*).

5. *men that lust for plunder*: the N.E.B. has taken the last two words of the previous verse, and put them with this verse. They are more traditionally translated 'mountains of prey' or 'everlasting mountains'. *swoon away*: Hebrew 'slept their sleep' which is usually taken to refer to the sleep of death.

8. *out of heaven*: although God's battle-quarters are set up in Zion (verse 2), heaven is where God holds his court (see Ps. 82) and passes sentence. 1 Kings 8: 27–30 describes the connection between God's earthly and heavenly dwellings.

9. *rising in judgement*: cp. Ps. 82: 1.

10. *Edom shall confess thee*: the more familiar rendering is 'the wrath of man shall praise thee' – 'Edom' and 'man' have the same consonants in Hebrew. Both the traditional translation and the N.E.B. translation make the same point, that God's warlike activity is directed towards the establishment of true justice in the world, and that rebellious men and nations will accept this justice. It is possible that Edom (to the south) and Hamath (to the north) denote the whole world.

11f. The surrounding nations are probably addressed, and urged to pledge their loyalty to God. ✶

HAS GOD FORGOTTEN TO BE GRACIOUS?

77

I cried aloud to God,   1
I cried to God, and he heard me.
In the day of my distress I sought the Lord,   2
and by night I lifted*a* my outspread hands in prayer.
I lay sweating and nothing would cool me;
I refused all comfort.
When I called God to mind, I groaned;   3
as I lay thinking, darkness came over my spirit.
My eyelids were tightly closed;   4

[a] I lifted: *prob. rdg.; Heb. om.*

I was dazed and I could not speak.
5 My thoughts went back to times long past,
    I remembered forgotten years;
6 all night long I was in deep distress,
    as I lay thinking, my spirit was sunk in despair.

7 Will the Lord reject us for evermore
    and never again show favour?
8 Has his unfailing love now failed us utterly,
    must his*a* promise time and again be unfulfilled?
9 Has God forgotten to be gracious,
    has he in anger withheld his mercies?
10 'Has his right hand', I said, 'lost its grasp?
    Does it hang powerless,*b* the arm of the Most High?'

11 But then, O LORD, I call to mind thy deeds;*c*
    I recall thy wonderful acts in times gone by.
12   I meditate upon thy works
        and muse on all that thou hast done.
13 O God, thy way is holy;
    what god is so great as our God?
14 Thou art the God who workest miracles;
    thou hast shown the nations thy power.
15 With thy strong arm thou didst redeem thy people,
    the sons of Jacob and Joseph.

16   The waters saw thee, O God,
        they saw thee and writhed in anguish;
        the ocean was troubled to its depths.
17 The clouds poured water, the skies thundered,

[a] his: *so Pesh.; Heb. om.*
[b] lost . . . powerless: *prob. rdg.; Heb. unintelligible.*
[c] *Prob. rdg.; Heb.* then I call to mind the deeds of the LORD, for.

thy arrows flashed hither and thither.
The sound of thy thunder was in the whirlwind,[a]   18
thy lightnings lit up the world,
earth shook and quaked.
Thy path was through the sea, thy way through mighty   19
waters,
and no man marked thy footsteps.
Thou didst guide thy people like a flock of sheep,   20
under the hand of Moses and Aaron.

✻ The nature of the distress referred to in verse 2 cannot be ascertained. Perhaps it was a national calamity which affected the psalmist deeply, whether he was an ordinary Israelite, or a representative figure, such as the king. In any case, later users of the psalm, whether individuals or congregations, have been able to gain help for their special problems from it. The text vividly describes the anguish which the psalmist is experiencing, and his perplexity that things seem to have turned out contrary to his understanding of God's power and promises. However, he finds comfort in remembering God's mighty works in the past, and he never loses his conviction that God's ways will ultimately be vindicated.

1. *I cried aloud to God . . . he heard me:* this appears to contradict what immediately follows, in which the psalmist voices his sense of isolation from God. It is probably best regarded as a summary of the message of the whole psalm.

2. The verse emphasizes the remarkable persistence of the psalmist, who is convinced that the answer to his problem lies with God, however far off God may seem to be.

3. *I groaned:* possibly a description of anguish caused by reflection on the enormous difference between God's mighty deeds in the past, and the psalmist's present humiliation. The psalmist's mental anguish also seems to affect him physically.

[a] *Or* in the chariot-wheels.

4. *My eyelids were tightly closed:* the N.E.B. translation continues the description, begun in verse 3, of the psalmist's anguish. The more traditional rendering – 'thou holdest mine eyes' – implies that God prevents the psalmist from sleeping.

5. *I remembered forgotten years:* Hebrew 'years of long ago', which is better parallelism with *times long past.* The psalmist probably thinks of better days in the past.

7–10. Underlying the seemingly hopeless questions expressed in these verses is probably the conviction that the answer to them is 'No!'.

7. *reject us: us* here and in verse 8 is not in the Hebrew, although it is a fair interpretation of the original.

8. *unfailing love . . . failed:* this word-play is not in the Hebrew, but it brings out the idea of *ḥesed* as unfailing, covenant love (see on Ps. 51: 1).

10. *'Has his right hand . . . Most High?':* the N.E.B. footnote, 'Heb. unintelligible', is not entirely fair, although the Hebrew is admittedly very difficult. The rendering of the Authorized Version 'And I said, This *is* my infirmity: *but I will remember* the years of the right hand of the most High' gives the sense that the psalmist must bear his present anguish, but will console himself by thinking about God's past triumphs. In this case, verse 10 is already partly an answer to the questions posed in verses 7–9. The N.E.B. translation makes verse 10 continue these questions, but is forced to alter the text of verse 11*a* (whose substantial accuracy is not in doubt) in order to emphasize that verses 11–20 are an answer to these questions. Verses 11–20 recall the great acts of God in the past, and express the basis of the psalmist's hope.

13. *thy way is holy:* the meaning is probably that God acts in accordance with his holy purposes for the world, even if these involve the punishment of Israel.

15. *the sons of Jacob and Joseph:* there may be a reference here to the northern kingdom, Israel; but more likely the verse refers to the redemption of the whole Israelite nation in the exodus.

16–20. The deliverance at the Red Sea is alluded to, but the allusion is enriched by traditional (mythological) phrases (verses 17f.) which describe the spectacular occurrences in nature which were believed to accompany God's mighty works in the world, and which showed that God was the lord of creation.

19. *Thy path was through the sea . . . no man marked thy footsteps:* although God's action at the Red Sea was concrete, its nature was not comprehended by man. Similarly, God's ways in the present time of doubt and anxiety must be trusted.

20. *flock of sheep:* this intimate picture contrasts with the cosmic imagery of the preceding verses, and re-affirms God's continuing tender care for his people. ✻

HE REMEMBERED THAT THEY WERE ONLY
MORTAL MEN

78

✻ It is impossible to be certain about the date or original setting of this psalm. Basically, it recalls the history of Israel from the exodus from Egypt, to the establishment of Jerusalem and the house of David. Because it contains no reference to the division of the kingdom after the death of Solomon (but see note on verse 67), some interpreters date it before the death of Solomon (e.g. around 930 B.C.). Other commentators argue that the style of presentation and interpretation of the history is similar to that found in parts of Deuteronomy. Because Deuteronomy is usually associated with the reform of Josiah (2 Kings 23f.; 621 B.C.) they date the psalm shortly before the exile. The text also raises other questions which cannot be answered conclusively. Are the references to the exodus, the plagues and the wilderness wanderings (verses 12–31, 40–51) based on the written accounts of these events in Exodus and Numbers, or do the references in the psalm represent an independent (perhaps early oral) form of tradition about these happenings? If the psalm was originally composed for the instruction of the people at a religious festival, which festival was it?

If these and other questions cannot be answered with certainty, the theological message of the psalm is clear. The psalmist recalls several moments of past history as being 'a story with a meaning' (verse 2). He seeks to 'expound the riddle' (verse 2) that not only do generations of Israelites who were not themselves directly involved in God's saving acts go their own way and not God's way, but that the generations who *were* witnesses of the saving acts turned their backs on God, also. But in this, the psalm deals not with something peculiarly Israelite, but with something well known to the modern religious reader, if he ponders how often he turns away from God after having been the recipient of divine mercies. Yet God's mercies can outlast human inconstancy.

The final verses (65–72) mention how God has chosen Zion (Jerusalem) and David. The original purpose of these verses may have been to vindicate the claim of Jerusalem, as opposed to other holy places, to be the only sanctuary truly favoured by God. ✻

1   Mark my teaching, O my people,
    listen to the words I am to speak.

2   I will tell you a story with a meaning,
    I will expound the riddle of things past,

3   things that we have heard and know,
    and our fathers have repeated to us.

4   From their sons we will not hide
    the praises of the LORD and his might
    nor the wonderful acts he has performed;
    then they shall repeat them to the next generation.

5   He laid on Jacob a solemn charge
    and established a law in Israel,

which he commanded our fathers
    to teach their sons,
that it might be known to a future generation,   6
    to children yet unborn,
and these would repeat it to their sons in turn.
He charged them to put their trust in God,   7
to hold his great acts ever in mind
    and to keep all his commandments;
not to do as their fathers did,   8
a disobedient and rebellious race,
a generation with no firm purpose,
with hearts not fixed steadfastly on God.

* 1–8. The psalmist explains the purpose of his psalm.

1. *Mark my teaching . . .:* the opening verse is reminiscent of the wisdom teaching, e.g. in the book of Proverbs, although it is not clear whether the psalmist is himself a wisdom teacher, or merely employing a typical formula.

2. *story with a meaning:* the Hebrew *māshāl* is often translated as 'proverb' or 'parable'. Perhaps a basic part of its meaning is that of comparison between two things, and hence in the present psalm, past history will be related so as to be compared with, and shed light on, current happenings. *riddle of things past:* the riddle, or enigma, is that past generations that were particularly favoured by God, were disobedient to him. For the words riddle and *māshāl*, see also Ps. 49: 4, and compare the phrases with which that psalm begins.

5. *He laid on Jacob:* Jacob is here a name for Israel. The *solemn charge* and *law* may refer either to the law given to the Israelites at Mount Sinai or to the charge that parents should teach their children about the saving acts of God (Deut. 6: 20–5). *

9   The men of Ephraim, bowmen all and marksmen,
        turned and ran in the hour of battle.
10   They had not kept God's covenant
     and had refused to live by his law;
11   they forgot all that he had done
     and the wonderful acts which he had shown them.

12   He did wonders in their fathers' sight
        in the land of Egypt, the country of Zoan:
13   he divided the sea and took them through it,
     making the water stand up like banks on either side.
14   He led them with a cloud by day
     and all night long with a glowing fire.
15   He cleft the rock in the wilderness
     and gave them water to drink, abundant as the sea;
16   he brought streams out of the cliff
     and made water run down like rivers.
17   But they sinned against him yet again:
     in the desert they defied the Most High,
18   they tried God's patience wilfully,
     demanding food to satisfy their hunger.
19   They vented their grievance against God and said,
     'Can God spread a table in the wilderness?'
20   When he struck a rock, water gushed out
     until the gullies overflowed;
     they said, 'Can he give bread as well,
     can he provide meat for his people?'
21   When he heard this, the LORD was filled with fury:
     fire raged against Jacob,
     anger blazed up against Israel,
22   because they put no trust in God

and had no faith in his power to save.

Then he gave orders to the skies above   23
    and threw open heaven's doors,

he rained down manna for them to eat   24
and gave them the grain of heaven.

So men ate the bread of angels;   25
he sent them food to their heart's desire.

He let loose the east wind from heaven   26
and drove the south wind by his power;

he rained meat like a dust-storm upon them,   27
flying birds like the sand of the sea-shore,

which he made settle all over the camp   28
    round the tents where they lived.

So the people ate and were well filled,   29
for he had given them what they craved.

Yet they did not abandon their complaints[a]   30
even while the food was in their mouths.

Then the anger of God blazed up against them;   31
    he spread death among their stoutest men
    and brought the young men of Israel to the ground.

* 9–31. Rebellion against God in the wilderness wanderings.

9–11. The reference to the *men of Ephraim* is puzzling, and
we know nothing about the occasion which is here mentioned.
It may give the reason why the tribe of Ephraim was rejected
in favour of the tribe of Judah (verse 67), or may be a comment
on an otherwise unknown incident from the time of the
psalmist or a later editor. In the total context of the psalm, the
verses mean that the Ephraimites were defeated in battle,
because persistent disregard of God made it impossible for them
to look to him for strength and encouragement, and the
rejection of Ephraim (verse 67) is thus anticipated.

[a] *Or* craving.

12. *He did wonders:* a reference to the plagues in Egypt, which are mentioned more fully in verses 43–51. In what follows, the lessons of history are more important than the mere recalling of the events. *Zoan* is one of the names for the capital of Egypt at the time of the exodus. It does not occur in the accounts in the book of Exodus. It was probably in the north-west part of the Nile delta.

13. *stand up like banks:* a similar phrase occurs in Exod. 15: 8 in the song of triumph which is possibly the oldest account in the Old Testament of the Red Sea deliverance.

14. The pillars of cloud and fire (Exod. 13: 21, 'by day a pillar of cloud to guide them ... by night a pillar of fire to give them light') are symbols for God's presence among his people, and of his guidance and protection.

15f. Exod. 17: 6 and Num. 20: 8–13 describe the miraculous provision of water by God.

18. *they tried God's patience:* cp. Exod. 17: 2–7. The idea that the Israelites *tried* or tested God is prominent in the psalms (cp. 95: 9). Here, it probably means more than *tried God's patience*. The Israelites no doubt did this, but they also sought to put to the test God's ability to work greater miracles than they had already seen (verse 20, and cp. Gideon's 'tests' with the fleece, Judg. 6: 39). This attitude towards God involved human arrogance – the idea that man can taunt or cajole God into obeying human orders – and was undoubtedly the downfall of the Israelites concerned.

20. *bread ... meat ...:* the manna and quails (Exod. 16).

21. *fire raged:* these words may be connected with the incident related in Num. 11: 1–3.

22. Perhaps only one thing grieves God more than when his people disbelieve his *power* to save them – when they disbelieve his desire to save them.

23. *Then he gave orders:* it seems surprising that, after all, God should grant the unworthy requests of the Israelites, and the Authorized Version softens the apparent difficulty with its translation 'Though he had commanded ...'. However, we

should follow the N.E.B. here. God's acts of grace cannot always appear to be logical to human understanding.

24. Cp. John 6: 31.

25. *bread of angels*: literally, 'bread of mighty ones'. The N.E.B. translation contrasts mortal man with the mighty heavenly beings, and thus emphasizes God's grace in providing for the Israelites food normally reserved for higher beings.

26–31. The account of the sending of the quails seems to be close to Num. 11: 31–3. With verse 30 compare Num. 11: 33, and the spreading of *death among their stoutest men* (verse 31) most probably matches the second half of Num. 11: 33. The passage in Numbers gives no reason for the onset of the divine punishment, unless we infer that it was because of the people's greed. Here, according to the N.E.B. text (verse 30), the granting of the wishes of the people did not stop their complaints. They therefore judged themselves by expressing their ingratitude to God, while at the same time seizing what he gave. ✳

In spite of all, they persisted in their sin   32
and had no faith in his wonderful acts.

So in one moment he snuffed out their lives   33
  and ended their years in calamity.

When he struck them, they began to seek him,   34
they would turn and look eagerly for God;

they remembered that God was their Creator,   35
that God Most High was their deliverer.

But still they beguiled him with words   36
and deceived him with fine speeches;

they were not loyal to him in their hearts   37
nor were they faithful to his covenant.

Yet he wiped out their guilt   38
and did not smother his own[a] natural affection;

[a] his own: *prob. rdg.; Heb. om.*

often he restrained his wrath
and did not rouse his anger to its height.

39   He remembered that they were only mortal men,
who pass by like a wind and never return.

✶ 32–9. The account in these verses of the inconstancy and
fickleness of the Israelites, involving temporary repentance
(verses 34f.), and the (self-)delusion of noble sentiments and
words (verse 36), can only have been written by one who knew
these things from his own life and the lives of his fellow-
citizens. This passage describes religious failure, modern as well
as ancient, and saw that it was the key to Israel's history. It
expresses the attitude of the eternal God towards transient
humanity (verse 39).

33. *snuffed out their lives:* the reference is probably to the
wilderness generation, none of whom lived to enter the
promised land (Num. 14: 22f.).

35. *God was their Creator:* the text has 'rock' but the same
consonants may be read with the meaning *Creator.* This
provides a good parallel to *deliverer* (and on *deliverer* see Ps.
19: 14). ✶

40   How often they rebelled against him in the wilderness
and grieved him in the desert!

41   Again and again they tried God's patience
and provoked the Holy One of Israel.

42   They did not remember his prowess
on the day when he saved them from the enemy,

43   how he set his signs in Egypt,
his portents in the land of Zoan.

44   He turned their streams into blood,
and they could not drink the running water.

45   He sent swarms of flies which devoured them,

and frogs which brought devastation;
    he gave their harvest over to locusts   46
and their produce to the grubs;
he killed their vines with hailstones   47
    and their figs[a] with torrents of rain;
he abandoned their cattle to the plague[b]   48
    and their beasts to the arrows of pestilence.
He loosed upon them the violence of his anger, 49
wrath and enmity and rage,
launching those messengers of evil
to open a way for his fury.   50–51
He struck down all the first-born in Egypt,
the flower of their manhood in the tents of Ham,
not shielding their lives from death
but abandoning their bodies to the plague.

✳ 40–51. The psalmist returns to his meditation upon the past history of Israel, and reflects upon the plagues in Egypt. The account of the ten plagues in Exod. 7: 14 – 12: 36 is usually held to be a combination of two or three separate literary traditions; see the commentary on Exodus in this series, pp. 40f. The tradition of the plagues in Ps. 78 shows signs of independence from the traditions in Exodus. The order of the plagues is different, the Hebrew word rendered *locusts* (verse 46) is not found in the Exodus account, neither is the word rendered *torrents of rain* (verse 47). If the N.E.B. translation of verses 50f. is correct, it appears that the deaths of the first-born were due to plague. The earliest accounts of the exodus were probably included in hymns of praise for the deliverance (cp. Exod. 15) and verses 40–51 stem from a hymnic tradition independent of the traditions contained in the book of Exodus. It has been said

[a] *Lit.* sycomore-figs.   [b] *So one MS.; others* hail.

that worship is the best cure for self-pity, and many problems in the religious life may derive from a lack of contact with a worshipping community, whose hymns of praise recall God's mercies. The failures of ancient Israel may also have been due to a neglect of these means of grace (verses 42f.).

41. *tried God's patience:* see note on verse 18.

44. The psalm's version of the first plague is closer to the P account than to the J account (see Exod. 7: 19 and the commentary on Exodus, p. 46), for it envisages that more waters than merely those of the Nile are turned to blood.

45. *swarms of flies:* the fourth plague, Exod. 8: 20-32. *frogs:* the second plague, Exod. 8: 1-15.

46. *locusts . . . grubs:* the eighth plague concerns grubs; cp. Exod. 10: 1-20 where the N.E.B. renders the word here translated *grubs* as 'locusts'. It is difficult to determine whether the *locusts* of our psalm are a separate plague, not recorded in Exodus.

47. *hailstones . . . torrents of rain:* the seventh plague, Exod. 9: 13-26, is a plague of hailstones. Again, it is difficult to determine whether the *torrents of rain* is the same, or a separate plague. The Hebrew word occurs only here in the Old Testament and is traditionally taken to be frost or lumps of ice.

48. *cattle to the plague:* the Massoretic Text (see *The Making of the Old Testament*, p. 135) supported by most of the versions has 'hail' instead of *plague*. The N.E.B., which follows one ancient Hebrew manuscript, brings the verse close to the fifth plague, Exod. 9: 1-7. *arrows of pestilence:* the Hebrew *resheph* is normally taken to mean 'thunderbolt' but a god of pestilence, Resheph, was known in ancient Canaan (and cp. Ps. 76: 3).

49-51. A description of the tenth plague. *their bodies to the plague:* the Hebrew word for plague occurs in Exod. 9: 3 as a description of the cattle-plague of the fifth plague, so that some renderings (see the Revised Version footnote) relate the phrase to cattle-plague. If this is right, the text is in some disorder. The N.E.B. has re-arranged verses 50f. for the sake of greater clarity in translation. *

But he led out his own people like sheep   52
and guided them like a flock in the wilderness.
He led them in safety and they were not afraid,   53
and the sea closed over their enemies.
He brought them to his holy mountain,   54
the hill which his right hand had won;
he drove out nations before them,   55
he allotted their lands to Israel as a possession
and settled his tribes in their dwellings.
Yet they tried God's patience and rebelled against him;   56
they did not keep the commands of the Most High;
they were renegades, traitors like their fathers,   57
they changed, they went slack like a bow.

    They provoked him to anger with their hill-shrines   58
    and roused his jealousy with their carved images.
When God heard this, he put them out of mind   59
and utterly rejected Israel.

    He forsook his home at Shiloh,   60
the tabernacle in which he dwelt among men;
he surrendered the symbol of his strength[a] into   61
      captivity
    and his pride into enemy hands;
he gave his people over to the sword   62
    and put his own possession out of mind.
Fire devoured his young men,   63
and his maidens could raise no lament for them;
his priests fell by the sword,   64
and his widows could not weep.

      [a] the symbol of his strength: *lit.* his strength.

* 52–64. God's mercy and Israel's stubbornness continue to the occupation of the promised land.

54. *his holy mountain:* Hebrew 'his holy border'. It is not clear whether the reference is to the border of the holy land in the first part of the verse, and to the hill country in the second part, or whether, as in the N.E.B., a particular mountain, Mt Zion (Jerusalem), is meant; and cp. Ps. 2: 6.

55. *allotted:* cp. Josh. 23: 4.

58. A new form of rejection of God was that the Israelites turned to other gods who had done nothing, and could do nothing, for them.

59–62. The humiliation of Israel by the Philistines is referred to, which culminated in the destruction of the sanctuary of Shiloh (verse 60; cp. Jer. 7: 12) and the capture of the Ark, the *symbol of his strength* (verse 61; cp. 1 Sam. 4). The fact that God allowed the Ark, the symbol of his war-like presence in battle, to be captured, foreshadowed the loss of Jerusalem itself in 587 B.C.

63f. The actual events here described are either not otherwise recorded, or are highly poetic descriptions of what happened during the wars with the Philistines. *

65 Then the Lord awoke as a sleeper awakes,
    like a warrior heated with wine;
66 he struck his foes in the back parts
    and brought perpetual shame upon them.
67 He despised the clan of Joseph
    and did not choose the tribe of Ephraim;
68 he chose the tribe of Judah
    and Mount Zion which he loved;
69 he built his sanctuary high as the heavens,
    founded like the earth to last for ever.
70 He chose David to be his servant
    and took him from the sheepfolds;

he brought him from minding the ewes   71
to be the shepherd of his people Jacob;[a]
and he shepherded them in singleness of heart   72
and guided them with skilful hand.

✵ 65–72. God vindicates his people, and chooses Zion and David.

65. *awoke:* see on Ps. 44: 23. *like a warrior heated with wine:* or possibly, 'shouting with wine'. This is a bold metaphor, possibly taken from the divine warrior theme of ancient Canaanite literature. The victories of David, and possibly also of Saul and Jonathan, are alluded to.

67. *clan of Joseph:* the traditional Hebrew text has 'tent' or 'tabernacle' of Joseph, and most commentators see here a further reference to the rejection of Shiloh, which was in the hill country of Ephraim, the territory of the house of Joseph. If the N.E.B. is correct, the reference could be to the final destruction of the northern kingdom, Israel, in 721 B.C.

69. The psalmist describes the impregnable nature of Jerusalem and its sanctuary, and expresses his confidence in its durability. However, our psalm was clearly written before Jerusalem fell in 587 B.C. as indeed it did again in A.D. 70. Had the psalmist lived to see these catastrophes, he would have agreed that the pattern of human rebellion, divine punishment and divine grace, which is the theme of the psalm, had not ended with the reign of David. He would have extended his meditation on the 'riddle' of Israel's history so as to include the destruction of Jerusalem as another deliberate surrender by God of a symbol of his strength. But if the just and forgiving mercy of God can outlast the stubbornness of man (verses 38f.), then this psalm is not only a story of human folly, it is a psalm of hope. ✵

[a] *Prob. rdg.; Heb. adds* and Israel his possession.

HOW LONG, O LORD?

79

1 O God, the heathen have set foot in thy domain,
    defiled thy holy temple
and laid Jerusalem in ruins.

2   They have thrown out the dead bodies of thy servants
        to feed the birds of the air;
    they have made thy loyal servants carrion for wild
        beasts.

3 Their blood is spilled all round Jerusalem like water,
    and there they lie unburied.

4   We suffer the contempt of our neighbours,
    the gibes and mockery of all around us.

5 How long, O LORD, wilt thou be roused to such fury?
    Must thy jealousy rage like a fire?

6 Pour out thy wrath over nations which do not know thee
and over kingdoms which do not invoke thee by name;

7 see how they have devoured Jacob and laid waste his
        homesteads.

8   Do not remember against us the guilt of past
        generations
    but let thy compassion come swiftly to meet us,
        we have been brought so low.

9 Help us, O God our saviour, for the honour of thy name;
    for thy name's sake deliver us and wipe out our sins.

10 Why should the nations ask, 'Where is their God?'
    Let thy vengeance for the bloody slaughter of thy
        servants
    fall on those nations before our very eyes.

Let the groaning of the captives reach thy presence   11
    and in thy great might set free death's prisoners.
As for the contempt our neighbours pour on thee, O Lord,   12
    turn it back sevenfold on their own heads.
Then we thy people, the flock which thou dost   13
      shepherd,
    will give thee thanks for ever
and repeat thy praise to every generation.

* This psalm is traditionally, and commonly, connected with
the destruction of Jerusalem by the Babylonions in 587 B.C.
Although the language of the psalm is so strong that only a
disaster on the scale of that in 587 would fit, it is to be noted
that there is nothing in the psalm itself which explicitly refers
to the Babylonian destruction, and there are possibly references which argue against such an equation (see the commentary
on verses 1f.). We may say that the connection is not unlikely,
but also not demonstrable. The psalmist asks God to avenge
the disaster that has befallen Israel, but so that God's honour
and integrity are upheld.

    1. *domain:* the whole land, and, in particular, Jerusalem.
defiled: if the reference is to 587 B.C. when the temple was
destroyed, *defiled* seems to be a weak sentiment. However, to
the Hebrews, the fact that heathens had entered the most holy
place would possibly be more abhorrent than the fact that the
building had been destroyed.

    2f. The decent treatment of human remains is a universal
concern, as much in the present as in the past (and cp. Ps. 141:7);
the revulsion expressed in these verses is thus understandable.
If the Babylonians were responsible for such atrocities in 597
or 587 B.C., the fact is not mentioned in the relevant biblical
historical passages, 2 Kings 24: 8 – 25: 21; Jer. 39: 1–10. *loyal
servants:* the victims include good and bad Israelites alike.

Loyalty to God's covenant does not bring immunity from tribulation (see further on verses 5–8). Part of these verses is quoted in 1 Macc. 7: 17.

5–8. These verses show that both the immediate cause and the ultimate cause of Israel's plight are recognized. The immediate cause is the ruthless action of a people or peoples more powerful than Israel (verse 7) who do not recognize God (verse 6). The ultimate cause is God himself who has permitted, or initiated, Israel's humiliation, as a punishment for the unfaithfulness of past generations (verses 5, 8. Note also that verse 9*b* recognizes the guilt of the present generation).

5. *jealousy:* God is jealous for, rather than jealous of, his people and Israel is his special possession. His action to bring back Israel to full obedience is drastic indeed.

6. *Pour out thy wrath:* perhaps an understandable reaction to the events. If the people of the covenant have suffered thus for their sins, what should be the fate of those outside the covenant?

9–13. The question raised by these verses is whether the psalmist wishes God to vindicate Israel for Israel's satisfaction, or for God's. Again, the human desire to be vindicated is most understandable, but the psalmist goes further than this. For atrocities to go unpunished (verse 10) and for Israel to continue in humiliation, is to suggest to the world the impotence of God. More important than the restoration of Israel's pride is the honouring of God's name (verse 9).

11. *groaning of the captives:* if the primary reference is to the Babylonian exile, conditions as such do not seem to have been unduly harsh. However, all exile from home is a bitter experience (cp. Ps. 137). *death's prisoners:* probably those exiles who have nothing to hope for but death.

13. *the flock which thou dost shepherd:* cp. Ps. 77: 20. This phrase is a recognition that in spite of all Israel's difficulties, God is still actively guarding those for whom he is jealous (verse 5). ✳

MAKE THY FACE SHINE UPON US THAT WE
MAY BE SAVED

80

Hear us, O shepherd of Israel,   1
who leadest Joseph like a flock of sheep.
   Show thyself, thou that art throned on the
     cherubim,
   to Ephraim and to Benjamin.   2
   Rouse thy victorious might from slumber,[a]
   come to our rescue.
   Restore us, O God,   3
and make thy face shine upon us that we may be
     saved.

   O LORD God of Hosts,   4
how long wilt thou resist thy people's prayer?
   Thou hast made sorrow their daily bread   5
and tears of threefold grief their drink.
Thou hast humbled us before our neighbours,   6
and our enemies mock us to their hearts' content.
   O God of Hosts, restore us;   7
make thy face shine upon us that we may be saved.

Thou didst bring a vine out of Egypt;   8
thou didst drive out nations and plant it;
thou didst clear the ground before it,   9
so that it made good roots and filled the land.
The mountains were covered with its shade,   10
   and its branches were like those of mighty cedars.
It put out boughs all the way to the Sea   11
   and its shoots as far as the River.

[a] from slumber: *prob. rdg.; Heb.* and Manasseh.

12   Why hast thou broken down the wall round it
        so that every passer-by can pluck its fruit?
13   The wild boar from the thickets gnaws it,
            and swarming insects from the fields feed on it.
14   O God of Hosts, once more look down from heaven,
        take thought for this vine and tend it,
15   this stock that thy right hand has planted.*a*
16   Let them that set fire to it or cut it down
        perish before thy angry face.
17   Let thy hand rest upon the man at thy right side,
        the man whom thou hast made strong for thy service.
18   We have not turned back from thee,
        so grant us new life, and we will invoke thee by name.
19   LORD God of Hosts, restore us;
        make thy face shine upon us that we may be saved.

✻ It is difficult to be certain which national calamity originally
called forth this psalm, and in any case, the psalm was probably
used during many calamities after the one which first inspired
it. The mention of the tribes of Ephraim, Benjamin and
Manasseh (verse 2, and see the N.E.B. footnote) may indicate
that the psalm originated among these tribes in the north, or
that the psalm was composed in Jerusalem after these northern
tribes were overrun by the Assyrians, say, 732–722 B.C., and
constituted a prayer for their restoration. Whatever the
original setting, verses 8–19 suggest that a restoration of all
Israel is earnestly desired. A refrain occurs in verses 3, 7 and 19,
and possibly (with variations) in verse 14. The refrain expresses
faith in God's power to restore his people, but the psalmist is
puzzled that God does not seem to choose to act. This
combination of faith and uncertainty is well known to the

[a] *Prob. rdg.; Heb. adds* and on the son whom thou hast made strong for
thy service (*cp. verse 17*).

156

servants of God in every generation. The psalmist, however, does not turn back from God (verse 18) and maintains his faith that God's ways will ultimately be vindicated.

1. *shepherd . . . who leadest:* the use of the words *shepherd, Joseph, leadest,* indicates that the psalmist has in mind the exodus deliverance (cp. Pss. 78: 52; 81: 4f.). That was in the past; *leadest* asserts the psalmist's faith that in spite of appearances to the contrary, God is still leading his people (see Ps. 79: 13). *Show thyself:* demonstrate your power in saving and restoring your people. (Cp. Ps. 94: 1.) *cherubim:* winged creatures whose artistic representations were thought to constitute the throne of the invisible God (cp. 1 Sam. 4 :4; 1 Kings 8 : 6f.; and see further on Ps. 99: 1). Here, they symbolize God's kingship in heaven and his presence among his people.

2. For metrical reasons, the N.E.B. has taken the first part of verse 2 with verse 1, and altered Manasseh to *from slumber* (i.e. *mnšh* to *mšnh*). *Ephraim . . . Benjamin:* possibly all the ten northern tribes are meant, or merely the rump of the hill country of Ephraim, which was all that remained of the northern kingdom in the second half of the eighth century (2 Kings 15: 29).

3. *make thy face shine:* grant us your blessing. Cp. Num. 6: 25. A shining face is a sign of favour.

4. *O LORD God of Hosts:* see Ps. 24: 10. *resist:* the Hebrew normally means to burn in anger against, but it is here taken to be a different verb with the sense of 'was hard'. Because he has not granted the request of his people, God is thought to be displeased. This may well be an unworthy notion about the nature of God; it is by no means a merely primitive or ancient view of God.

5. *tears of threefold grief:* tears by the bucketful.

6. *Thou hast humbled us:* the nature of the humiliation is not clear, though possibly the Hebrew literally translated as 'thou hast made us an occasion of strife among our neighbours' suggests that neighbouring states were quarrelling over Israelite territory.

8–13. The allegory of the vine. Israel's history is here presented in almost fable-like language.

8f. The image of Israel as a vine is common in the Old Testament (cp. Isa. 5: 1–7). The description of the clearing of ground and the transplanting of a vine is an allegory of the exodus, and of the occupation of Canaan. The allegory stresses the divine character of these events.

10. The mighty growth of the vine probably refers to the full flowering of the Israelite empire in the time of David.

11. *Sea . . . River:* the Mediterranean Sea and the River Euphrates.

12. *Why hast thou broken down:* the psalmist in no way imagines that having planted his vine, God abandoned it. Its protective wall has been broken down by God himself, even if he has used the agency of surrounding nations. (For the same view, see verses 5 and 6: 'Thou hast made . . . Thou hast humbled . . .') The psalmist is therefore not praying to an absent deity, but to God, whose hand is seen in Israel's catastrophes. *pluck its fruit:* the taking of Israelite territory may be meant.

13. *wild boar:* an unclean animal (Lev. 11: 7), and here, a symbol for Israel's enemies. *swarming insects:* the exact zoological reference is unknown, but this is also a symbol for enemies.

14. *once more look down:* the N.E.B. implies (against verses 5, 6, 12) that God has withdrawn his concern for Israel. The traditional rendering 'relent [turn again]: look down from heaven' fits the general sense of the psalm better. God is not being asked to cease his indifference but to change his attitude.

15. *this stock:* the meaning of the Hebrew is uncertain, but if this word is a noun, then *stock* is the best rendering. The remainder of the verse, which the N.E.B. puts into the footnote, is an anticipatory reference to the king in verse 17.

17. *man at thy right side:* probably the king. Cp. Ps. 110: 1. *man whom thou hast made strong:* the Hebrew has 'son of man'. Although the phrase 'son of man' may mean simply 'man', the fact that here the full phrase 'son of man' is used of the king

may have suggested to Christ something of his role as son of
man, especially in view of the New Testament references to
vine imagery (Mark 12: 1–12; John 15: 1–16), a theme of this
psalm. In its present context, the phrase suggests a contrast
between the human frailty of the king (he is born of human-
kind) and the fact that God has made him strong for his service.
This last thought is a ground for confidence in the God who
will surely fulfil his promises to his people and his anointed
king. It also serves as confidence for the church throughout
the ages, whose king is God's chosen one. ✶

LISTEN TO ME, O ISRAEL

81

Sing out in praise of God our refuge,[a]   1
    acclaim the God of Jacob.

Take pipe and tabor,   2
take tuneful harp and lute.

Blow the horn for the new month,   3
    for the full moon on the day of our pilgrim-feast.

This is a law for Israel,   4
    an ordinance of the God of Jacob,

laid as a solemn charge on Joseph   5
    when he came out of Egypt.[b]

When I lifted the load from his shoulders,   6
his hands let go the builder's basket.

When you cried to me in distress, I rescued you;   7
    unseen, I answered you in thunder.

I tested you at the waters of Meribah,
where I opened your mouths and filled them.[c]

[a] *Or* strength.
[b] *Prob. rdg.; Heb. adds* I hear an unfamiliar language.
[c] *Line transposed from end of verse 10.*

16*a*   I fed Israel*b* with the finest wheat-flour
          and satisfied him*c* with honey from the rocks.

8   Listen, my people, while I give you a solemn charge –
       do but listen to me, O Israel:

9   you shall have no strange god
       nor bow down to any foreign god;

10   I am the LORD your God
        who brought you up from Egypt.*d*

11   But my people did not listen to my words
       and Israel would have none of me;

12   so I sent them off, stubborn as they were,
        to follow their own devices.

13   If my people would but listen to me,
       if Israel would only conform to my ways,

14   I would soon bring their enemies to their knees
       and lay a heavy hand upon their persecutors.

15   Let those who hate them*e* come cringing to them,
       and meet with everlasting troubles.*f*

✻ The subject-matter of this psalm lacks a central point of
focus. It begins with an exhortation to the people to praise God
at a festival (verses 1–5), recalls some of the great moments of
Israel's deliverance from Egypt, with God speaking in the first
person (verses 6–12), and ends with a plea by God to his people
to turn back to him (verses 13 to the end). Some interpreters
suggest that the psalm is made up of two originally separate

[*a*] *Verse transposed.*
[*b*] I fed Israel: *prob. rdg.; Heb.* He fed him.
[*c*] *So one MS.; others* you.
[*d*] *See note on verse 7.*
[*e*] those . . . them: *prob. rdg.; Heb.* those who hate the LORD.
[*f*] *Verse 16 transposed to follow verse 7.*

units, verses 1–5(6) and 7–16. Whether or not this is so, it is possible to give the psalm a unified interpretation. Its occasion is probably the Feast of Tabernacles held in September/October (see verse 3) at which the law was read (verse 8) and the people were exhorted to renew their trust in God. But so as to emphasize that such renewal of trust is no formality, the psalm contains a note of warning (verses 11f.), and a promise that only the unwillingness of the people to trust fully – together with the responsibilities and inconveniences that that may imply – hinders a reversal of Israel's present condition. A date for the psalm is almost impossible to determine.

1. *God our refuge:* God who protects, or who gives us strength (see the footnote).

2. *Take pipe:* it is not clear in the Hebrew whether an actual instrument, or singing, is meant. *tabor:* a type of small drum, perhaps used to accompany a pipe. *lute:* a direct fore-runner (in the Middle Ages) of the guitar. It is not known whether the Hebrew word denotes an instrument whose strings were stopped by the left hand and plucked with the right, or whether is was a smaller type of harp or lyre.

3. *new month . . . full moon:* see Lev. 23: 23–43 where a complex festival is commanded beginning on the first day of the seventh month (new moon) and continuing through to the beginning of the feast of Tabernacles on the fifteenth day. According to Deut. 31: 10f. the law was to be read at the *pilgrim-feast* of Tabernacles every seven years (see verses 8f.).

4. *This is a law:* i.e. the observance of the festival.

5. *Joseph:* the northern tribes only may be meant, but probably the reference is to the whole nation, Israel. The final sentence of the verse is difficult, and is relegated to the footnotes by the N.E.B. If it is retained, it must either be rendered 'where (i.e. in Egypt) I heard an unfamiliar language', or taken with verse 6 where it could be an introduction to the speech with which verse 6 begins.

6. *load . . . builder's basket:* the oppression in Egypt.

7. *When you cried to me:* either during the time of slavery in

Egypt (Exod. 2: 23), or at the approach of the Egyptians at the Red Sea (Exod. 14: 10). *I answered you:* possibly, the incident of Exod. 14: 24 is meant. *I tested you:* Exod. 17: 1–7. *where I opened:* the N.E.B. has transposed this line from verse 10, and has then added verse 16 to follow immediately. While it is possible that better sense is thus produced at this point in the psalm, the conclusion of the psalm is considerably weakened (see on verse 15).

16. *I fed Israel:* see Deut. 32: 13f.

8. *Listen, my people:* this is reminiscent of many passages in Deut., e.g. 6: 4.

9. *no strange god:* see the prohibition in the ten command-ments, Exod. 20: 3; Deut. 5: 7.

10. *I am the LORD your God:* see Exod. 20: 2; Deut. 5: 6. Verses 9 and 10 are either a deliberate allusion to the ten commandments, or indicate that the commandments were read publicly at the festival, perhaps together with other laws. God's claim to deserve the undivided loyalty of his people is based on his gracious act when he *brought you up from Egypt.* The laws are to be obeyed, not in order to earn God's grace, but because God has already acted graciously, and will continue to do so.

11. *But my people did not listen:* verses 11 and 12 may refer to specific incidents in the wilderness or to a wider sweep of Israelite history.

13f. Again, it is not clear whether a specific calamity is meant here, or whether this is a general statement. The promise would be appropriate to either.

15 (and 16). The transference of verse 16 to follow verse 7 and 10*c* necessitates two changes in the N.E.B. to verse 15*a*, and an exceedingly free rendering of 15*b*. Although difficult, the Hebrew may be translated literally 'Let those who hate the LORD cringe before him, let this be so as long as they live. But he (God) will feed him (Israel) with the finest wheat, and I will satisfy you with honey from the rock.' In this case, the psalm ends with an assurance that God will destroy all who

oppose him, but will bless his own people. If elsewhere in the
psalm the blessing is conditional (verses 13f.), this is perhaps
only because it would be harmful to receive blessing where
blessing is unrecognized. *

GODS YOU MAY BE, YET YOU SHALL DIE AS
MEN DIE

82

God takes his stand in the court of heaven 1
    to deliver judgement among the gods themselves.

How long will you judge unjustly 2
    and show favour to the wicked?
You ought to give judgement for the weak and the 3
      orphan,
    and see right done to the destitute and
    downtrodden,
you ought to rescue the weak and the poor, 4
    and save them from the clutches of wicked men.
But you know nothing, you understand nothing, 5
    you walk in the dark
    while earth's foundations are giving way.
This is my sentence: Gods you may be, 6
    sons all of you of a high god,[a]
yet you shall die as men die;[b] 7
princes fall, every one of them, and so shall you.

Arise, O God, and judge the earth; 8
    for thou dost pass all nations through thy sieve.

* At first sight, this is a perplexing psalm. Who are the gods
whom God judges, and what is the occasion of the judgement?

    [a] *Or* of the Most High.   [b] *Or* as Adam died.

The traditional explanation is that human judges in Israel are meant, but though this makes sense of verses 2–5, it hardly does justice to verses 6f. Similarly, the view that the gods are the rulers of foreign nations who are oppressing Israel hardly makes sense of verses 2–5. The most likely explanation is that the gods are the heavenly beings, each of whom controls the destiny of a nation (see Deut. 32: 8). In this case, the psalm asserts the power of the God of Israel over these other 'gods' (cp. Ps. 95: 3). Sentence is passed on them (verses 6f.) because they have forfeited the right to be gods – they have not protected the weak from the strong (verses 2–5). Only the universal rule of God will bring true justice to the nations (verse 8). With the whole psalm, cp. Ps. 58: 1–2.

1. *court of heaven*: the Hebrew, 'assembly of God', perhaps conveyed the idea that it was God's own court or assembly. (Cp. Job 1–2; 1 Kings 22: 19.) *among the gods*: see above. The word *among* is ambiguous, and probably does not mean deciding between rival claims that gods might have. More likely, God, surrounded by his heavenly court, rises to pronounce judgement on the gods of the nations.

2–4 sum up the case against the accused gods. In Old Testament teaching, not only is God himself expected to perform the acts which the gods fail to do (Ps. 10: 14–18) but like action is expected of the king (Jer. 22: 1–4). Similar teaching can be found in ancient Near Eastern texts outside the Bible:

'Thou judgest not the cause of the widow,
        Nor adjudicat'st the case of the wretched.'
(J. B. Pritchard, *Ancient Near Eastern Texts*, p. 149.)

5. The failure of the accused gods results from their ignorance; but the implication is that they should have known better, and meanwhile the perversion of justice undermines the moral order upon which life on earth is dependent.

6f. Belief in a number of gods was almost universal among Israel's neighbours, and where the Old Testament itself assumes the existence of other gods, it does not go into the question of whether they were created by the God of Israel.

Probably, the first step towards reconciling belief in the unique-
ness of the God of Israel with the acknowledgment of the
existence of other gods, was to regard the other gods as part of
the heavenly court over which God presided as king (Ps. 95:3).
Later, probably during the sixth century, Israelite teachers
thought more deeply about the idea of God as creator of the
world, and came to deny that other gods had any real existence
(Ps. 115: 3–8); such gods were merely the work of human
hands and ideas. The purpose of the present passage is to
declare that the accused gods are the servants of the God of
Israel, ruling over nations only with his permission; but they
have now forfeited the moral right to power and authority,
and they are condemned. *sons . . . of a high god:* this difficult
phrase probably means no more than that the gods are gods
indeed. If the N.E.B. footnote is correct, however, the 'Most
High' is probably a title of the God of Israel (Ps. 83 : 18 and cp.
on Ps. 57: 2), and then the gods are created by him.

8. The psalm concludes with a prayer that what has been
decided in the heavenly court may be accomplished on earth,
so that all nations may benefit from true justice. *pass . . . through
thy sieve:* an expression for judgement. The traditional translation 'you shall inherit all nations' may be paraphrased 'all the
nations belong to you', a further expression of God's supremacy in the world. *

LET THEM LEARN THAT THOU ALONE ART LORD

83

Rest not, O God;   1
O God, be neither silent nor still,
for thy enemies are making a tumult,   2
and those that hate thee carry their heads high.
They devise cunning schemes against thy people   3
and conspire against those thou hast made thy treasure:

4   'Come, away with them,' they cry,
         'let them be a nation no longer,
     let Israel's name be remembered no more.'

5   With one mind they have agreed together
     to make a league against thee:

6   the families of Edom, the Ishmaelites,
         Moabites and Hagarenes,

7   Gebal, Ammon and Amalek,
         Philistia and the citizens of Tyre,

8   Asshur too their ally,
     all of them lending aid to the descendants of Lot.

9   Deal with them as with Sisera,
         as with Jabin by the torrent of Kishon,

10   who fell vanquished as Midian*ᵃ* fell at En-harod,*ᵇ*
         and were spread on the battlefield like dung.

11   Make their princes like Oreb and Zeeb,
         make all their nobles like Zebah and Zalmunna;

12   for they said, 'We will seize for ourselves
         all the pastures of God's people.'

13   Scatter them, O God, like thistledown,
         like chaff before the wind.

14   Like fire raging through the forest
     or flames which blaze across the hills,

15   hunt them down with thy tempest,
         and dismay them with thy storm-wind.

16   Heap shame upon their heads, O LORD,
         until they confess the greatness of thy name.

17   Let them be abashed, and live in perpetual dismay;
         let them feel their shame and perish.

[a] as Midian: *transposed from previous verse.*
[b] En-harod: *prob. rdg., cp. Judg. 7: 1; Heb.* Endor.

So let them learn that thou^a alone art LORD,   18
    God Most High over all the earth.

* In this psalm, many nations have banded together for the
purpose of utterly destroying Israel. It is to be noted that no
actual attack is mentioned. So many different historical settings
for the psalm have been proposed, that it is clear that we
cannot be dogmatic about its date and setting. It is possible
that the nations are symbols for all that is in opposition to the
will of God, and the psalm may be interpreted as a prayer for
the coming of God's kingdom. Though the psalmist prays for
the humiliation of those who threaten Israel, his ultimate
desire is that these enemies should 'confess the greatness of
thy name' (verse 16).

    1. *Rest not*: do not remain inactive or indifferent.

    2. *thy enemies*: it is not so much that Israel's enemies are also
God's enemies, but that God's enemies are also Israel's
enemies; for Israel is an actual example in the world of God's
grace and mercy, and an affront to those who would rather
trust in human power. *carry their heads high*: a sign of arrogance. For the whole verse cp. Ps. 2: 1–3.

    3. *hast made thy treasure*: literally 'thy treasured ones'. God's
protection and special favour are meant.

    4. *'Come . . . no longer'*: an expanded paraphrase of the
Hebrew 'they say, "Come, let us annihilate them from being
a nation"'.

    6–8. The names of the allies against Israel. *families of Edom*:
Hebrew 'tents of Edom'. *Ishmaelites . . . Hagarenes*: the *Hagarenes* lived, according to 1 Chron. 5: 10 (Hagarites), east of
Gilead, in Transjordan. It is not clear whether, by *Ishmaelites*,
an identifiable society, or a general term, perhaps meaning
traders or tent-dwellers, is meant.

    7. *Gebal* probably denotes not the ancient Phoenician city
of that name, but a region in the neighbourhood of Petra,

[a] *So some MSS.; others add* thy name.

occupied by a partly-settled people. *Amalek* was another
partly-settled people, occupying regions to the south of
Jordan.

8. *Asshur too their ally:* the might of Assyria appears to be
lent to the coalition, whose leaders, the *descendants of Lot*, are
Ammon and Moab (cp. Gen. 19: 36–8). It is impossible to
know whether Assyria was, at the time of the psalm's composition, a great power or a moderate power, nor is it clear
why Assyria should want to assist the coalition against Israel.
It remains a possibility that the nations who oppose Israel are
in fact symbols for what opposes the kingdom of God as
represented by Israel.

9–11. *Deal with them:* the psalmist bases his prayer for
deliverance on a number of past victories for Israel, in which
God's part was particularly conspicuous. In the battle against
Sisera and Jabin (Judg. 4f.), the *torrent of Kishon* had miracu-
lously swept away the enemy forces. In Gideon's fight against
Midian (Judg. 7) the Israelite army numbered only 300,
although, according to the tradition, Israel could have put
32,000 men into the field. For the fate of Oreb, Zeeb, Zebah
and Zalmunna, see Judg. 7: 25; 8: 4–21. The text is in some
disorder in the Hebrew; see the N.E.B. footnotes.

12. *for they said:* the N.E.B. refers these words to the enemies
mentioned in verse 11; but it is possible that the enemies of
verses 2–8 expressed the sentiments in verse 12. *pastures of
God's people:* literally 'God's pastures'; i.e. God's own land.

13–18. In highly poetic language (verses 13–15) the psalmist
asks God to act against the nations, so that by recognizing the
shame of their rebellion (verses 16f.) they will either turn to
God or perish. Just as Ps. 82 described the judgement of the
gods, so this psalm prays for judgement on the nations. *God
Most High:* see on Ps. 82: 6f. ✻

HOW DEAR IS THY DWELLING-PLACE

84

How dear is thy dwelling-place,   1
    thou LORD of Hosts!
I pine, I faint with longing   2
    for the courts of the LORD's temple;
my whole being cries out with joy
    to the living God.
Even the sparrow finds a home,   3
    and the swallow has her nest,
where she rears her brood beside thy altars,
    O LORD of Hosts, my King and my God.
Happy are those who dwell in thy house;   4
    they never cease from praising thee.
Happy the men whose refuge is in thee,   5
    whose hearts are set on the pilgrim ways[a]!
As they pass through the thirsty valley   6
    they find water from a spring;
and the LORD provides even men who lose their way
    with pools to quench their thirst.[b]
So they pass on from outer wall to inner,   7
and the God of gods shows himself in Zion.

O LORD God of Hosts, hear my prayer;   8
    listen, O God of Jacob.
O God, look upon our lord the king   9
    and accept thy anointed prince with favour.

[a] are set . . . ways: *or* high praises fill.
[b] they find . . . thirst: *prob. rdg.; Heb. obscure.*

10   Better one day in thy courts
          than a thousand days at home;
      better to linger by the threshold of God's house
          than to live in the dwellings of the wicked.
11   The LORD God is a battlement and a shield;
          grace and honour are his to give.
      The LORD will hold back no good thing
          from those whose life is blameless.

12   O LORD of Hosts,
      happy the man who trusts in thee!

⋆ Although this psalm describes the privilege of those who
either serve and worship regularly in the Jerusalem temple, or
who are able to visit it as pilgrims, we have no certain information that the psalmist himself was a pilgrim or temple official.
Neither is there any evidence that the psalm was a liturgy used
by pilgrims. It is impossible to date the psalm. Some regard it
as composed before the exile, because of the possible mention
of the king (verse 9), while others argue that only after the
exile could one speak of the altars (in the plural) of the temple
(verse 3). Whatever its age or original setting, the psalm is a
timeless expression of the ultimate satisfaction of pilgrimage,
and the privilege of worship in the narrower sense of prayer
to God, and the sense of his presence.
      1. *LORD of Hosts:* see on Ps. 24: 10.
      2. *courts of the LORD's temple:* the Jerusalem temple
possessed a number of courts and forecourts. Whether pilgrims were allowed to live in these courts is not clear; the
verse may mean no more than that the psalmist longs to stand
in the temple precincts, contemplating the building which
marks the most hallowed parts of God's house. *the living God:*
the psalmist does not necessarily believe that God's presence is
more 'concentrated' in Jerusalem than elsewhere; but the
temple, with its worship and traditional associations, enables

the psalmist to focus his thoughts on *the living God* in a way not possible elsewhere. Cp. Ps. 42: 2.

3. The N.E.B. translation rightly indicates that the birds do not nest upon the altars but *beside thy altars*, e.g. in roofs near the altars. The language conveys the idea of God's protection for weak and small members of the created order. Some interpreters take *beside thy altars* with verse 4, e.g. 'beside thy altars, they (the worshippers) never cease from praising thee'.

4. *Happy are those who dwell:* most probably the officials of the temple who reside in the temple precincts, although to *dwell in thy house* may be a way of saying 'to worship in God's house' (cp. Ps. 23: 6).

5. *whose hearts . . . pilgrim ways:* Hebrew 'highways are in their hearts', which can be taken as 'highways (to Zion) are in their hearts (i.e. desires)' or 'highways (i.e. pilgrim ways) are in their hearts (i.e. desires)'. The N.E.B. footnote has 'high praises' for *pilgrim ways*, the Hebrew word basically meaning 'to cast up'. Some interpreters alter the word slightly to produce the sense 'confidence is in their hearts'.

6. *thirsty valley:* Hebrew 'valley of (or, to) Baca'. The word *bākā* is connected by many commentators with a word meaning 'balsam tree', and the point is made that the balsam tree grew in arid, waterless places. Although there is some doubt as to the presence of balsam trees in the geographical area of ancient Israel, the occurrence of the word for 'thirst' in the next contrasting phrase of this verse leads many to understand the valley of Baca as representing, or being the name of, an arid valley through which pilgrims passed. The rendering in the Book of Common Prayer 'vale of misery' ultimately rests on the Hebrew verb *bākāh* 'to weep'. It is not impossible that already in ancient times the name 'Baca' was connected with 'weeping' and that the verse symbolized the trials that beset the servants of God in their pilgrimage of life. *the LORD provides . . . to quench their thirst:* Hebrew 'the early rain clothes it even with pools', both of which renderings make sense if 'it'

is taken to mean the arid valley. The pilgrims are refreshed on their journey by the sight of the effect of the early rains (October–December). The N.E.B. footnote unfairly describes the Hebrew as obscure, and the N.E.B. rendering, though in the spirit of the psalm, is highly conjectural.

7. *from outer wall to inner:* the N.E.B. translation is a description of the progress of the pilgrim through the fortifications of Jerusalem. The traditional rendering 'from strength to strength', which is just as possible, would denote the growing expectation of the pilgrim as he neared his goal, and perhaps also a swelling in the numbers of pilgrims as all roads lead to Jerusalem. *God of gods . . . in Zion:* the N.E.B. translation raises the interesting question how and when the *God of gods shows himself in Zion*, and although the traditional interpretation is not without difficulty, the general sense is better preserved by a rendering such as 'every one of them appears before God in Zion'.

8. *hear my prayer:* the traditional division of the Hebrew text separates verse 8 from verse 9 by *Selah* (possibly a congregational response). If verse 8 is separate, then it is a prayer for a profitable pilgrimage, or the pilgrim's first prayer spoken in the temple precincts. The N.E.B. follows the view that verses 8f. constitute a prayer for the king, whose favour with God is desired for the good of both king and nation.

9. *O God . . . the king:* Hebrew either 'O God, our shield, look' or 'O God, look upon our shield (i.e. the king)'. The second half of the verse *thy anointed prince* (although the Hebrew lacks 'prince', and a high priest could conceivably be meant) suggests that 'shield' is a term for the king in his role as the defender of the nation, as well as the weak of the nation (cp. Ps. 82: 3–5).

10. The mere fact of being in the temple precincts constitutes an experience whose quality is more than the rest of a lifetime can match. Thus the psalmist contrasts this happy moment with what he knows must normally be his lot. *the wicked, in* (or better, 'among') whose *dwellings* the psalmist

must live, may be Israel's heathen neighbours, or more probably, Israelites who do not care for God, and who would not
fit the description of the servant of God in Ps. 15. Cp. also
Ps. 27: 4.

11. *battlement:* clearly, God's protection is meant.

12. *happy the man:* this is not simply a description of a man's
inner feelings, but a recognition of how fortunate is the man
whose trust in God endures, nourished by the privileges of
pilgrimage, worship and prayer, and constant even when he
has to pass through the 'thirsty valley'. ✳

DELIVERANCE IS NEAR

85

Lord, thou hast been gracious to thy land   1
  and turned the tide of Jacob's fortunes.
  Thou hast forgiven the guilt of thy people   2
  and put away all their sins.
  Thou hast taken back all thy anger   3
  and turned from thy bitter wrath.

  Turn back to us, O God our saviour,   4
and cancel thy displeasure.
Wilt thou be angry with us for ever?   5
Must thy wrath last for all generations?
Wilt thou not give us new life   6
that thy people may rejoice in thee?
O Lord, show us thy true love   7
and grant us thy deliverance.

Let me hear the words of the Lord: 8
are they not[a] words of peace,
  peace to his people and his loyal servants

[a] of the Lord: are they not: *prob. rdg.; Heb.* of God the Lord.

and to all who turn and trust in him[a]?

9 Deliverance is near to those who worship him,
   so that glory may dwell in our land.

10   Love and fidelity have come together;
     justice and peace join hands.

11   Fidelity springs up from earth
     and justice looks down from heaven.

12   The LORD will add prosperity,
     and our land shall yield its harvest.

13   Justice shall go in front of him
     and the path before his feet shall be peace.[b]

* At first sight, this psalm seems to date from after the exile. The writer gives thanks for a great deliverance, most likely the return from exile (verses 1–3). He then pleads to God to reverse the present fortunes of the people of God (verses 4–7). A divine oracle (verses 8–13), perhaps delivered by a prophet or a priest, assures the people of God's blessing. Although it cannot be proved that verses 1–3 refer to the return from the Babylonian exile, this is the most likely hypothesis; however, the occasion of distress in verses 4–7 cannot be identified. In its timeless aspect, the psalm develops from the apparent contradiction between a certainty in God's promises and the present fortunes of the people of God, a sublime picture of the blessings to come when God's rule is unalterably established.

1–3. The language of the opening verses is reminiscent of Ps. 126 and Isa. 40–55. In Ps. 126: 1, 'turned the tide of Zion's fortune' is probably a reference to the return to Jerusalem from the Babylonian exile. *Jacob* is frequently a name for God's people in Isa. 40–55 (e.g. 40: 27; 41: 8), and in Isa. 40: 2 Israel is told that God no longer regards his people as culpable for

[a] and to all . . . him: *so Sept.; Heb.* and let them not lose hope.
[b] and the path . . . peace: *prob. rdg.; Heb.* so that he may put his feet to the way.

their sins. All this suggests that verses 1–3 refer to the Babylonian exile, either by original intention, or by the reapplication of a general psalm to a particular event. *turned from thy bitter wrath:* although the Old Testament may use such phrases to describe the misfortunes of Israel, it is acknowledged that God is never angry with his people without cause, and that his anger is followed by grace when Israel is ready to receive it.

4–7. Many commentators have suggested that when the exiles returned to Jerusalem, some time between 540 and 516 B.C., the harsh conditions (cp. Hag. 1: 5–11) dampened their great enthusiasm, and called forth this psalm. Although this is possible, one wonders whether such returned exiles could say 'Thou hast taken back all thy anger' (verse 3) and then so quickly add *Wilt thou be angry with us for ever?* (verse 5). Perhaps we should assume a somewhat longer passage of time between the situations of verses 1–3 and 4–7.

6. *give us new life:* possibly, restore the material of our life (cp. Ezek. 37: 3–14; and cp. Ps. 16: 11).

7. *show us thy true love: true love* (Hebrew *ḥesed*) is often translated as 'steadfast love' or 'covenant love'. The thought here may be that this love has remained constant towards Israel, even if not apparent. The prayer is for a visible token of this abiding love.

8. The words of assurance that follow may be spoken by a priest or prophet conveying the divine word. *and to all who turn and trust in him:* the Hebrew 'but do not let them turn back to folly' arises because the word *kislah* (N.E.B. *trust in him*) can mean either 'confidence' or 'stupidity'. It is a matter of individual judgement whether one feels that there is a note of warning in verse 8 (i.e. following the Hebrew as translated above), or whether the promises are unconditional (as implied by the N.E.B.).

9. *so that glory may dwell in our land: glory* is probably 'God's glory' here, an expression for God's presence among his people (Ezek. 43: 1–4). It is not clear whether the verse

implies that God's glory (i.e. presence) is for the moment absent from Israel (i.e. the exiles have returned but the temple is not yet rebuilt). In Isa. 60: 2 and 62: 2 'glory' may mean the manifestation of God's presence and kingdom in the latter days. Ezek. 10: 18f. describes the removal of the glory (i.e. presence) of God from the Jerusalem temple.

10f. The hoped-for blessing is now described as though it were already present. *Love, fidelity, justice* and *peace* are personified, and their joining together symbolizes the desired age. Possibly, *love* and *justice* are divine attributes, while *fidelity* and *peace* are the human responses, heaven and earth joined together (verse 11).

12. The image of material provision, especially in the form of abundant harvests, continues the description of the hoped-for blessing. Cp. Ps. 72: 16f.

13. As the climax to the psalm, God is pictured as himself coming among his people, although the mystery of such a happening is preserved by the divine coming being implied rather than stated explicitly. *Justice* is pictured as an outrider or herald. The Hebrew 'and will set his steps in the way' may imply that justice will prepare a path for God to follow, but this is not easy, and hence the N.E.B. implies that *peace* will also accompany justice in the vanguard of the procession. The Hebrew word for *peace* implies not merely absence of war, but prosperity, and right relations between men and men, and men and God.

The psalm, as it progresses, looks forward increasingly to the final establishment of God's eternal rule. It is not surprising that the Christian Church has seen in the psalm a picture only fully realized in the Incarnation. *

GIVE ME PROOF OF THY KINDNESS

86

Turn to me, LORD, and answer;   1
  I am downtrodden and poor.
Guard me, for I am constant and true;   2
save thy servant who puts his trust in thee.
O Lord my God,[a] show me thy favour;   3
  I call to thee all day long.
  Fill thy servant's heart with joy, O Lord,   4
for I lift up my heart to thee.
Thou, O Lord, art kind and forgiving,   5
  full of true love for all who cry to thee.
  Listen, O LORD, to my prayer   6
    and hear my pleading.
    In the day of my distress I call on thee;   7
    for thou wilt answer me.

  Among the gods not one is like thee, O Lord,   8
  no deeds are like thine.
All the nations thou hast made, O Lord, will come,   9
will bow down before thee and honour thy name;
  for thou art great, thy works are wonderful,   10
  thou alone art God.

  Guide me, O LORD,   11
that I may be true to thee and follow thy path;
  let me be one in heart
  with those who revere thy name.
I will praise thee, O Lord my God, with all my heart   12
  and honour thy name for ever.

    [a] my God: *transposed from previous verse.*

13   For thy true love stands high above me;
thou hast rescued my soul from the depths of Sheol.

14 O God, proud men attack me;
    a mob of ruffians seek my life
      and give no thought to thee.

15 Thou, Lord, art God, compassionate and gracious,
    forbearing, ever constant and true.

16   Turn towards me and show me thy favour;
grant thy slave protection
    and rescue thy slave-girl's son.

17 Give me proof of thy kindness;
    let those who hate thee see to their shame
that thou, O LORD, hast been my help and comfort.

* This psalm appears to be a prayer for deliverance from a particular danger (verse 14), but we need to be aware of the way a poet may use vivid metaphor. We cannot identify either the psalmist or his troubles. The psalmist implores God to give a proof of his kindness that will be seen by the psalmist's adversaries (verse 17). In the course of his prayer, the psalmist utters many statements about God's mercy and power, and he expresses his certainty (verse 9) that all the nations of the world will one day acknowledge the lordship of the God of Israel.

It is impossible to date the psalm, or to identify the psalmist and his troubles. Many commentators have noted similarities of language between this psalm and other psalms (with verse 4*b* compare 25: 1; with verse 2 compare 25: 20) but it is going too far to claim that Ps. 86 is merely a mosaic of excerpts from other psalms. It expresses its own particular piety, especially in the use of the phrase 'thy servant' for the psalmist, and the phrase 'O Lord' for God, conveying the sense that God is the psalmist's master and protector. Much psalm poetry depends for its effect on familiar phrases, hence the frequent similarity of psalm phrases.

1. *Turn to me:* Hebrew 'incline thine ear', a common phrase in prayers for help, asking for God's special attention to the psalmist's plight. *downtrodden and poor:* it has been suggested that these words denote a particular 'party' within Israel; however, the N.E.B. translation rightly implies that the phrase describes the psalmist's present state.

2. *constant and true:* two words are used to translate the Hebrew *ḥasid*, 'godly or pious one'. The Hebrew word *ḥesed* denotes God's unfailing love (cp. verse 5 'true love') and a *ḥasid* is one who seeks to respond to this love. Possibly, there is a covenant background here; God's unfailing love has established his covenant, and has brought the psalmist into it. The words 'O thou my God' or 'thou art my God' are embedded in the phrase *save thy servant who puts his trust in thee*, but are rightly transferred to the beginning of verse 3.

3. *all day long:* that is, constantly.

4. *thy servant:* this could mean the king, but most commentators consider this psalm to have been composed after the exile. *I lift up my heart:* in prayer.

5. *full of true love:* the psalmist expresses not a pious hope, but a conviction based on his contemplation of Israel's past history, especially that relating to the initiative of God's love in establishing his covenant with Israel.

7. *In the day of my distress:* this phrase probably refers not to the particular day, but to the general time of distress. *thou wilt answer me:* again, this is more than a pious hope (see note on verse 5) and leads on to the psalmist's assertions about God's greatness (verses 8–10).

8. *Among the gods:* the psalmist is aware that surrounding nations worship other gods, but his contemplation of Israel's history convinces him that they have no power compared with that of the God of Israel.

9. *All the nations thou hast made:* some commentators transfer the words 'thou hast made' to the end of verse 8, which would then read 'no deeds are like thine which thou hast done' and verse 9 would accordingly lack its statement about God's

control of other nations in history. However, this latter thought is not foreign to the Old Testament (Amos 9: 7) and forms a fitting introduction to the declaration that the nations will *bow down before thee and honour thy name*. Verses 8–10 are one of the noblest expressions of the incomparability of God in the Old Testament. They form the basis of the psalmist's hopes for deliverance.

11. *Guide me . . . that I may be true to thee:* the psalmist acknowledges that he needs God's help, not only for deliverance from his troubles, but also in order to be God's loyal servant. *let me be one in heart . . . revere thy name:* Hebrew 'to fear thy name'. As it stands, the Hebrew means that the psalmist asks God to make him wholehearted in his devotion to God. Some ancient versions, followed by some modern commentators, read 'let my heart rejoice to fear thy name'; and it may be the unusual idea in the Hebrew of uniting the heart in the sense of uniting all the powers of the personality, that has led the N.E.B. to translate by *those who revere thy name*, thus giving a different slant to the verb 'unite'.

13. *stands high above me:* the N.E.B. tries to bring out the contrast in the Hebrew between *high* and *depths of Sheol*. It is possible that the first phrase should be rendered 'thy true love is great towards me' in which case there would be no *high–depths* contrast. *from the depths of Sheol:* the psalmist may be recalling an occasion when he came very close to death.

14. *proud men:* they are arrogant, and have little respect for God. *mob of ruffians:* it does not follow that these are non-Israelites. The Old Testament contains many references to Israelites who are not god-fearing, and indifference or hostility to true religion is not a modern innovation. *mob* does not convey the idea of an organized assembly, which is implicit in the Hebrew.

15 seems to be a quotation from the first part of Exod. 34: 6, the words pronounced by God when he showed his glory to Moses. We can only guess at the thoughts which the words would evoke for the psalmist – the evidence in past history of

God's faithfulness to his character and promises, and perhaps
the afflictions of Moses in God's service.

16. *slave-girl's son*: a servant born of a slave-girl was per-
manently bound to his master (Exod. 21: 4); thus the psalmist
conceives his relation to God.

17. *proof of thy kindness*: probably deliverance from the
present troubles.

Throughout the psalm there is a tension between the
psalmist's conviction that God is faithful and true, and his
earnest prayer for deliverance. Why does he need to pray so
earnestly if his confidence in God is so great? The psalmist may
not receive precisely the deliverance that he desires, but if not,
he will understand more fully that God's faithfulness to his
servants in this world cannot always be expressed in action as
they would desire. The servant of God then as now must often
suffer at the hands of enemies, but the fellowship with God
resulting from his earnest prayer will be the best answer to
that prayer. *

GLORIOUS THINGS ARE PROCLAIMED OF YOU,
O CITY OF GOD

87*ᵃ*

The LORD loves the gates of Zion   1–2
    more than all the dwellings of Jacob;
        her*ᵇ* foundations are laid upon holy hills,
    and he has made her his home.*ᶜ*   4–5
I will count Egypt*ᵈ* and Babylon among my friends;
Philistine, Tyrian and Nubian shall be*ᵉ* there;

[a] *The text of this psalm is disordered, and several verses have been re-
arranged.*
[b] *Prob. rdg.; Heb.* his.
[c] his home: *prob. rdg.; Heb.* most high.
[d] Egypt: *Heb.* Rahab.
[e] *Prob. rdg.; Heb. adds* this one was born (*cp. verse 6*).

and Zion shall be called a mother[a]
in whom men of every race are born.
6 The LORD shall write against each in the roll of
nations:
'This one was born in her.'
7 Singers and dancers alike all chant[b] your praises,
8 proclaiming glorious things of you, O city of God.

* The N.E.B. footnote, that 'the text of this psalm is disordered', is based on two main points. First, the psalm begins
in Hebrew 'his foundations are laid upon holy hills' with no
antecedent for 'his'. Second, it is difficult to trace a clear line
of thought through the psalm. The N.E.B. re-ordering of the
verses is 2, 1, 5b, 4, 5a, 6, 7, 3, but other re-arrangements have
been suggested, and it is clear that such suggestions are no
more than intelligent guesses on the basis of what seems to be
logical to various translators or commentators. However,
while accepting that the beginning of the psalm is difficult, we
should remember that what is logical to us may differ from
what was acceptable to an ancient poet. To avoid complica-
tion, the commentary accepts the N.E.B. order of the verses.
What emerges from the Hebrew as well as all the proposed
reconstructions is that Zion is praised as the city chosen by
God. The psalmist looks forward to the time when the nations
of the world will be reconciled to each other by a common
loyalty to Zion and its God. For Christians, it is the heavenly
Jerusalem (Zion) that is the symbol of the triumph of the
kingdom of God in reconciling the nations of the world. It is
impossible with certainty to date the psalm, or to suggest its
setting in the life of Israel. In any case, its meaning would not
necessarily be enhanced if we knew these facts; the message
transcends time and place.

1f. *gates of Zion:* the entire city. *dwellings of Jacob:* either

[a] a mother: *so Sept.; Heb. om.*
[b] all chant: *prob. rdg.; Heb. all my springs.*

other cities or other sanctuaries of Israel. *holy hills:* either the several hills on which Jerusalem was built or a reference to popular belief that God or the gods dwelt on holy mountains. With verses 1f. cp. Isa. 2: 1–4.

4f. *made her his home:* Hebrew (of 5*b*) 'and he who has established her is the Most High' or 'and the Most High has himself established her', either of which would make good sense with the N.E.B.'s rearrangement. The title 'Most High' is often associated with Jerusalem (cp. Ps. 46: 4). The N.E.B. 'probable reading' is unnecessary, and it is not clear why the footnote has 'most high' without capitals. *I will count Egypt:* God speaks in the first person. *among my friends:* 'among those who know me', perhaps in the sense of 'those who acknowledge my power, and who pledge their loyalty to me'. *shall be there:* shall be regarded as citizens of Zion. *Egypt . . . Babylon . . . Philistine . . .:* who is meant? The reference could be to the peoples of the known world – Mesopotamia (*Babylon*), Upper and Lower Egypt (*Egypt, Nubian*), the rest of Palestine (*Philistine*) and Syria (*Tyrian*), but this is not an exhaustive reference to the known world. Alternatively, the passage has been explained as referring to Jews in exile in the lands mentioned. This, if correct, would give the psalm a different meaning from that outlined above. However, the straightforward meaning of the text suggests nations, and not Jews exiled among nations. *Zion shall be called a mother . . .:* the N.E.B. gives a free rendering of the difficult Hebrew: 'with regard to Zion it shall be said, each one was born in her'. The N.E.B. phrase 'men of every race' appears to support the interpretation of the psalm which is indicated above.

6. *roll of nations:* see Isa. 4: 3; Ezek. 13: 9, where there are apparent references to rolls of names of citizens.

7. *Singers and dancers . . .:* some interpreters see here a reference to a procession, perhaps at a ceremony to commemorate the bringing of the Ark to Jerusalem (2 Sam. 6), but singing and dancing were common features of Israelite worship. *chant your praises:* this is a conjectural emendation of the

Hebrew 'all my springs are in you' which may refer to Zion
as the source of all blessedness, when its God is universally
recognized. ✶

88

1 O LORD, my God, by day I call for help,*a*
  by night I cry aloud in thy presence.
2 Let my prayer come before thee,
  hear my loud lament;
3 for I have had my fill of woes,
  and they have brought me to the threshold of Sheol.
4 I am numbered with those who go down to the abyss
  and have become like a man beyond help,
5 like*b* a man who lies dead*c*
  or the slain who sleep in the grave,
  whom thou rememberest no more
  because they are cut off from thy care.
6 Thou hast plunged me into the lowest abyss,
   in dark places, in the depths.
7 Thy wrath rises against me,
  thou hast turned on me the full force of thy anger.*d*
8 Thou hast taken all my friends far from me,
  and made me loathsome to them.
  I am in prison and cannot escape;
9 my eyes are failing and dim with anguish.
  I have called upon thee, O LORD, every day
  and spread out my hands in prayer to thee.

[a] I call for help: *prob. rdg.; Heb.* my deliverance.
[b] *So some MSS.; others* among.
[c] who lies dead: *prob. rdg.; Heb. obscure.*   [d] anger: *or* waves.

Dost thou work wonders for the dead?   10
Shall their company rise up and praise thee?
Will they speak of thy faithful love in the grave,   11
    of thy sure help in the place of Destruction*a*?
Will thy wonders be known in the dark,   12
    thy victories in the land of oblivion?

But, LORD, I cry to thee,   13
    my prayer comes before thee in the morning.
Why hast thou cast me off, O LORD,   14
    why dost thou hide thy face from me?
I have suffered from boyhood and come near to death;   15
    I have borne thy terrors, I cower*b* beneath thy blows.
    Thy burning fury has swept over me,   16
        thy onslaughts have put me to silence;
    all the day long they surge round me like a flood,   17
    they engulf me in a moment.
Thou hast taken lover and friend far from me,   18
        and parted me from*c* my companions.

✶ This is a psalm of unrelieved gloom and anguish; even the
one phrase which might lighten it – 'the God who saves me' –
is awkwardly placed in verse 1, and emended by the N.E.B.
(see footnote). Some have supposed that its 'happy' ending is
lost, but it is arguable that the psalm is of more value without
such an ending. However we interpret it: whether we regard
it as an expression of Israel's feeling of hopelessness during the
Babylonian exile, or as the prayer of one who has been plagued
by illness from his youth, the remarkable thing is that the
psalm has been included in the Psalter at all. Yet here it stands,
and it is a testimony to the realism of the psalmists. By

[*a*] *Heb*. Abaddon.
[*b*] I cower: *so Vulg.; Heb. unintelligible.*
[*c*] parted me from: *prob. rdg., cp. Pesh.; Heb. unintelligible.*

including this psalm in their collection, they have warned all
who follow the God of Israel that faith may one day come up
against an impenetrable mystery of unrelieved distress; they
have also given hope, for if this happens, the psalm is a reminder that the one whose experience it matches is not the first or
the only believer to have suffered thus. Furthermore, this one
experience is not the only valid clue to the reality of God in
the world, for though the individual may even die with dis-
appointed hope, the community of faith which has included
this psalm in its scriptures lives on in hope. The date and circumstances of the psalm are impossible to determine.

1. *I cry aloud in thy presence:* though the psalmist receives no
answer that he can recognize, he does not doubt that he is
somehow in God's presence. The Hebrew of verse 1 is literally
'LORD, the God who saves me, by day I call, by night before
thee.'

2. *loud lament:* in Hebrew this is a ringing cry, here, one of
anguish and sorrow.

3. *I have had my fill of woes:* we cannot be certain of the
nature of the woes; they may have been physical but we cannot rule out the possibility that they were mental and spiritual.
The Hebrew is literally 'My soul has been sated with troubles',
and although 'soul' is sometimes a way of saying 'I', it can
also denote the spiritual and emotional life of a person.
threshold of Sheol: again, we do not know whether this is an
illness which has brought the psalmist close to death, or
whether he is so spiritually and emotionally weary that he
would happily die.

4f. If the psalmist is *numbered with those who go down to the
abyss* (another word which indicates 'death') by his neighbours and family, this will increase his depression and despair;
moreover, if the psalmist's own belief is that God remembers
no more those *who sleep in the grave* (but cp. Ps. 139: 8; Amos
9: 2) and that such people are *cut off from thy care,* his plight
will be the more desperate. But he does not lose all hope, and
continues to pray.

6–9. The psalmist now asserts that God himself has brought about his troubles, though we cannot tell what these are. His eyes may be *failing and dim* with old age, but the cause is given as *anguish* (verse 9), probably caused by loss of hope; physical eyesight is probably not meant. Whether the psalmist's *loathsome* presence is physical illness or deformity, we cannot tell. It is possible that the psalmist's *friends* have gone *far from* him (verse 8) because they regard him as a sinner punished by God's *wrath*, but the psalmist neither confesses sin, nor asserts innocence. Perhaps the friends showed themselves to be no friends in time of need, thus increasing the psalmist's isolation and his feeling of being *in prison* with no one, God or man, to help. *prison* may be another way of saying 'Sheol'. With these verses cp. Job 19: 13–20.

10–12. The questions addressed to God in these verses seem to imply the answer 'No!' It is not that God cannot, but that he does not, work in the shadowy existence that is beyond death. The logic is then clear: if God will not perform a miracle for the psalmist beyond the grave, he must do it while the psalmist yet lives. *Shall their company rise up?*: *company* is the N.E.B. rendering of *repaim*, often rendered as 'shades'. Although the scientific etymology of the word is uncertain (N.E.B. implies 'to be united') the *repaim* are the inhabitants of the underworld, mere shadows of their former selves, unable to *rise up and praise thee*, having forgotten God's *wonders* and *victories* that he has achieved in the world of living men.

13–18. The psalmist renews his general complaint; as long as he has life, he will do what those in the land of death cannot do – pray to God especially *in the morning* hour when the return of light gives hope for deliverance.

15. The N.E.B. does not fully bring out the force of the Hebrew, which is that continually since *boyhood* the psalmist has *suffered* and come *near to death*. The exact meaning of the word translated *I cower beneath thy blows* is uncertain.

16f. The imagery of damage done by raging flood waters

187

is used to express the psalmist's feelings of God's animosity to him.

18. The bitterest part of his complaint is that he finds himself absolutely alone; he is separated from human support and comfort, and though God is not absent, the divine presence is a terrifying and threatening force.

Taken by itself, this is an alarming psalm, but as pointed out in the introduction, it represents only one part of the spectrum of religious insight contained in the Psalter. Although we know little about why the psalms are arranged in their present order, we should note that the despair of this psalm may be answered by the confident opening of the next. *

WHERE ARE THE FAITHFUL PROMISES GIVEN TO DAVID?

89

* The subject-matter of the psalm can be divided into three main sections: (a) verses 5–18, which assert God's power as creator and ruler of the world, and express the good fortune enjoyed by Israel as 'the people who have learnt to acclaim' God (verse 15); (b) verses 19–37 which describe the covenant which God made with David and his successors; (c) verses 38–51 which describe a situation which seems to contradict the divine promises made to David and his dynasty, leading to a prayer that God will quickly restore the Davidic throne.

Scholars have not been able to reach any general agreement about either the literary unity of the psalm, or its setting in the life and history of Israel. If verses 38–45 are taken to be a reference to the Babylonian exile, there is a problem that possibly in verses 47–51, the king himself speaks in the first person. This king could be Jehoiachin (see 2 Kings 25: 27–30), but we must admit that we know nothing about the opportunities that he might have had for the sort of prayer and worship implied in this psalm. On the view that it is the king speaking in verses 47–51, other interpreters have taken verses 38–45 to refer to a catastrophe other than the Babylonian exile (e.g. the Assyrian invasion of 701 B.C. or the invasion of Shishak (1 Kings 14: 25–8)). Another view is that verses 38–45 refer not to an historical catastrophe, but to a ritual humiliation of the king in the temple.

In its present position in the Psalter, the psalm constituted for Jews after the Babylonian exile a prayer for the restoration of the Davidic kingship, and later, this hope became a messianic hope. Its permanent value is that it constitutes a prayer for the establishment of God's rule among men, and Christians will see the beginnings of the answer to that prayer in the life and continuing influence of Jesus Christ. ✲

I will sing the story of thy love, O LORD,*a* for ever; 1
I will proclaim thy faithfulness to all generations.
Thy true love is firm as the ancient earth,*b* 2
thy faithfulness fixed as the heavens.
The heavens praise thy wonders, O LORD, 5*c*
   and the council of the holy ones exalts thy
      faithfulness.
In the skies who is there like the LORD, 6
   who like the LORD in the court of heaven,
   like God who is dreaded among the assembled holy 7
      ones,
great*d* and terrible above all who stand about him?
O LORD God of Hosts, who is like thee? 8
Thy strength*e* and faithfulness, O LORD, surround thee.

[a] thy love, O LORD: *so Sept.; Heb.* the LORD's acts of love.
[b] Thy . . . earth: *prob. rdg.; Heb.* Thou hast said for ever true love shall be made firm.
[c] *Verses 3 and 4 transposed to follow* servants *in verse 19.*
[d] great: *so Sept.; Heb.* often.
[e] Thy strength: *prob. rdg.; Heb. obscure.*

9   Thou rulest the surging sea,
     calming the turmoil*ᵃ* of its waves.
10   Thou didst crush the monster Rahab with a mortal
         blow*ᵇ*
     and scatter thy enemies with thy strong arm.
11   Thine are the heavens, the earth is thine also;
     the world with all that is in it is of thy foundation.
12   Thou didst create Zaphon and Amanus;*ᶜ*
     Tabor and Hermon echo thy name.
13   Strength of arm and valour are thine;
     thy hand is mighty, thy right hand lifted high;
14   thy throne is built upon righteousness and justice,
     true love and faithfulness herald thy coming.

15   Happy the people who have learnt to acclaim thee,
     who walk, O LORD, in the light of thy presence!
16   In thy name they shall rejoice all day long;
     thy righteousness shall lift them up.
17   Thou art thyself the strength in which they glory;
     through thy favour we hold our heads high.
18   The LORD, he is our shield;
     the Holy One of Israel, he is our king.

* 1f. *I will sing the story: story* has no equivalent in the
Hebrew; at best it is an unnecessary word in the translation,
and at worst it is misleading if it suggests that God's love is not
known at first hand by the psalmist. *love* is the Hebrew *ḥesed*
(see Ps. 86: 2). *to all generations:* the N.E.B. is ambiguous in a
way that the Hebrew is not. The Hebrew can only mean that
through all generations, that is, as long as the psalmist lives, he
will *proclaim thy faithfulness.* This is because God's love and

[a] turmoil: *prob. rdg.; Heb. obscure.*
[b] with a mortal blow: *lit.* like one wounded *or* slain.
[c] Amanus: *prob. rdg.; Heb.* right hand *or* south.

faithfulness have not merely been demonstrated in Israel's past history but are built into the very fabric of the *heavens* and *earth*. The N.E.B. has omitted the puzzling 'I said' (not 'Thou hast said' as in the footnote). The N.E.B. rendering (see footnote) transposes verses 3f. to a quite logical position in the middle of verse 19. But they may equally well be read with verses 1f. as a summary of the major themes of verses 5–37.

5–18. God, the lord of the world and the lord of Israel.

5. The praise of God is not uttered by Israel alone, but also by *The heavens* (that is, the angels, stars and other heavenly bodies; cp. Ps. 79: 1) and *the council of the holy ones* which surrounds God as a court surrounds an earthly king (see 1 Kings 22: 19; Isa. 6: 1–9; Job 1f. and Ps. 82).

6f. continue the theme of the heavenly court and declare that God is its incomparable head.

9. *the surging sea* is a symbol for all that threatens to destroy the ordered world, but such is God's power that he calms its turmoil.

10. *Rahab*, which perhaps would remind the Hebrew user of this psalm of the verb 'to act arrogantly or boisterously', is a name for Egypt (Isa. 30: 7; 51: 9–11 and Ps. 87: 4), and as such alludes to God's victory over the Egyptians and the Red Sea at the exodus. Rahab may also be the name of a water-monster, known in popular stories about the struggle between forces of order and forces of (watery) chaos prior to the creation of the world. Thus verses 9 and 10 will express God's power over the destructive forces in nature, and the nations of the world. Cp. also Ps. 74: 13.

12. *Zaphon and Amanus:* the N.E.B. assumes that we have a reference to popular mythology, in which certain mountains were believed to be the abode of God or the gods. This is possible, and if correct, the name *Amanus* will have been corrupted into the Hebrew word for 'right hand' when the mythology of Amanus was forgotten. The Amanus range are a south-eastern branch of the Taurus Mountains, dividing Syria from Cilicia and Cappadocia. *Zaphon* was also to the north of

Israel. *Tabor* was in Galilee, at the north-east corner of the
valley of Jezreel, while *Hermon* dominates the view from
northern Israel of the Anti-Lebanon range. The verses probably express God's lordship over mountains, holy and spectacular alike. If we accept the traditional rendering 'north and
south', then the reference is to the furthest extremities of the
world.

13f. The *arm* and *right hand* of God symbolize his power and
his readiness to use it. Some interpreters see in *true love* and
faithfulness, angels which attend upon God; but this seems unlikely in view of the parallel statement that God's *throne is
built upon righteousness and justice* (and cp. Ps. 85: 10f.).

15–18. The privileged position of Israel is stressed. They
have *learnt to acclaim* God. They rejoice in his name and glory
in his strength.

18. The N.E.B. takes the words *shield* and *king* as references
to God. Some interpreters render the verse 'Our shield (i.e.
our king; see on Ps. 84: 9) belongs to the LORD, our king
(belongs) to the Holy One of Israel.' If this latter translation is
correct (but we cannot decide this for certain) it strengthens
the position of those who maintain that the psalm (or this part
of it) was written before the exile. ✻

19   Then didst thou announce in a vision
      and declare to thy faithful servants:
3   I have made a covenant with him I have chosen,
        I have sworn to my servant David:
4   'I will establish your posterity for ever,
      I will make your throne endure for all generations.'
      I have endowed a warrior with princely gifts,
    so that the youth I have chosen towers over his people.
20   I have discovered David my servant;
        I have anointed him with my holy oil.
21   My hand shall be ready to help him

and my arm to give him strength.
No enemy shall strike at him   22
  and no rebel bring him low;
  I will shatter his foes before him   23
  and vanquish those who hate him.
My faithfulness and true love shall be with him   24
and through my name he shall hold his head high.
  I will extend his rule over the Sea   25
  and his dominion as far as the River.
He will say to me, 'Thou art my father,   26
  my God, my rock and my safe refuge.'
And I will name him my first-born,   27
  highest among the kings of the earth.
  I will maintain my love for him for ever   28
  and be faithful in my covenant with him.
  I will establish his posterity for ever   29
  and his throne as long as the heavens endure.
If his sons forsake my law   30
  and do not conform to my judgements,
  if they renounce my statutes   31
  and do not observe my commands,
I will punish their disobedience with the rod   32
  and their iniquity with lashes.
Yet I will not deprive him of my true love   33
  nor let my faithfulness prove false;
  I will not renounce my covenant   34
  nor change my promised purpose.
I have sworn by my holiness once and for all,   35
  I will not break my word to David:
his posterity shall continue for ever,   36
his throne before me like the sun;

37   it shall be sure for ever as the moon's return,
      faithful so long as the skies remain.[a]

* 19-37. The covenant with David.

For this whole section, see 2 Sam. 7: 4-17, although the
literary connection, if any, between the two passages is not
certain.

19. *announce in a vision:* probably to Nathan (2 Sam. 7: 4).
thy faithful servants: either the whole Israelite people, or the
prophets.

3f. *him I have chosen . . . my servant David:* for *servant* see
2 Sam. 7: 5, 8. *chosen* may be inferred from 2 Sam. 7: 8. The
words 'chosen' and 'servant' occur in Isa. 42: 1 of the servant
of the LORD, and in Isa. 41: 8 of Israel. They are not therefore
exclusively royal titles. *I have endowed* resumes the second half
of verse 19.

20. *I have discovered:* see 1 Sam. 16: 11-13, where the gift of
God's spirit to David is linked to the anointing.

22. *shall strike at him and no rebel bring him low:* the meaning
of the verb translated *shall strike at him* is uncertain and it is
arguable that *rebel* is not a clear translation. Possibly, we should
render *strike at* by 'outwit'. David did suffer from blows by
enemies (cp. 2 Sam. 15-18; 20) but was not finally outwitted.
'Wicked man' is probably better than *rebel*.

24. *hold his head high:* Hebrew 'his horn (possibly meaning
'his strength' or 'royal power') shall be exalted'.

25. *the Sea:* probably the Mediterranean. *the River*
(Hebrew 'rivers'): probably the Euphrates.

26. *'Thou art my father':* the king stands in a special relationship to God, being regarded as his adopted son (see on Ps.
2: 7).

27. *first-born:* see on Ps. 2: 7. The first-born son had certain
privileges among a man's children.

30-4. The conditions of the covenant (cp. 2 Sam. 7: 12-16).
Just as a father punishes his son without the father-son rela-

[a] so long . . . remain: *prob. rdg.; Heb.* a witness in the skies.

194

tionship ceasing to exist, so disobedient kings will be punished
(and probably the people of Israel along with them) without
the covenant being annulled.

35–7. The promises to David and his posterity are re-
affirmed. *

Yet thou hast rejected thy anointed king,   38
    thou hast spurned him and raged against him,*a*
thou hast denounced the covenant with thy servant,   39
defiled his crown and flung it to the ground.
Thou hast breached his walls   40
and laid his fortresses in ruin;
all who pass by plunder him,   41
and he suffers the taunts of his neighbours.

    Thou hast increased the power of his enemies   42
        and brought joy to all his foes;
    thou hast let his sharp sword be driven back   43
        and left him without help in the battle.

    Thou hast put an end to his glorious rule*b*   44
and hurled his throne to the ground;
thou hast cut short the days of his youth and vigour   45
and covered him with shame.

How long, O Lord, wilt thou hide thyself from sight?   46
    How long must thy wrath blaze like fire?
Remember that I shall not live for ever;*c*   47
hast thou created man in vain?
What man shall live and not see death   48
or save himself from the power of Sheol?
Where are those former acts of thy love, O Lord,   49

[a] raged against him: *or* put him out of mind.
[b] his glorious rule: *prob. rdg.; Heb.* from his purity.
[c] live for ever: *prob. rdg.; Heb. obscure.*

those faithful promises given to David?

50   Remember, O Lord, the taunts hurled at thy servant,[a]
how I have borne in my heart the calumnies of the
nations;[b]

51   so have thy enemies taunted us, O LORD,
taunted the successors of thy anointed king.

52   Blessed is the LORD for ever.
                       Amen, Amen.

✳ 38. *Yet thou hast rejected:* rightly or wrongly, the psalmist
asserts that God has indeed broken the promises which have
just been enumerated. We naturally ask what sort of situation
would occasion such an accusation against God. In spite of the
difficulties of the king appearing to speak in verses 47–51, the
view that the psalmist is referring to the destruction of the
temple in 587 B.C. and to the Babylonian exile is a powerful one.
What other catastrophe would invite the conclusion that God
was not merely punishing a disobedient king, but that he had
broken his promise 'I will not renounce my covenant' (verse
34)? This question demands an answer, whatever interpretation of the psalm is advanced.

40. *Thou hast breached his walls:* that is, the walls of defences
in the land.

41. *the taunts of his neighbours:* probably the neighbouring
peoples such as Moab, Ammon and Edom.

44. *Thou hast put an end to his glorious rule:* the strength of
the language in this verse suggests that the king has not merely
lost a battle, but that the institution of monarchy has ceased to
exist.

45. *thou hast cut short:* either a reference to the death of the
king, or to his capture and imprisonment while still young.

46–51. A prayer for restoration.

[a] *So some MSS.; others* servants.
[b] the calumnies . . . nations: *prob. rdg.; Heb.* all of many peoples.

46. *How long, O LORD, wilt thou hide thyself:* cp. Ps. 79: 5.

47. *hast thou created man in vain?:* it is difficult to see what sense the N.E.B. has, and the Hebrew should perhaps be taken as a statement parallel to the first part of the verse 'and how transient are all men whom thou hast created'.

48. *What man shall live:* we have an argument similar to that in Ps. 88: 10–12, that if God's redemption is not seen in this world, it will not be seen in the land of the dead.

50f. *Remember, O Lord, the taunts:* the traditional Hebrew text and two of the ancient versions have 'the taunts hurled at thy servants'. The singular in the N.E.B. rendering depends on a number of other Hebrew manuscripts and one ancient version. If we accept 'servants' it is slightly easier to maintain a consistent interpretation throughout the psalm. Verses 38–45 will refer to the Babylonian exile, and the speaker in verses 46–51 will not be the king, but a representative Israelite who looks for the restoration of the Davidic monarchy. This interpretation would still be possible if we read *servant*, though less likely in view of verse 39, where 'servant' must refer to the king. An important factor is how we understand the phrase in verse 51 rendered by the N.E.B. as *successors of thy anointed king*. The N.E.B. rendering would further allow the view that it is not necessarily the king speaking in these concluding verses. The successors could be elders or priests in charge of the community after the exile, who are taunted by the enemies of Judah that the house of David has vanished for ever. However, some experts support the translation 'they taunt thy anointed king at every step'.

There is no one interpretation of the psalm's original cultic and historical setting that can be maintained without straining some part of the text, but this does not invalidate its permanent insights which are explained above.

52. This verse is the doxology which concludes the third book of the Psalter; cp. Pss. 41: 13; 72: 18f. and 106: 48. *

BOOK 4

TEACH US TO ORDER OUR DAYS RIGHTLY

90

1 Lord, thou hast been our refuge
    from generation to generation.
2   Before the mountains were brought forth,
    or earth and world were born in travail,
from age to age everlasting thou art God.
3   Thou turnest man back into dust;
    'Turn back,' thou sayest, 'you sons of men';
4   for in thy sight a thousand years are as yesterday;
5   a night-watch passes, and thou hast cut them off;
    they are like a dream at daybreak,
    they fade like grass which springs up[a] with the
        morning
    but when evening comes is parched and withered.
7 So we are brought to an end by thy anger
    and silenced by thy wrath.
8   Thou dost lay bare our iniquities before thee
    and our lusts in the full light of thy presence.
9   All our days go by under the shadow of thy wrath;
    our years die away like a murmur.[b]
10 Seventy years is the span of our life,
    eighty if our strength holds;[c]
    the hurrying years are labour and sorrow,
    so quickly they pass and are forgotten.

[a] *Prob. rdg.; Heb. adds* and passes away.
[b] a murmur: *or, with some MSS.,* a task interrupted.
[c] *Or* eighty at the most.

Who feels the power of thy anger,   11
    who feels thy wrath like those that fear thee?
Teach us to order our days rightly,   12
    that we may enter the gate of wisdom.
        How long, O LORD?   13
    Relent, and take pity on thy servants.
Satisfy us with thy love when morning breaks,   14
    that we may sing for joy and be glad all our days.
Repay us days of gladness for our days of suffering,   15
    for the years thou hast humbled us.
Show thy servants thy deeds   16
    and their children thy majesty.
May all delightful things be ours, O Lord our God;   17
    establish firmly all we do.*ᵃ*

✻ This psalm can be divided into two main sections. In verses
1–12, the psalmist describes the eternal nature of God and the
frailty and transience of man. Man's life-span is not only a
mere moment in comparison with God's eternity, but man's
frailty includes his sinful nature, and this is exposed to God's
righteous anger. In verses 13–17 there is a prayer for deliverance. The nature of the affliction is not specified, but it does
not seem to be the sort of catastrophe implied, for example, in
Pss. 88 and 89. Yet it may be as difficult to cope with a small
amount of affliction spread over many years as with an intense
calamity. The psalmist is aware that God's punishment is
deserved (verse 8), but it is his recognition of God's power
over against human frailty that gives him the boldness to seek
from God a taste of joy before his short human span comes to
its end. Scholars regard this as a psalm composed after the
exile, though criteria for dating are hardly present in the text.
    1. *our refuge*: or 'our dwelling-place', according to another

[a] *So some MSS.; others add* on us, and establish firmly all we do.

ancient textual tradition. Either phrase expresses God's protection of his people from one *generation* to another *generation.*

2. *Before the mountains were brought forth:* the creation is described in terms of the labour of childbirth (cp. Job 38: 8) and
for this reason, N.E.B. takes the verb translated *were born in
travail* as a passive. Traditionally, the phrase has been given an
active sense with God as subject: 'you brought forth earth and
world'. The intention is not to imply that God is to be
compared with a human parent, but to stress that he is prior
to the material world in time.

3. *Thou turnest man back into dust:* God both bestows and
withdraws the life-force which makes man a living person as
opposed to lifeless matter. '*Turn back,*' *thou sayest:* this is most
naturally a complementary way of expressing what is said in
the first half of the verse, but some commentators understand
it as a command to new generations to be born.

4-6. The N.E.B. rendering of a difficult passage cuts across
the traditional verse division. The general meaning is, however, clear. From God's standpoint, outside of time, a human
life lasts no longer than grass which is at its best for less than a
day. This does not mean that God has no other interest in
humanity. Indeed, God has given to man a position of dignity
and stewardship in creation (see Ps. 8: 3-8).

7. *So we are brought to an end:* two problems face the inter-
preter here: first, what is the meaning of *So*; second, what is
the meaning of *brought to an end*? The N.E.B. rendering appears
to suggest that men die because of God's *anger* and *wrath*, and
verse 7 is a pivot verse which links the sentiments about man's
frailty (verses 3-6) with the descriptions of God's anger (verses
8-9). However, verse 10 clearly states that man has a natural
limited life span, independent of God's anger and wrath,
although a further problem of interpretation lies in verse 11.
Some interpreters take the *we* in verse 7 to refer to Israel,
and suggest that a specific experience in Israel's past history is
meant, but this hardly makes sense of the 'our' in verse 10. A

consistent interpretation can be obtained if we take the word translated *So* as 'surely' and understand *brought to an end* in the sense that God's justified anger contributes towards, but is not the main cause of, the loss of a man's powers as he grows older. Verses 3–6 are best taken as a statement of the transience of human life; verses 7–9 as a statement of man's moral frailty, which exposes him to God's justified anger.

8. *our iniquities:* it is not easy to translate the range of terms for moral fault and guilt from one language to another, but possibly underlying the Hebrew word for *iniquities* is the idea of awareness of false or impure motives in an act of wrong-doing. *our lusts:* the Hebrew may be rendered literally as 'secret sins'. What we hide from others is open to the *full light of thy presence.*

9. *die away like a murmur:* i.e. as a murmur or whisper fades away from human hearing, so does human life fade away. Another suggestion, in addition to the footnote, is 'like a spider's web'.

10. *Seventy years is the span of our life:* for the ancient Israelite, this is not a normal or average span, but the span of a fortunate man. If it is unusual to live for 70 years, and exceptional to live to 80, the shortness of life for the average person is thus further emphasized.

11f. *Who feels the power of thy anger?:* the point and force of the question are not clear. The N.E.B. seems to be a rhetorical question which states that *those that fear* God are most aware of his *anger* and *wrath.* Another possibility is that verses 11 and 12 go together, with verse 11 'Who feels the power of thy anger, and thy wrath so that he fears thee?' being a question implying the answer 'No one!'. This is then a fitting introduction to the prayer in verse 12 *Teach us to order our days rightly,* i.e. grant us that wisdom which begins with the fear of thee, so that we may use our short life to best effect.

13–17. A prayer for relief.
Although we cannot identify the suffering from which relief

is sought, the prayer is one of readiness to continue as faithful
servants of God even if no relief comes. The psalmist and his
company long to *sing for joy* and *be glad*, perhaps in celebration
of seeing God's *deeds* and *majesty* (verse 16). It is to be observed
that these verses seem to express a different mood from verses
1–12. While the opening section of the psalm speaks generally
about the human condition, verses 13–17 seem to refer to a
more particular, though unidentifiable, situation. See also
Ps. 13.

17. *May all delightful things:* or 'May the graciousness of the
Lord our God be upon us.' *

I WILL SATISFY HIM WITH LONG LIFE

91

1   You that live in the shelter of the Most High
       and lodge under the shadow of the Almighty,

2   who say, 'The LORD is my safe retreat,
       my God the fastness in which I trust';

3   he himself will snatch you away
       from fowler's snare or raging tempest.

4   He will cover you with his pinions,
       and you shall find safety beneath his wings;

5   you shall not fear the hunters' trap[a] by night
       or the arrow that flies by day,

6   the pestilence that stalks in darkness
       or the plague raging at noonday.

7   A thousand may fall at your side,
       ten thousand close at hand,
       but you it shall not touch;
       his truth[b] will be your shield and your rampart.[c]

[a] the hunters' trap: *lit.* the scare.   [b] *Or* his arm.
[c] his truth . . . rampart: *transposed from end of verse 4.*

With your own eyes you shall see all this;   8
    you shall watch the punishment of the wicked.

For you, the Lord is a*a* safe retreat;   9
you have made the Most High your refuge.

No disaster shall befall you,   10
no calamity shall come upon your home.

For he has charged his angels   11
    to guard you wherever you go,
    to lift you on their hands   12
for fear you should strike your foot against a stone.

You shall step on asp and cobra,   13
you shall tread safely on snake and serpent.

Because his love is set on me, I will deliver him;   14
I will lift him beyond danger, for he knows me by
    my name.

    When he calls upon me, I will answer;   15
I will be with him in time of trouble;
    I will rescue him and bring him to honour.

I will satisfy him with long life   16
to enjoy the fullness of my salvation.

✻ The main problem of this psalm is to explain the changes of
person in the traditional Hebrew text. Verses 14–16 are in the
first person, which can only be God himself. Verses 1–13 have
two abrupt changes, which the N.E.B. rendering has oblitera-
ted. Thus verse 2 is literally 'I shall say, "The Lord is my safe
retreat"' and verse 9 is literally 'for thou, Lord, art my safe
retreat, thou hast made the Most High thy refuge'. The
interpretation of these changes of person affects our view of
the original setting of the psalm. If we follow the traditional
Hebrew text in verses 2 and 9*a*, then we must suppose that

[*a*] *Prob. rdg.; Heb.* my.

verse 1 is either a declaration by a cultic official or an assertion of faith by the psalmist, verse 2 is spoken by the psalmist, and verses 3–8 spoken by the cultic official. Verse 9a is then an affirmation of the psalmist, with verses 9b–13 the reply of the cultic official. Finally, an oracle of acceptance is declared in God's name (verses 14–16). On this view, the psalm may derive from an 'entrance liturgy' (cp. Pss. 15, 24) or may concern a person seeking asylum in the temple. An alternative interpretation associates Pss. 90–2 together, taking 90 as a prayer for deliverance from exile, 91 as the divine assurance that Israel will be safe when calamity falls upon Babylon, and 92 as the thanksgiving for deliverance. Whatever view we take of this psalm considered in isolation, we must remember that it follows several psalms which have spoken of God punishing and casting off his people. The amazing confidence expressed in Ps. 91 that 'No disaster shall befall' the psalmist (verse 10) must both temper, and be tempered by, the somewhat different view expressed in Pss. 88–90.

1f. *You that live:* in order to remove the abrupt transition to the first person in verse 2 (see above) the N.E.B. constructs a long sentence whose main clause is not reached until verse 3. It is more likely that the psalm begins with the simple statement 'He that lives in the shelter . . . dwells under the shadow of the Almighty.' In English, such a statement is a tautology, but in Hebrew poetry it is common to assert something by saying it twice. In the opening two verses, we have four different names for God, as well as four words for his protection. *the Most High* is usually regarded as the name for the deity worshipped in Jerusalem before the city's conquest by David, while *the Almighty* may be connected with the name by which the patriarchs worshipped God (Exod. 6: 2–3). It is difficult to know precisely what associations the names had for the psalmist. See also on Ps. 7: 17.

3. *fowler's snare or raging tempest:* the first phrase probably refers to man-made danger, and the second to natural danger.

4. *He will cover you:* the psalmist uses the image of the bird

protecting its young; cp. Ps. 17: 8. The last line of the Hebrew
is transposed by the N.E.B. to follow verse 7 (see the footnote)
but it is by no means clear that this is correct.

5f. *hunters' trap by night . . . arrow that flies by day:* the
psalmist may be referring to man-made chance dangers,
against which a man cannot protect himself, and in verse 6,
pestilence that stalks may be natural dangers against which a man
cannot protect himself. There may be some personification of
pestilence, if the verb translated *stalks* does not simply mean
'spreads'. Some interpreters see a reference to demonic or
magical forces in whose power Israelites believed.

7f. *A thousand may fall:* the reference is possibly to a battle,
but probably also to the various calamities previously mentioned in verses 3, 5 and 6. The point seems to be (verse 8) that
death from disaster is God's *punishment of the wicked* and that
the psalmist will be spared this.

9. On the change of person in the traditional Hebrew text
see above. Verses 9*b*–13 repeat the main point of verses 3–7.

11. *he has charged his angels:* see Gen. 24: 7, 40 and Exod.
23: 20 for other references to the guiding and protecting func-
tions of angels, and cp. Ps. 34: 7; Matt. 4: 6; Luke 4: 10.

13. *asp and cobra . . . snake and serpent:* instead of the Revised
Version 'lion and adder' and 'the young lion and the serpent'. It is not easy to identify these creatures, which in any
case are symbolic of enemies and dangers. The N.E.B. gives a
more plausible imagery.

14–16. God's promise.

14. *Because his love is set on me:* literally, 'because he
attaches himself to me'. *for he knows me by my name:* the name
is also an expression of God's character (Exod. 33: 19 – 34: 9),
and is known only because God has revealed it.

15f. The intimate relationship which exists between the
psalmist and God will result in prayers for help answered, and
a long life of rich fulfilment. ✻

IT IS GOOD TO GIVE THEE THANKS

92

1   O LORD, it is good to give thee thanks,
     to sing psalms to thy name, O Most High,

2   to declare thy love in the morning
     and thy constancy every night,

3   to the music of a ten-stringed lute,
     to the sounding chords of the harp.

4   Thy acts, O LORD, fill me with exultation;
     I shout in triumph at thy mighty deeds.

5   How great are thy deeds, O LORD!
     How fathomless thy thoughts!

6   He who does not know this is a brute,
     a fool is he who does not understand this:

7   that though the wicked grow like grass
     and every evildoer prospers,
       they will be destroyed for ever.

8 While thou, LORD, dost reign on high eternally,

9   thy foes will surely perish,[a]
     all evildoers will be scattered.

10 I lift my head high, like a wild ox tossing its horn;
     I am anointed richly with oil.

11   I gloat over all who speak ill of me,
  I listen for the downfall of my cruel foes.

12   The righteous flourish like a palm-tree,
     they grow tall as a cedar on Lebanon;

13   planted as they are in the house of the LORD,
     they flourish in the courts of our God,

14   vigorous in old age like trees full of sap,

     [a] *So Sept.; Heb. adds* for behold thy foes, O LORD.

luxuriant, wide-spreading,
eager to declare that the LORD is just,   15
the LORD my rock,[a] in whom there is no
   unrighteousness.

＊ This psalm describes the joy which that person has who not
only believes in God's just government of the world, but who
witnesses the reward of righteousness and the punishment of
wickedness. This joy demands its expression in praise and
worship, and if the psalmist seems to be filled with self-
righteousness, especially towards his enemies (verse 11), it is
perhaps because he cannot understand why men wish to
ignore God's just government of the world (verse 6) and its
blessings for mankind. The psalm is not about the psalmist; it
begins and ends with God, and its central assertion is that God
reigns 'on high eternally' (verse 8). Although many interpreters argue that the psalmist has been delivered from adversity, it is not obvious that this is so. A date for the psalm can
hardly be fixed.

   1. *it is good:* appropriate to God's greatness and man's
dependence. *to sing psalms:* psalms in the general sense of songs
of praise.

   3. *ten-stringed lute:* see the comment on Ps. 81: 2.

   4. *Thy acts . . . mighty deeds:* these probably include God's
works both in creation and in history.

   5. *How fathomless thy thoughts:* if the psalmist could stand
in God's place, he would no doubt see the reason why things
happen as they do. As it is, the psalmist is prepared to trust
where he does not understand, certain that God's ways will be
vindicated (verse 15).

   6–9. *He who does not know this:* to trust in God's ways is not
a matter of intelligence, but of worldly commonsense, which
ultimately affects the action of the *fool*, who sees only the out-
ward prosperity of the *evildoer*, and not his certain fate at the

[a] *Or* creator.

hands of the just and mighty Lord of the world (verses 7–9).
The N.E.B. footnote is misleading. The full passage in Hebrew
is '(for) behold thy foes, O LORD, thy foes will surely perish'.
This repetitive style is common in Hebrew poetry, and is
found in Ps. 93: 3.

10. *I lift my head high:* the traditional Hebrew text is usually
rendered 'thou hast lifted my head high' which is then interpreted in terms of the psalmist's deliverance from his enemies.
wild ox: a symbol of strength and vigour. *I am anointed richly:*
an anointing to a public office is a possible, but not the only,
meaning (it could denote anointing with oil at a feast). We
probably have here another symbol for vitality, or spiritual
blessing.

11. *I gloat over: gloat* is an unnecessarily emotive translation
of a verb which need mean no more than that the psalmist
witnesses the downfall of his enemies.

13f. The phrases *house of the LORD* and *courts of our God*
may indicate worship and devotion in the temple on the part
of the faithful. Just as trees planted in the temple area grow tall
and fine, so true worshippers live long and flourish; and cp.
Ps. 1: 3.

15. The prosperity of the psalmist is something that he
wishes to share with others, as he is *eager to declare that the
LORD is just,* and as he tries to be a living witness to the
righteous principles according to which God governs the
world. ✶

THE LORD IS KING

93

1 The LORD is king; he is clothed in majesty;
the LORD clothes himself with might and fastens on his
belt of wrath.

2 Thou hast fixed the earth immovable and firm,
thy throne firm from of old;

from all eternity thou art God.[a]

O LORD, the ocean lifts up, the ocean lifts up its 3
    clamour;
    the ocean lifts up[b] its pounding waves.
The LORD on high is mightier far 4
than the noise of great waters,
mightier than the breakers of the sea.

Thy law stands firm, and holiness is the beauty of thy 5
    temple,
    while time shall last, O LORD.

✻ The interpretation of this psalm depends on the translation
of verse 1, and whether there are allusions in verses 3f. to
popular myths about the 'battle for kingship' between forces
personifying the storm and the seas. Then, if there are such
allusions, how are they to be interpreted? Because the phrase
'The LORD is king' (verse 1) resembles the phrases 'Absalom
is king' (2 Sam. 15: 10) and 'Jehu is king' (2 Kings 9: 13),
and because in both these passages the person named has *just*
become king, some interpreters wish to render verse 1 of our
psalm 'The LORD has become King.' It is then suggested that
at an annual festival (possibly Tabernacles) the renewal of
God's kingship was somehow enacted or celebrated, with
Ps. 93 as part of the liturgy. If verses 3f. are further regarded as
alluding to the 'battle for kingship' theme from popular
mythology, the psalm and its accompanying ceremony will be
a way of declaring God's sovereign supremacy over all other
gods, as well as over the whole world. Although the questions
raised by such an interpretation are too large for discussion
here, it would be fair to describe this approach as not proven.
If it were proven, it would add nothing to the theology of the
psalm, though it would tell us something about the cultic life

[a] God: *so Targ.; Heb. om.*
[b] the ocean lifts up: *or* let the ocean lift up.

of ancient Israel. On any view, the psalm declares that God has existed 'from all eternity' (verse 2), that he rules the world of nature, and that he upholds morality and righteousness (verse 5).

1. *The LORD is king:* this rendering leaves open the possibility that by some ritual act the kingship of God has been declared anew. If this were correct, it would not imply that God had ceased to be king. The Christian affirmation each Easter day 'Christ is risen' does not mean that the resurrection is repeated annually! The Revised Standard Version 'The LORD reigns' places the emphasis more forcefully upon God's eternal exercise of kingly power. *he is clothed in majesty:* a complicated image which contains the ideas of being majestic and of being clothed after the manner of kings. *clothes himself with might . . . wrath:* in the traditional interpretation of the Hebrew there is only one explicit object, *might,* to go with the two verbs *clothes himself* and *fastens on his belt.* The N.E.B. gets a second object, *wrath,* from the following clause in the Hebrew. The second occurrence of *clothes* may be due to an ancient copying mistake, in which case 1*b* can be rendered 'the LORD fastens on might like a belt' or we can render the Hebrew as 'the LORD clothes himself; he fastens on might like a belt'. 1*b* seems to assert that God is ready to act powerfully to uphold his rule. *Thou hast fixed the earth:* although the Israelites believed that the sun went round the earth (Ps. 19: 5f.), the reference here is to the fact that no force can shake the ordered world which God has created.

2. *thy throne firm:* that is, God's rule and the moral order that it implies are also unshakeable. *from all eternity:* God is without beginning.

3f. *O LORD, the ocean lifts up:* Hebrew tenses in the psalms are notoriously difficult to translate. In this verse they appear to say 'the ocean lifted up, the ocean lifted up . . . the ocean lifts up' (i.e. continues to lift up) or 'let the ocean lift up' (cp. N.E.B. footnote). If we follow what the tenses appear to indicate, we might say that the past tenses refer to God sub-

duing the waters at creation or to the battle for kingship motif
from popular mythology. However, certainty is impossible
here. The verses make a contrast with verse 2. The raging of
forces of nature, and perhaps of foreign nations, cannot defeat
the rule and order of *The LORD on high*, who is *mightier far
than the . . . waters.*

5. *Thy law:* Hebrew 'testimonies' or 'decrees', what is
uttered or commanded by God. See further on Ps. 119. *stands
firm:* or 'is trustworthy'. *holiness is the beauty:* a difficult phrase
in the Hebrew, which perhaps means that the greatest splendour which the temple can have is the holiness of the lives of
those whose prayers are said in it, and whose praise to God is
directed towards it. Alternatively, it is the holiness of God
which is the beauty of the temple. ✳

HAS THE TEACHER OF MANKIND NO KNOWLEDGE?

94

O LORD, thou God of vengeance,	1
thou God of vengeance, show thyself.	
Rise up, judge of the earth;	2
punish the arrogant as they deserve.	
How long shall the wicked, O LORD,	3
how long shall the wicked exult?	
Evildoers are full of bluster,	4
boasting and swaggering;	
they beat down thy people, O LORD,	5
and oppress thy chosen nation;	
they murder the widow and the stranger	6
and do the fatherless to death;	
they say, 'The LORD does not see,	7
the God of Jacob pays no heed.'	
Pay heed yourselves, most brutish of the people;	8

you fools, when will you be wise?

9   Does he that planted the ear not hear,
he that moulded the eye not see?

10   Shall not he that instructs the nations correct them?
The teacher of mankind, has he no*a* knowledge?

11   The LORD knows the thoughts of man,
that they are but a puff of wind.

12 Happy the man whom thou dost instruct, O LORD,
and teach out of thy law,

13   giving him respite from adversity
until a pit is dug for the wicked.

14 The LORD will not abandon his people
nor forsake his chosen nation;

15   for righteousness still informs his judgement,*b*
and all upright men follow it.

16   Who is on my side against these sinful men?
Who will stand up for me against these evildoers?

17 If the LORD had not been my helper,
I should soon have slept in the silent grave.

18   When I felt that my foot was slipping,
thy love, O LORD, held me up.

19   Anxious thoughts may fill my heart,
but thy presence is my joy and my consolation.

20   Shall sanctimonious calumny call thee partner,
or he that contrives a mischief under cover of law?

21   For they put the righteous on trial*c* for his life
and condemn to death innocent men.

[a] no: *prob. rdg.; Heb.* om.
[b] for . . . judgement: *prob. rdg.; Heb.* for judgement will return as far as righteousness.
[c] they put . . . trial: *prob. rdg.; Heb.* they cut the righteous.

But the LORD has been my strong tower,   22
    and God my rock of refuge;
our God requites the wicked for their injustice,   23
   the LORD puts them to silence[a] for their misdeeds.

✻ This is a remarkable psalm in which the psalmist is sustained in his troubles as much by intellectual convictions as by his traditional belief in God. A question which affects the interpretation is the identity of the oppressors mentioned in verses 4–7, 16. One view is that they are foreign nations which oppress Israel during the Babylonian exile. Although this is possible, and although the psalm could appropriately be used on any occasion when foreign nations had the upper hand over Israel, it is more likely that the oppressors are rulers of Israel who care nothing for God. The psalmist seems to live at a time when those in authority are using the law to govern in a way contrary to God's commandments (verses 4–7, 20); they even justify their deeds by reference to divine standards (verse 20*a*). But their basic philosophy is that God has no effective power or interest to prevent them from carrying out their policies (verse 7).

The psalmist is thus faced with a situation familiar to religious people in many societies and in many ages. In a nominally religious society, the rulers act according to secular principles, and the committed believer finds himself in conflict with laws which contradict what he regards as divine or supreme law. Religion seems powerless to prevent the course which the rulers follow. In this situation, the psalmist finds consolation in three ways. First, he asserts his intellectual conviction that the God who is the creator of mankind (verses 8f.), the instructor of the nations and the 'teacher of mankind' (verse 10) *does* take heed, and will uphold justice. Second, he takes comfort in his belief that there will still be found among the people 'upright men' who will follow righteousness (verse 15); third,

[a] *So some MSS.; others repeat* puts them to silence.

he remembers how the 'presence' of God in his own life gives him 'joy' and 'consolation' (verse 19). Nevertheless, the whole psalm is a prayer that the God who avenges wrong (verse 1) will act decisively.

It has sometimes been thought that this psalm consists of several, originally separate, parts; but its inner unity suggests that this is unnecessary. Its themes, also, could have been relevant to so many periods of Israel's history, that the discovery of its 'original setting' would hardly affect its permanent meaning.

1. *God of vengeance:* or 'God who avenges wrongs', the wrongs being the breaking of the law. *show thyself:* it is not clear whether the psalmist desires a supernatural demonstration of divine power, a final ending or re-ordering of the world, or the re-establishment of God's rule in Israel by more 'natural' means, such as the replacement of corrupt rulers by god-fearing ones. The means are less important than the desire.

2. *Rise up:* the image of the judge rising to deliver sentence.

3. *the wicked:* this may be a reference to wicked persons in general, and to the unjust rulers complained of elsewhere in the psalm, in particular.

4. *full of bluster:* this is no veiled practice of injustice; the oppressors speak openly and proudly of what they are doing.

6. *they murder the widow:* cp. Ps. 82: 3f.

7. *the God of Jacob pays no heed:* if these are the actual words of the evildoers, as opposed to a summary by the psalmist of their attitude, then perhaps in the phrase *God of Jacob* the evildoers are denying that Israel is a special people with a special law, and are asserting that Israel should be governed like any other nation. Alternatively, the verse denies that God can have any concern for the world.

8. *most brutish of the people:* cp. Ps. 92: 6. It is not necessarily lack of intelligence that is criticized here, but a 'closed' and short-sighted use of intelligence.

9. *Does he that planted:* perhaps the evildoers believe in God

but regard him as powerless or disinterested. The psalmist
invites them to think out the implications of their belief.

10. *he that instructs the nations:* a bold statement that God is
somehow involved in the affairs of all the nations of the earth.

11. *the thoughts of man: thoughts* is here 'plans' and 'schemes'
of men. These fail time and again because of the fallibility of
the 'thinkers'. Cp. 1 Cor. 3: 20.

12. *Happy the man:* 'happy' in the sense of 'fortunate'
(1: 1 and 119: 1). *instruct*, the same word as in verse 10, has the
sense of instructing by leading and disciplining. *thy law:* cp.
Ps. 119: 1. Here, the term probably includes actual laws, as
well as general teaching.

13. *giving him respite from adversity:* either, enabling him to
avoid adversity, or, giving him serenity when experiencing
adversity. *until a pit is dug:* until injustice is punished; a
'hunting' metaphor.

15. *for righteousness still informs his judgement:* if the N.E.B.
is right here, then we have a surprising statement which
implies that some people thought that God might have abandoned justice. It is more likely that the Hebrew should be
interpreted as 'judgement will once again (i.e. in the (near)
future) be equitable'.

16. *Who is on my side:* a rhetorical way of saying that only
God is on the side of the psalmist, and that he is to be relied
upon, a point which is then asserted in verse 17.

17. *the silent grave:* that is, the grave where all is silent.

20. *Shall sanctimonious calumny:* Hebrew 'shall throne of
destruction' (or 'throne of bluster') call thee partner?' Presumably this refers to rulers who use their position to practise
injustice and who expect to enjoy divine acquiescence. It also
suggests an alien power, possibly that of death. *under cover of
law:* or 'against thy law'.

21. *put the righteous on trial:* or 'attack the life of the
righteous'.

22. *has been my strong tower:* has been, and still is.

23. *requites . . . puts them to silence:* the tenses are difficult.

The N.E.B. states a general certainty on the part of the psalmist. It is also possible to render the verbs in the future, thus expressing the psalmist's belief that God will answer his prayer. ✲

IF ONLY YOU WILL LISTEN TO HIS VOICE!

95

1 Come! Let us raise a joyful song to the LORD,
    a shout of triumph to the Rock of our salvation.

2 Let us come into his presence with thanksgiving,
    and sing him psalms of triumph.

3 For the LORD is a great God,
    a great king over all gods;

4 the farthest places of the earth are in his hands,
        and the folds of the hills are his;

5 the sea is his, he made it;
    the dry land fashioned by his hands is his.

6 Come! Let us throw ourselves at his feet in homage,
    let us kneel before the LORD who made us;

7   for he is our God,
    we are his people, we the flock he shepherds.[a]
    You shall know[b] his power today
        if you will listen to his voice.

8 Do not grow stubborn, as you were at Meribah,[c]
        as at the time of Massah[d] in the wilderness,

9 when your forefathers challenged me,
    tested me and saw for themselves all that I did.

[a] his people . . . shepherds: *so one MS., cp. Ps. 79: 13; others* the people of his shepherding and a flock.
[b] You shall know: *prob. rdg.; Heb. om.*
[c] *That is* Dispute.   [d] *That is* Challenge.

For forty years I was indignant   10
with that generation, and I said:
They are a people whose hearts are astray,
and they will not discern my ways.
As I swore in my anger: 11
    They shall never enter my rest.

✷ It seems clear from its subject-matter that Ps. 95 is to be
associated with public worship. Verses 1f constitute an invitation to worship, verses 3–5 declare that God, as mighty
creator, is one to whom worship is due, and verses 6–7a invite
Israel to worship not merely the creator, but the God who has
an intimate relationship with his people. Verses 7b–11 (or 8–11
depending on translation and interpretation) are a warning to
the worshippers to learn the lessons contained in the traditions
about Israel's wilderness wanderings. If the worshippers are
people 'whose hearts are astray' (verse 10) then their worship
will be rejected as surely as those Israelites were rejected who
did not enter the promised land (verse 11).

It is impossible to fix a date or 'original setting' for the
psalm.

1. *Come!*: motion is not implied here; the word perhaps
has the same force as 'come on!' It also anticipates 'come' in
verse 2. *a shout of triumph*: the verb is used of acclamation at
coronations. *Rock of our salvation*: *Rock* is a divine title as
in Ps. 89: 26. It also suggests refuge and security; and see also
Ps. 18: 2.

2. *come into his presence*: probably, enter the temple. *psalms
of triumph*: including, possibly, some of the book of psalms,
but not necessarily restricted to these.

3. *a great God*: as verses 4f. show, verse 3 is asserting much
more than that the God of Israel is an outstanding God among
many others. Taken together, verses 3–5 are a claim that God
is the only effective God, and *a great God* should perhaps be
regarded as a superlative: 'the supreme God'. The mention of

all gods does not imply that the phrase could not have originated in Israel. Israelites were aware of the fact that other peoples worshipped their own deities. Verses 4f. imply that these deities were not the creative and sustaining forces of the world.

4. *farthest places . . . folds:* the traditional Hebrew text has 'depths of the earth' and (possibly) 'heights of the mountains', 'heights' or *folds* being renderings of a Hebrew word of uncertain etymology. The sense of the verse (and the verse following) is that God's power extends to every part of the world.

7. The N.E.B. follows many commentators in assuming (i) that 7*b* was originally identical with Ps. 100: 3*c* and (ii) that part of 7*c* has been lost. The two suggestions are not unconnected, because acceptance of the first makes it easier to sustain the second. The N.E.B. is only one possible way of restoring the missing part of 7*c*, if anything is in fact missing. The traditional rendering with its skilful and bold poetic imagery 'we are the people of his pasture and the sheep of his hand. O that today you will listen to his voice!' is at least as plausible as the alternative represented in the N.E.B.

8–11. See Exod. 17: 1–7; Num. 20: 1–13 and Deut. 6: 16 for the incidents alluded to. The incidents involve rebellion, dispute and testing. Our verses here show how the traditions about Israel's past history were used for meditation and instruction (see also Ps. 78).

11. *They shall never enter my rest:* see Num. 14: 21–4. *rest* denotes perhaps not only the resting-place for Israel after the wilderness wanderings, but God's final 'resting-place' in Jerusalem (Ps. 132: 8). In Heb. 3: 7 – 4: 11 the 'rest' is understood as a sabbath rest, an expression denoting God's salvation in Jesus Christ. *

THE LORD IS KING

96

Sing a new song to the LORD;   1[a]
  sing to the LORD, all men on earth.
Sing to the LORD and bless his name,   2
  proclaim his triumph day by day.
    Declare his glory among the nations,   3
      his marvellous deeds among all peoples.
Great is the LORD and worthy of all praise;   4
  he is more to be feared than all gods.
    For the gods of the nations are idols every one;   5
    but the LORD made the heavens.
      Majesty and splendour attend him,   6
      might and beauty are in his sanctuary.

    Ascribe to the LORD, you families of nations,   7
ascribe to the LORD glory and might;
    ascribe to the LORD the glory due to his name,   8
bring a gift and come into his courts.
      Bow down to the LORD in the splendour of holiness,[b]   9
      and dance in his honour, all men on earth.
Declare among the nations, 'The LORD is king.   10
  He has fixed the earth firm, immovable;
  he will judge the peoples justly.'
Let the heavens rejoice and the earth exult,   11
    let the sea roar and all the creatures in it,
    let the fields exult and all that is in them;   12
    then let all the trees of the forest shout for joy

[a] *Verses 1–13: cp. 1 Chr. 16: 23–33.*
[b] the splendour of holiness: *or* holy vestments.

13   before the LORD when he comes[a] to judge the earth.
      He will judge the earth with righteousness
         and the peoples in good faith.

✵ The N.E.B. footnote indicates that Ps. 96 is repeated in
1 Chron. 16: 22–33, where it forms part of the praise that was
offered to God on the occasion of David bringing the Ark of
the Covenant to Jerusalem. Whether this tradition in 1 Chron.
16 rests on any solid foundation, that is, whether Ps. 96 was
actually connected with any annual ceremony commemorat-
ing the bringing of the Ark to Jerusalem, is impossible to say.
Many commentators describe the psalm, along with 47, 93,
97–9, as an enthronement psalm, but the nature and occasion
of the enthronement to which they refer remain hypothetical.
It is clear, however, that these psalms celebrate, in similar
language, the universal kingship of God. In addition 96: 13;
97: 5 and 98: 9 speak of the 'coming' or the 'approach' of
God to judge the world. These three psalms thus not only
proclaim God's universal rule, but look forward in eager
anticipation to its effective consummation.

   1. *a new song*: at Isa. 42: 10 the same phrase refers to a song
to be sung in celebration of the divine 'coming', which will
deliver the people from the Babylonian exile. In the present
context, it perhaps reminds Israel that God constantly does
marvellous things, for which 'new' songs are appropriate,
even if God is praised in traditional and familiar songs. *all men
on earth*: Hebrew 'all the earth'. Who is being addressed? One
possibility is that in verses 1–6, Israel the people of God is
addressed, while in verses 7–10, the command is to the nations
of the world; or verses 1f may be a general command to all
peoples, with verses 3–6 narrowed to a command to Israel.

   2. *bless his name*: give thanks to God for what he is, and has
done. *proclaim his triumph day by day: day by day* must be taken
with *proclaim. his triumph* may be either a specific act (such as

[a] *So many MSS.; others repeat* when he comes.

the return from exile, if the psalm was composed after the exile) or may also include daily manifestations of grace witnessed variously by many different people.

3. *Declare his glory:* cp. Ps. 19: 1, where the phrase is linked to the manifestation of God's glory in the natural order.

4. *he is more to be feared:* verses 4f. express in different words the belief stated in Ps. 95: 3–5.

5. *the gods of the nations are idols:* Ps. 96 goes further than Ps. 95. If other gods exist, their power is nothing, and the worship of them is futile. See comment on the futility of idols in Isa. 40: 18–20.

6. The probable meaning is that *Majesty, splendour, might* and *beauty* are personified, and seem to be God's royal attendants at his court, both in his heavenly sanctuary and in his temple which symbolizes his earthly dwelling.

7. *Ascribe to the LORD:* Ps. 29: 1f. contains another, and perhaps older, form of these verses. The nations of the world are summoned to pledge their obedience to the only true God of the world.

8. *bring a gift:* just as tribute (the same word as 'gift') is brought to earthly kings, so the nations are summoned to bring tokens of their obedience, probably into the courts of the temple.

9. *the splendour of holiness:* the Hebrew phrase is notoriously difficult, and its interpretation is partly dependent on whether the word traditionally rendered 'fear' or 'tremble' before him is translated *dance* as in the N.E.B. Many recent commentators have argued for the translation 'Bow down to the LORD at his appearing in holiness' to which 'tremble before him' is a fitting parallel. However, the word 'theophany' which is then introduced into the discussion to describe the 'appearing' is by no means free of difficulty. What was the nature of God's 'appearing' at the theophany? Was it symbolically enacted in the temple, or have we rather to do with the future longed-for coming of God to consummate his rule? So much is obscure, that it is perhaps safer to follow the two N.E.B. suggestions: *splendour of holiness* which perhaps means splendour of a holy

occasion rich in symbols of the holy, or (see footnote) 'holy vestments' or garments, worn on this special occasion by the representatives of the nations. See also the comments at Ps. 29:2.

10. *The LORD is king:* see Ps. 93: 1f. Perhaps the rulers of the nations who were summoned to Jerusalem are now to return to their peoples and there to proclaim God's kingship.

11–13. The *sea* which, in Ps. 93: 3f. seemed to roar in futile opposition to God's rule, is now to lend its voice to the swelling song of joy in which everything in earth and heaven joins, as God *comes to judge the earth.* His judgement will no doubt involve punishment, and the destruction of evil, but even those who are deeply hurt by it, will acknowledge that it is done in *righteousness* and *good faith.* God will perform for his world what man is powerless to achieve. ✳

THE LORD IS KING

97

1 The LORD is king, let the earth be glad,
   let coasts and islands all rejoice.
2 Cloud and mist enfold him,
      righteousness and justice
      are the foundation of his throne.
3 Fire goes before him
   and burns up his enemies[a] all around.
4 The world is lit up beneath his lightning-flash;
   the earth sees it and writhes in pain.
5 The mountains melt like wax as the LORD approaches,
   the Lord of all the earth.
6 The heavens proclaim his righteousness,
   and all peoples see his glory.

[a] burns . . . enemies: *or, with slight change,* blazes on every side.

Let all who worship images, who vaunt their idols,   7
    be put to shame;
bow down, all gods,*ᵃ* before him.

Zion heard and rejoiced, the cities of Judah were glad   8
    at thy judgements, O LORD.
For thou, LORD, art most high over all the earth,   9
    far exalted above all gods.

The LORD loves*ᵇ* those who hate evil;   10
    he keeps his loyal servants safe
    and rescues them from the wicked.
A harvest of light is sown for the righteous,   11
    and joy for all good men.
You that are righteous, rejoice in the LORD   12
    and praise his holy name.

✶ Many of the themes already discussed in Pss. 93 and 96 are
to be found in Ps. 97, as well as Pss. 98 and 99, but the present
psalm presents one difficult problem, which arises from the
tenses of verses 3–7. In the Hebrew verse 3 has imperfect or
future tenses (it could therefore be rendered 'fire *shall go*
before him') whereas in verses 4–6 the tenses are perfects ('the
world *was* lit up . . .'). In verse 7, the verbs can be taken as
imperatives (as in the N.E.B.) or as future tenses ('all who
worship images . . . will be put to shame'). If the perfects of
verses 4–6 are translated as referring to a past event, some
commentators assert that they describe a symbolic perfor-
mance in worship of God's 'coming'. Another view is that
the recent deliverance from the Babylonian exile is alluded to.
It is also possible to take the perfects as perfects of certainty,
that is, as describing the future coming of God to establish his
rule universally. In the face of so much possible difference of

[a] bow . . . gods: *or* all gods bow down . . .
[b] The LORD loves: *prob. rdg.; Heb.* Lovers of the LORD.

interpretation, it is foolish to be dogmatic. At least it can be said for certain that the language of the psalm resembles that of parts of Pss. 18 and 77, and it may be that our psalmist is using traditional language about God's past saving acts, especially at the exodus (Ps. 77: 16–18), to describe a future and final coming.

1. *The LORD is king:* see Ps. 93: 1. *coasts and islands:* cp. the similar phrases in Isa. 42: 10. The Hebrew is literally 'many islands', the whole phrase probably denoting the furthest parts of the world.

2. *Cloud and mist:* in his true being, God is hidden from man, and cannot be seen; only indirectly can his approach be recognized (verses 4f.). *righteousness and justice:* cp. Ps. 89: 14.

3. *Fire:* is a common Old Testament symbol for the holy presence of God (Exod. 3: 2).

4. *The world is lit up:* in the N.E.B. this seems to be a general statement which implies the awe for God felt by men when they see lightning. This may be right, although it is possible to take verse 4 closely with verse 5, linking it with God's approach. Cp. also Ps. 29: 8f.

5. *The mountains melt:* a vivid image which indicates how impermanent the world is compared with the reality of God. *as the LORD approaches:* Hebrew 'before the LORD'. It is not clear whether the psalmist is simply using traditional language to make a general point about the contrast between God and the world, or whether the final coming of God in judgement is envisaged. *Lord of all the earth:* further identifies who the Lord is who now approaches.

6. *The heavens proclaim:* heavenly forces are often figuratively called upon to witness God's covenant with his people, especially if Israel breaks the covenant (Deut. 4: 26; Isa. 1: 2). Here, the heavens are to proclaim that God's rule is righteous; this will be openly seen by *all peoples. glory:* cp. Ps. 96: 3.

7. *Let all who worship images:* or 'all who worship . . . will be put to shame'. No substitutes for the divine will be able to endure the awesome reality of God. Cp. Heb. 1: 6.

8. *Zion heard:* it is not easy to relate the past tenses to an actual event, although some interpreters see a reference to the impending return from the Babylonian exile. The tenses could be taken as perfects of certainty, as in the N.E.B. in verses 4–6; i.e. 'Zion hears'.

10–12. *The LORD loves:* the traditional Hebrew text, which has 'You who love the LORD, hate evil! He keeps . . .', is as possible as the emended text followed by the N.E.B. It constitutes encouragement to those who are faithful to God to trust in his ultimate triumph over evil. In either case, these final verses speak of the reward to be received by the righteous, a reward which includes their joy in seeing the God whom they worship vindicated in the eyes of the world. *

HE COMES TO JUDGE THE EARTH

98

Sing a new song to the LORD,   1
    for he has done marvellous deeds;
his right hand and holy arm have won him victory.

    The LORD has made his victory known;   2
    he has displayed his righteousness to all the nations.

        He has remembered his constancy,   3
        his love for the house of Israel.
All the ends of the earth have seen
    the victory of our God.

    Acclaim the LORD, all men on earth,   4
    break into songs of joy, sing psalms.

    Sing psalms in the LORD's honour with the harp,   5
    with the harp and with the music of the psaltery.

        With trumpet and echoing horn   6
acclaim the presence of the LORD our king.
Let the sea roar and all its creatures,   7

the world and those who dwell in it.
8   Let the rivers clap their hands,
     let the hills sing aloud together
9   before the LORD; for he comes
         to judge the earth.
     He will judge the world with righteousness
     and the peoples in justice.

✻ Ps. 98 resembles Ps. 96, and, to a lesser extent, Ps. 97. Verses 4–9, like verses 7–13 of Ps. 96, call upon men and the forces of the natural world to join in praise of God, the righteous judge and king, who is to judge the world (verse 9). In verses 1–3, the same problems occur as in Ps. 97: 8f. What is the past victory that is referred to? Is it an allusion to the exodus, to the return from the Babylonian exile, or what? As in the case of Ps. 97 a dogmatic answer is impossible, but this does not rob the psalm of its value as a hymn of praise, appropriate to many individual and corporate occasions.

1. *Sing a new song:* see Ps. 96: 1. *marvellous deeds:* these could include the works of creation, or the exodus, or the return from exile. *right hand . . . holy arm:* a figurative reference to divine power which alone has achieved victory. The 'strong hand' of God was the source of victory at the time of the exodus (Exod. 13: 9).

2. The use together of *victory* and *righteousness* indicates that, in this context, *righteousness* has the sense of vindicating or upholding what is right.

3. *All the ends of the earth have seen:* exactly how and when, again, is not clear.

4–9. See on Ps. 96: 7–13. The singing and music are appropriate to occasions of great rejoicing, and together with the *trumpet and echoing horn* (verse 6) recall the way in which a monarch was acclaimed at his accession (1 Kings 1: 39f.). The *psaltery* (verse 5) was a stringed instrument with its sound board behind and parallel to the strings, which were plucked.

It is not certain from the Hebrew whether the reference here
is to a musical instrument, or to accompanied singing. Compared with Ps. 96: 7–13, these verses lack the specific reference
to people coming into God's presence with gifts; but we may
assume from verse 6 that the psalm invites worship from those
who have already come into the holy place. *

THE LORD OUR GOD IS HOLY

99

The LORD is king, the peoples are perturbed;   1
he is throned on the cherubim, earth quivers.

  The LORD is great in Zion;   2
  he is exalted above all the peoples.
They extol his[a] name as great and terrible;   3
he is holy, he is mighty,   4
  a king who loves justice.

Thou hast established justice and equity;
thou hast dealt righteously in Jacob.
  Exalt the LORD our God,   5
    bow down before his footstool;
    he is holy.

  Moses and Aaron among his priests,   6
    and Samuel among those who call on his name,
called to the LORD, and he answered.
  He spoke to them in a pillar of cloud;   7
they followed his teaching and kept the law he gave them.
Thou, O LORD our God, thou didst answer them;   8
thou wast a God who forgave all their misdeeds
  and held them innocent.

[a] *Prob. rdg.; Heb.* thy.

9   Exalt the LORD our God,
          bow down towards his holy hill;
          for the LORD our God is holy.

✶ Ps. 99 resembles Pss. 93 and 97, by opening with the
declaration 'The LORD is king.' However, it says nothing
about the creation of the world, and nothing about God
coming to judge the world, although God is described as 'a
king who loves justice' (verse 4). It has a reference to the
earlier traditions of Israel (verses 6–8) which are treated with
the same freedom as in Ps. 78. The background to the psalm
may be a covenant ceremony, although the text does not refer
directly or obviously to such a ceremony, neither does it describe past universal manifestations of God's power and justice.
Throughout, God's eternal rule is assumed, and users of the
psalm are summoned to 'bow down' to the one who is 'holy'.
There may be two parts, verses 1–5 and 6–9, each ending with
a similar refrain; or the phrases 'he (or God) is holy' in verses
4, 5 and 9 may mark differing parts of the psalm. The refrain
could be a link phrase, binding the poetry together.

   1. *The LORD is king:* see Ps. 93: 1. *the peoples are perturbed:*
all the peoples of the world, who tremble with fear when they
realize the facts of God's kingship, and consider his justice and
holiness. *throned on the cherubim:* the cherubim are either the
winds or storm-clouds personified, on which, according to
Ps. 18: 10, God 'rode', or they are part of the furnishing
around the Ark of the Covenant, and were thought to provide
the throne of the invisible God (see 1 Kings 6: 23–8 and 8: 6f.).
In appearance, they were winged creatures with lion heads,
and cherubim were carved, for example, on the walls of the
temple (1 Kings 6: 29).
   3f. The N.E.B. somewhat alters the traditional grouping of
the Hebrew words, which is literally 'Let them (or, 'they
shall') praise thy great and terrible name; he is holy. The king
is mighty, he loves justice; thou hast established equity: justice

and righteousness hast thou wrought in Jacob.' This rendering is taken by some interpreters to include a refrain similar to those in verses 5 and 9. The N.E.B. reads more logically, but is not necessarily superior to the traditional rendering. *Jacob* refers to the whole Israelite community.

5. *footstool:* either the Ark, or the temple, or Jerusalem, or the whole earth, or any of these as is appropriate to the situation of the worshipper. Cp. Ps. 110: 1.

6–8. *Moses and Aaron . . . Samuel:* the Old Testament records incidents in which these great men interceded or mediated on behalf of others with God, as Moses did for those who refused to go up into Canaan at once (Num. 14: 13) or Aaron, to halt the plague (Num. 16: 46), or Samuel, with regard to the wicked people who had asked for a king (1 Sam. 12: 16–25). In Jer. 15: 1, however, God says that he will not be moved even by the intercession of Moses and Samuel. The treatment of these incidents is free in this psalm. Moses *can* be regarded as a priest (Exod. 24: 6) but this is not our first thought about his role; neither did God speak to Samuel in a *pillar of cloud* (verse 7). Some interpreters render the verse 'Moses, and Aaron his priest, and Samuel as one who calls on his name . . .' However, the main point is that intercession with God on behalf of sinners was effective in the past (verse 8) and will be in the present and future through the mediation of the successors of Moses, Aaron and Samuel. This teaching is thus a fitting prelude to the final refrain (verse 9) which bids mankind bow to the LORD, who *is holy*; for a desire to respect that holiness will be necessary on the part of all those who intercede with God, and who place their hope in the effectiveness of the intercession. ✻

KNOW THAT THE LORD IS GOD

100

Acclaim the LORD, all men on earth,   1
worship the LORD in gladness;

enter his presence with songs of exultation.

3 Know that the LORD is God;
he has made us and we are his own,
   his people, the flock which he shepherds.

4   Enter his gates with thanksgiving
      and his courts with praise.

   Give thanks to him and bless his name;

5 for the LORD is good and his love is everlasting,
   his constancy endures to all generations.

✱ From verses 2*b* and 4 it may be surmised that this psalm
was originally intended to be sung by worshippers as they
entered the Jerusalem temple. For countless generations of
Jews and Christians, it has been used to accompany the
entrance in heart and mind to the presence of God, for worship and thanksgiving.

   1. *Acclaim:* see also Ps. 98: 4, meaning probably, 'shout in
acclamation of your heavenly king'. *all men on earth:* although
the psalm appears to concentrate upon God's chosen people
(verse 3), the summons to worship is a universal summons.

   2. *worship the LORD: worship* is probably a correct paraphrase here of the Hebrew word traditionally rendered
'serve'. *songs of exultation:* the N.E.B. tries to bring out the
force of a Hebrew word which suggests uttering a glad shout.

   3. *Know that the LORD is God:* 'know that the LORD alone
is God' is the force of the Hebrew (cp. 1 Kings 18: 39). Some
interpreters suggest that we have here a liturgical affirmation
used in the renewal of the covenant with God. *Know* should
be interpreted in the widest possible sense. It involves intellectual conviction as well as action based on trust. *we are his
own:* a traditional Hebrew alternative text, reflected, for
example, in the hymn 'All people that on earth do dwell', is
'he it is who has made us and not we ourselves'. *his people:*
see Ps. 95: 7.

   4. *Enter his gates:* cp. Ps. 24: 7, 9. *bless his name:* see Ps.
96: 2. ✱

A NOTE ON FURTHER READING

For background and comparative material see J. B. Pritchard, *Ancient Near Eastern Texts* (3rd ed., Princeton University Press, 1969).

For introductory books on the psalms see C. F. Barth, *Introduction to the Psalms* (Blackwell, 1966); H. Ringgren, *The Faith of the Psalmists* (S.C.M. Press, 1963); C. Westermann, *The Praise of God in the Psalms* (John Knox Press, Richmond, Virginia, 1965).

For a more comprehensive and detailed commentary see A. A. Anderson, *Psalms*, New Century Bible (Oliphants, 1972). For a more conservative approach see D. Kidner, *Psalms*, Tyndale Old Testament Commentaries (Inter-Varsity Press, 1973–5). For an older, but extremely valuable, commentary see A. F. Kirkpatrick, *The Book of Psalms*, The Cambridge Bible for Schools and Colleges (Cambridge University Press, 1891–1901).

INDEX

Aaron 229
Absalom 65, 209
abyss, *see* deep
acrostic psalms 10
Ahimelech 22
Amalek 35, 168
Ammon 168
angel(s) 43, 145, 191f., 205, 221
animal symbolism 43, 47, 51, 91, 158, 205, 208
Arabia 35
Ark of the Covenant 6, 65, 85, 87, 91, 150, 183, 220, 228f.
Asaph 4f.
Assyria 7, 156, 168, 189

Baal 85, 129
Babel 26, 32
Babylon(ians) 126f., 153, 183, 189, 204, 213
Bashan 87, 90
Bathsheba 7, 17
Benjamin 91, 156

cherubim 157, 228
chosen people *see* covenant people
Christian interpretation 14f., 42, 92, 113, 159, 176, 182, 189, 210, 218, 230
coronation 1, 112, 226
covenant (covenant faith, Sinai covenant) 17, 46, 50, 52, 63, 67, 97–9, 110, 154, 179, 220, 224, 228, 230; with Abraham 81; with David 1, 8, 59f., 67, 113, 188, 194, 196
covenant people 66, 95, 127, 130, 230
curses 46f., 52f., 99

David 7, 17f., 20, 22, 28, 38, 40, 42, 50f., 54, 60, 65, 113, 140, 151, 158, 188, 194f., 197, 204, 220
David, author of psalms 2–4, 7, 16, 38, 42, 50f., 54, 65, 113, 117

David, house of 1, 56, 59, 113, 139, 188, 194f., 197
death 32, 40, 90, 122–4, 134, 186f., 200; *see also* Sheol
Deborah 86
deep 73, 77, 82, 90, 94, 110, 129, 187, 191, 209f., 222
demonic and other terrifying imagery 32, 43, 51, 96, 108, 121f., 205
Deuteronomy 139
Doeg 22
doubt 2, 92, 137, 185, 213
doxologies 3, 6, 116f., 197
drama (ritual) 77, 82, 189, 223

Edom 54f., 57, 135, 167, 196
Egypt 35, 86, 91, 113, 139, 144, 161f., 183, 191.
Elohistic Psalter 4f.
enemies, *see* evildoers
Ephraim 56, 143, 151, 156f.
eschatological pictures 77, 90, 182, 220–2
eternal life 100, 123; *see also* life after death
evildoers 6f., 22f., 26–8, 32f., 38, 43, 45–7, 50, 67, 69, 77, 85, 90, 95, 107f., 120f., 123, 127, 132f., 167, 172, 180f., 194, 205, 207, 213f.
exile, Babylonian 20f., 25, 27, 38, 58, 92, 102, 116, 120, 126–8, 154, 170, 174f., 183, 185, 188f., 196f., 199, 204, 213, 220, 223, 225f.
exodus 78, 86, 91, 138f., 144–8, 157f., 160, 191, 224, 226
Ezekiel 128

faith 2, 22–4, 28f., 35, 39, 65f., 79, 101, 119, 120f., 127, 156, 186, 204
fertility 72, 74, 79, 116, 176; *see also* harvest
festivals 33, 72, 90, 140, 160f., 209

Flood 25f.; *see also* deep
folly 25f., 95, 207
forgiveness 17, 19, 99
form criticism 7f.

Gibeon 66
Gideon 144, 168
Gilead 56, 167
glory 44, 77, 107, 123, 175f., 180, 221
God
  as creator 42, 72, 74, 129, 139,
    146, 165, 191f., 210f., 213, 217,
    226, 228
  as gardener 47, 74, 158
  as judge 46f., 53, 55, 67, 70, 102,
    131, 133f., 162, 164f., 205, 208,
    213f., 220, 222, 226, 228
  as shepherd 82, 139, 154, 157,
    218, 230
  as warrior 56, 73, 86, 134, 151
  kingdom of 1, 83, 167, 182
  kingship of 1, 7f., 43, 53, 81, 95,
    102, 113, 115, 128f., 132, 134,
    157, 164f., 176, 192, 207, 209f.,
    220, 222–4, 226, 228, 230
  majesty of, *see* God, kingship of
  presence of 19f., 36, 65f., 81, 85,
    101, 107, 120–4, 131f., 144, 170,
    175f., 186, 213, 230
  sovereignty of, *see* God, kingship
    of
  throne of 192, 228
  victory of 83, 88–91, 128, 182,
    225f.
  wrath of 55f., 130, 133, 154, 157,
    175, 200f., 210
gods (pagan) 44, 46, 148, 150,
  162–5, 179, 183, 191, 218, 221
Gunkel, H. 7

Hamath 135
harvest 74, 81f., 176
Hermon, Mt 87, 192
Hezekiah 113
holiness 87, 110, 138, 211, 221f.,
  224, 228f.
holy mountain(s) 150, 183, 191f.
Holy One of Israel 110, 192
hope 62, 89, 96, 106f., 110, 119, 138,
  151, 186

host of heaven (stars, sun, moon)
  74, 191, 210
humble (poor) 86, 104, 132, 179

Ishmael(ites) 35, 167
Israel (the people of God) 1, 7, 27,
  50f., 56, 59, 73, 78, 82, 91, 95, 107,
  120, 138, 141, 150, 153f., 167, 174f.,
  204, 213, 217; *see also* covenant
  people
Israel, land of (Canaan) 27, 35, 56,
  59, 78, 86f., 128, 148, 150, 153, 158,
  170, 177, 183, 218
Israel's history 1, 77f., 109, 132,
  137–9, 143–51, 156–8, 160–2, 228f.

Jabin 168
Jacob 27, 56, 133, 141, 174, 229
Jehoiachin 188
Jehu 209
Jeremiah 2, 92, 98
Jerusalem 6f., 9, 17, 20, 33, 38, 42f.,
  59, 73, 91, 126, 134, 139f., 150f.,
  153f., 156, 170, 172, 174f., 182f.,
  218, 220, 222, 229f.; *see also* Zion
Jesus Christ 19, 29, 38, 44, 92, 94,
  96, 98f., 159, 176, 189, 210, 218;
  see also Messiah
Jewish interpretation 6, 113, 189,
  230
Joab 54f.
Job 119f., 123
Jonathan 151
Jordan, river 56, 78, 129
Joseph 151, 161
Josiah 128, 139
Judah 55f., 65, 143, 197
Judas Iscariot 29
judgement (coming, final) 23, 36,
  132, 214, 220, 224, 226

king (of Israel) 1, 7f., 56–60, 65,
  67, 76, 112–16, 128, 137, 158f.,
  164, 170, 172, 179, 188f., 194, 196f.
Korah 33
Korah, sons of 3, 5

lament, individual 7f.
Law (of God) 2, 10, 141, 161f., 211,
  213–15

234